CW00404510

Images of Redemption

Images of Redemption:
Art, Literature and
Salvation

by

PATRICK SHERRY

T & T CLARK
A Continuum imprint
LONDON • NEW YORK

T&T CLARK LTD

A Continuum imprint

The Tower Building
11 York Road
London SE1 7NX, UK

370 Lexington Avenue
New York 10017–6503
USA

www.continuumbooks.com

Copyright © T&T Clark Ltd, 2003

All rights reserved. No part of this publication may be reproduced or transmitted in any form or by any means, electronic or mechanical, including photocopy, recording or any information retrieval system, without permission in writing from the publishers or their appointed agents.

British Library Cataloguing-in-Publication Data
A catalogue record for this book is available from the British Library

ISBN 0 567 08891 X (paperback)
ISBN 0 567 08894 4 (hardback)

Typeset by Fakenham Photosetting Ltd, Fakenham, Norfolk NR21 8NN
Printed and bound in Great Britain by Bookcraft, Midsomer Norton

Contents

Preface

Many artists and writers seem, at times, to be more concerned to depict the evil, ugliness, disorder, and unhappiness of a fallen world than to celebrate the beauty of creation. Whilst some of them just do this and, as it were, rub our noses in it, others do so as a prelude to showing us possibilities of liberation: for themes like achieving goals in the face of obstacles, overcoming hardship, return home from war or exile, learning through suffering, and indeed, more generally, what Shakespeare called 'the uses of adversity' are perennial ones in art and literature.

For religious believers the deepest forms of liberation are described in terms like 'salvation', 'enlightenment', 'release', and 'redemption' – what are called soteriological terms. There are many examples of art and literature that seek to convey such forms of liberation, especially in Christianity: I shall call them, following John W. Dixon, the 'arts of redemption'. They include works that express fundamental reactions like repentance and forgiveness, and ones that represent or describe possibilities of redemption being worked out in human lives. My purpose in this book is to consider such art and literature, and to see what light they shed on Christian teaching on salvation and redemption; thereby it may serve as an introduction to such teaching. I shall argue that in many cases art and literature are primary expressions of religious ideas, and that, therefore, they may give us a more immediate, and sometimes deeper, understanding of these ideas than is offered by theology. You may on occasion learn more about redemption from a novel than from a theological treatise.

I shall not attempt to give a comprehensive view of such art and literature or even to cover all genres equally, for my purpose is not to present a survey. Rather, I shall suggest a theological framework, that of the 'drama of redemption', and then offer some significant examples at each point and assess how they contribute to our religious understanding. The reader may well be able to think of other, and better, examples. As Ludwig Wittgenstein said in a very different context, in the Foreword to his *Philosophical Investigations*, 'I should not like my writing to spare other people the trouble of thinking. But, if possible, to stimulate someone to thoughts of his own.' In our case, however, it is more a matter of readers drawing on their own experience, imagination, and knowledge of art and literature, in order to further their religious understanding.

I am very grateful to Dr Francesca Murphy and Professor Richard Roberts for reading through earlier drafts of this work and making many helpful suggestions; and to Dr Marcel Sarot for inviting me to give a series of lectures and seminars at the University of Utrecht, and so giving me the opportunity to present some of the ideas in this book to a wider audience. Parts of chapters 5, 7, and 9 have been published previously in my articles: 'Redeeming the Past', *Religious Studies* vol. 34 (1998), pp. 165–75; 'Novels of Redemption', *Literature and Theology* vol. 14 (2000), pp. 249–60; and 'Saying and Showing: Art, Literature and Religious Understanding', *Modern Theology* vol. 18 (2002), pp. 37–48. I am grateful to Cambridge University Press, Oxford University Press, and Blackwell Publishers Ltd. for allowing me to use this material. I am also grateful to Methuen Publishing Ltd. for permission to quote from Michael Meyer's translation of *Brand* in Henrik Ibsen, *Plays: Five*.

CHAPTER ONE

Introduction: Art, Literature, and Redemption

The Arts of Redemption

Kierkegaard once used a variation of the story of the Sleeping Beauty to describe our understanding of traditional religious language. He wrote in his *Journal* for 1837:

> The old Christian dogmatic terminology is like an enchanted castle where the most beautiful princes and princesses rest in a deep sleep – it only needs to be awakened, brought to life, in order to stand in its full glory.[1]

I believe that Kierkegaard's remark is particularly applicable today to the language of soteriology, and that a consideration of how ideas of redemption, salvation, atonement and so on are communicated through art and literature may help in the restoration that he envisaged.

I was reminded of Kierkegaard's words a few years ago, when I was walking through the centre of a city where a street-evangelist was preaching: 'Only Jesus can save you. He has washed away your sins with his blood.' No one was listening to his message. At about the same time I read St Anselm's *Cur Deus Homo* and found much of it remote. Yet I continued to find the words of Isaiah on the Suffering Servant, and their use in the Church's

---

[1] Howard V. Hong and Edna Hong (eds.), *Søren Papers and Journals Kierkegaard's* iv (Bloomington, Ind., 1975), p. 461, §4774.

liturgy, very moving: unlike the evangelist and Anselm, they appealed to my heart and imagination. Moreover, a study which I was doing then of some Christians who were opposed to Hitler, and who paid for their resistance with their lives, seemed to provide some understanding of the idea of redemptive suffering – an idea with which I also found the Japanese novelist, Shusaku Endo, struggling in many of his works.

It seems, then, that literature, art, and history may help to provide a fresh understanding of religious ideas that have grown stale in the hands of preachers and theologians; and that such an understanding of concepts like redemption, salvation, and atonement may be particularly apposite at the present time. In a review of Pope John Paul II's book *Crossing the Threshold of Hope* in the *Independent* in 1994, Monica Furlong wrote (echoing what Dietrich Bonhoeffer had said fifty years earlier):

> If the Christian churches are to survive their present crisis then they need to find, as the early Christians did, new language and fresh thinking. Slapping down the old money – unity, salvation, hope, the Son of God, forgiveness – as if it is still legal tender, will not work. We bite the coin and find it counterfeit.

I am not sure that Furlong is fair to the Pope's book; but I think that she is right in suggesting that a lot of traditional concepts fail to 'touch down' (to use a favourite phrase of Ian Ramsey) in people's experience and understanding today. 'Salvation', in particular, is used as a short-hand term for something whose meaning is unclear to many people. I notice, too, that few sermons deal with the ideas I have mentioned. It is, of course, hard to discuss them in a few minutes – here, of all places, we need *depth*; but I suspect that there are some other reasons, that the topic is uncongenial because either many people think that they are fundamentally 'all right', so that they do not need 'redeeming' (whatever that is), or else they are in despair or at least do not understand how someone's death on a cross two thousand years ago can help with the manifold evils of human life. Nietzsche said famously of Christians that they do not look redeemed: but perhaps this is because they do not feel redeemed; and that, in turn, is partly, perhaps, because the world does not look redeemed.

Yet, despite all this, one can be profoundly moved, as I have suggested, by some of the words of the Bible and the liturgy, for instance 'despised and rejected of men, a man of sorrows, and acquainted with grief ... surely he hath borne our griefs, and carried our sorrows ... with his stripes we are healed' (Isa. 53.3–5). Such words seem to appeal to something deep within us. We may also, perhaps, remember here John Henry Newman's claim that the real cause of Christianity's success in the Roman Empire was 'the Image of Him who fulfils the one great need of human nature, the Healer of its wounds, the Physician of the Soul ...'[2] Or perhaps we are moved by the image of the Good Shepherd – which was one of the most popular ones in the earliest Christian art, found for example on the walls of the catacombs, an image, like Newman's 'Healer' and 'Physician', that conveys something of what Paul Evdokimov calls the tenderness of God.[3]

All this suggests that one answer to the difficulty raised by Furlong is to approach people through their hearts and imaginations. And an obvious way of doing this is through art and literature, specifically through what I shall call 'the arts of redemption', borrowing a phrase from John W. Dixon.

Dixon introduced this phrase as part of a general argument, that the different types of Christian art correspond to the principal events in the Christian drama. Thus he differentiates 'the arts of creation', which celebrate God's creation, 'the arts of image', which explore the structure of creation and seek to

---

[2] J.H. Newman, *An Essay in Aid of a Grammar of Assent*, 4th edn. (London, 1874), p. 464.
[3] Paul Evdokimov, *La femme et le salut du monde* (Paris, 1978), p. 167. He is echoing e.g. Isa. 66.13.

understand its parts and order, 'the arts of the fall', which investigate the tragic consequences of the fall and penetrate the nature
of our fallen existence, and 'the arts of redemption', in which 'the
artist is occupied with the redemptive act itself or the kind of
world that results from the transfiguration of creation in
redemption'.[4] Of course, one and the same individual may be
concerned with all these kinds of art:

> The artist lives within the natural order and his celebration
> of it makes the art of creation. He explores and analyzes it
> and makes the art of the image of God. He sees and mourns
> its brokenness and makes the art of the fall. He lives within
> its healing and makes the art of redemption.[5]

Of the last of these Dixon says,

> The art of redemption is art immediately under the grace of
> God. This art is not informed by the innocence of delight
> that characterizes the art of creation but by a glory trans-
> figured out of pain. Tragedy here has been redeemed and
> transformed, not obliterated or forgotten, but caught up in a
> new meaning and a new life; the city of God is not given but
> is arrived at on pilgrimage.[6]

As examples of this kind of art, Dixon instances Donatello's
pulpits, Michelangelo's and Titian's *Pietà*s, and Piero della
Francesca's *Resurrection*.[7] These examples indicate, I take it, that
such art need not actually portray ugliness or disorder, though it
may do so. What is essential for Dixon is transformation: '... the

[4] John W. Dixon, *Nature and Grace in Art* (Chapel Hill, 1964), p. 72. Further possible
categories might be the 'arts of Paradise' (which could include both those looking
back to a past Golden Age and those anticipating one to come), and the 'arts of
damnation'.
[5] Ibid., p. 195.
[6] Ibid., p. 78.
[7] Ibid., p. 155.

transfiguration of earth, the search for the grace beyond hope . . . the holiness of Christ penetrating the material and bringing into being the new earth.'[8]

I shall follow up later on what Dixon says, by discussing some other examples of the 'arts of redemption' (and not just examples drawn from painting and sculpture). But now let me say a little more about why this subject should concern us.

As Dixon's use of the term 'transfiguration' perhaps suggests, we are concerned with *vision*: the artist or writer may show us the possibility of a transformed world. Sometimes they may be illustrating a religious doctrine or a sacred text, but more often they are attempting to capture directly the religious meaning of the world and of events. Hence some works of art and of literature may be primary expressions of religious ideas (as contrasted with illustrations parasitic on something else). Thus Frank Burch Brown writes in a similar vein:

> The fact that the primary language of religion is markedly poetic, mythic, and otherwise aesthetic means it is with such language that theology repeatedly begins and that it is to such language that theology must often return.[9]

Such primary expressions may be found also in prayers, liturgies, and many parts of Scripture. For instance, the prayer 'Lamb of God who takest away the sins of the world, have mercy on us' (derived from John 1.29) may possibly be explained in terms of a doctrine of the Atonement, but it preceded any such doctrine. (A point worth making here is that there is no one 'official' doctrine of the Atonement: the early Church never defined one, as it did in the case of the doctrines of the Trinity and Incarnation.[10]) The

[8] Ibid., p. 199.

[9] Frank Burch Brown, *Religious Aesthetics: A Theological Study of Making and Meaning* (Princeton, 1989), p. 193.

[10] See John McIntyre, *The Shape of Soteriology: Studies in the Doctrine of the Death of Christ* (Edinburgh, 1992), ch.1, esp. pp. 1–16; and H.E.W. Turner, *The Patristic Doctrine of Redemption: A Study of the Development of Doctrine during the First Five Centuries* (London, 1952), p. 26.

relationship of the doctrinal formulations to the prayer is somewhat like that of a paraphrase to a poem. Now paraphrases, like illustrations, have their value. But they are secondary, in that they are parasitic on other things. I am arguing that in many cases the work of art or literature is primary. Our task is to see how such primary expressions contribute to religious understanding.

Those who ignore this primacy risk treating all religious art and literature merely as illustrations. They may also be in danger of trying to read a particular theology into a work of art or literature. This danger is noted by Stanley Cavell: writing of *King Lear* he observes that it is not 'illustrated theology', and asks 'which theology is thought to be illustrated, what understanding of atonement, redemption, etc., is thought to be figured?'[11]

The primacy of art and literature here derives, as we shall see, from their ability to show things and to express and communicate meanings directly, by themselves. But there is also another kind of primacy at stake, that of certain human reactions and behaviour. There are some fundamental responses like grief, guilt, repentance, expiation, and forgiveness, which are part of the texture of ordinary life. Such responses underlie both doctrine and theology: in medieval times the maxim 'first live, then philosophize' was often cited, a maxim which I would extend to include theologizing. Putting the point another way, one might say that experiences and behaviour underlie soteriologies: we are dealing here, or ought to be, with what is profound and moving in human life, and with the wisdom that is acquired from experience; and art and literature may have a role in conveying the relevant experiences and responses, and our reflections on them. Hence J.A.W. Bennett said towards the end of his study of the poetry of the Cross,

The deepening and revivifying of Christian belief is not always achieved by the theologians or philosophers. It is

---

[11] Stanley Cavell, 'The Avoidance of Love: A Reading of King Lear', in his *Must we Mean what we Say?* (New York, 1969), p. 301.

sometimes entrusted to poets: to a Dante, a Langland, a David Jones.[12]

The primacy of the responses and of their expression does not mean that their communication in art and literature is an easy matter: sometimes what Kierkegaard called 'indirect communication' may be appropriate or unavoidable. Besides the simple responses I have mentioned, we may have to reckon also with subtle psychological factors like unconscious motives and irrational forces. For their expression, imagery and symbolism may be especially appropriate. (Many people have pointed out that the traditional language of the theology of the Atonement is fraught with metaphors drawing on the legal system, the altar of sacrifice, the battlefield, and the slave-market.[13]) Often, too, the things that I have mentioned take a long time to develop and to manifest themselves in human life. Hence, I shall argue, narrative arts like novels and biographies are particularly appropriate here.

The primacy of the responses mentioned also means, I think, that we should not down-grade either the arts or the theology of Redemption, as if they were of secondary importance. In recent years Matthew Fox has conducted a polemic against the tradition of theology which emphasizes the Fall and Redemption, which he sees as stemming from St Augustine, in favour of what Fox calls 'Creation Spirituality'. The latter seeks to perceive and preach the 'original blessing' of creation, and to encourage a 'cosmic spirituality' which is concerned with the transfiguration of the whole world.[14] I accept the positive side of Fox's case, for I think that he has helped to rediscover an important aspect of the Christian tradition. But one can, I believe, accept this positive case without engaging in Fox's polemic. Dixon rightly sees that

[12] J.A.W. Bennett, *The Poetry of the Passion* (Oxford, 1982), p. 206.
[13] See Colin Gunton, *The Actuality of the Atonement: A Study of Metaphor, Rationality and Christian Tradition* (Edinburgh, 1988), pp. 16*ff*; and J.S. Whale, *Victor and Victim: The Christian Doctrine of Redemption* (Cambridge, 1960), pp. 36*f*, 69, 74.
[14] See, for example, Matthew Fox, *Original Blessing: A Primer in Creation Spirituality* (Santa Fé, 1983), pp. 46, 70*ff*.

there are both 'arts of creation' and 'arts of redemption'. One can easily think of some contrasts here: if Handel's *Messiah* and Bach's *St Matthew Passion* are examples of the latter, then Haydn's *Creation* seems an obvious example, as its title suggests, of Dixon's 'arts of creation'. Ulrich Simon sees Haydn's work as celebrating a 'sinless existence, in no need of atonement'[15]; seemingly unworried by predation in nature, 'Haydn sets wild animals and vermin within the harmony of the created world, following the poets with their adulation of the greatest predators.'[16] He does not concern himself with the wounding and war in nature which preoccupied St Paul in Romans 8.19–23, and which led Paul to extend the idea of liberation through Christ to all creation, not just human life.

Of course, Haydn also produced 'art of redemption', e.g. his *Seven Last Words from the Cross*. But some artists and writers have concentrated more on one kind of subject than another, for reasons of temperament, religious belief, or theology. Following Martin Green, we might distinguish here between 'devout humanists' and 'anti-humanists', the former category including those who celebrate human achievements and see them as possible means of divine grace, the latter category including those who make a sharp distinction between the 'natural' and the 'supernatural' and who tend to deprecate human nature and 'natural' goodness.[17] Matthew Fox would obviously come into Green's category of a 'devout humanist'. In terms of my contrast between Dixon's 'arts of creation' and 'arts of redemption', the 'devout humanist' is more interested in the former, the 'anti-humanist' in the latter. If we extend Green's categories to include artists and musicians as well as writers, then we have a contrast between those who celebrate the beauty of creation and those who discern both its fallenness and its possibility of redemption

[15] Ulrich Simon, *Atonement: From Holocaust to Paradise* (Cambridge, 1987), p. 12.
[16] Ibid., p. 15.
[17] Martin Green, *Yeats's Blessing on Von Hügel: Essays on Literature and Religion* (London, 1967), pp. 65–96.

(perhaps leading to a different kind of beauty). Theologically, we may contrast those like Matthew Fox, who stress the goodness of creation, with those who start from sin and redemption (seeing, perhaps, the development of the doctrine of Creation as posterior to God's 'creation' of his chosen people, Israel, by redeeming it from slavery in Egypt[18]). Of course, both Creation and Redemption have in common that they are modes of divine action.

When he introduces the phrase 'arts of redemption' Dixon warns against our seeking to *make* redemptive art: only God is the Redeemer, so all that we can do is to make an art that communicates what we experience of redemption. Otherwise, we just get more art of the fall, setting up false gods.[19] Dixon is evidently on the look-out here for anything that smacks of idolatry. A similar fear is evident in the work of some other Christian writers on aesthetics. Peter Taylor Forsyth, for example, writes, 'It is not so much that Art redeems as that it sustains us with the dream and the earnest of redemption'[20]; and Nathan Scott quotes a remark of I.A. Richards that poetry is 'capable of saving us', and sees it as exemplifying the Romantic tendency to make art into a religion.[21] Similarly, Nicholas Wolterstorff attacks Herbert Marcuse for finding saving liberation in art, and thus offering a surrogate for the Christian gospel of redemption and liberation.[22]

---

[18] A thesis championed particularly by Gerhard von Rad, e.g. in his *Old Testament Theology*, i, tr. D.M.G. Stalker (Edinburgh and London, 1962), pp. 136–9, though not universally accepted.

[19] Dixon, *Nature and Grace in Art*, p. 78.

[20] Peter Taylor Forsyth, *Religion in Recent Art* (London, 1901), p. 243. It is not clear how much weight Forsyth wishes to put on the metaphor of an 'earnest': properly speaking, it is something already realized now, though only partially. See also his *Christ on Parnassus* (London, 1911), pp. 224–5.

[21] Nathan A. Scott, Jr., *Rehearsals of Discomposure: Alienation and Reconciliation in Modern Literature* (London, 1952), p. 196.

[22] Nicholas Wolterstorff, *Art in Action: Toward a Christian Aesthetic* (Grand Rapids, 1980), iii.3.7. See also Leo Bersani, *The Culture of Redemption* (Harvard, 1990), esp. pp. 1–4, 20–1, for an attack, from a very different perspective, on the idea that art and literature can be redemptive.

Yet earlier on he himself has ascribed a redemptive significance to art: 'Art can serve as instrument in our struggle to overcome the fallenness of our existence, while also, in the delight it affords, anticipating the shalom that awaits us.'[23] This seems to suggest that, although art and literature cannot themselves redeem people, they may nevertheless be channels of grace (in the Orthodox Church icons are regarded as 'sacramentals'), and therefore have a redemptive function. Why should we set limits to the ways in which God may carry out His saving work? And why should we assume that only preachers and theologians can bring out the significance of Christ's redemption?

There are many examples one can quote of art and literature apparently liberating or enlightening people, and serving as channels of grace. John Stuart Mill was freed from a long depression through the delight which he found in Wordsworth's poetry.[24] Felix Mendelssohn wrote to Robert Schumann of Bach's chorale prelude '*Schmücke dich, o liebe Seele*', that 'if life were to deprive you of hope and faith, this one chorale would bring it all back again to you'.[25] Similarly, Vincent van Gogh described Rembrandt's religious paintings as 'metaphysical magic' to his friend Emile Bernard; he wrote also to his brother, Theo, about 'what Rembrandt has alone or almost alone among painters, that tenderness of the gaze ... that heartbroken tenderness, that glimpse of a superhuman infinitude...'; even when Rembrandt is true to nature, he says, 'he soars aloft, to the very highest height, the infinite ... Rembrandt is so deeply mysterious that he says things for which there are no words in any language.'[26] More generally, Dostoevsky said, in *The Idiot*, that 'Beauty will save the world and will rebuild its primordial image, of which the Creator saw that "it was good".' An enquiry into

---

[23] Wolterstorff, p. 84.

[24] John Stuart Mill, *Autobiography* (Oxford, 1971), pp. 88–90.

[25] Albert Schweitzer, *J.S. Bach*, i, tr. E. Newman (London, 1923), p. 245.

[26] *The Complete Letters of Vincent van Gogh* (Greenwich, CT, 1959), ii, p. 147; iii, pp. 187, 504.

how art and literature serve as channels of grace or instruments of redemption might throw some light, too, on the more general question of the nature of divine action.

Some Examples

Let us now consider a few more examples of the arts and literature of redemption, to flesh out Dixon's description. Most obviously, there are paintings and other depictions of the passion and death of Christ, including those in music, e.g. J.S. Bach's *Passions*. Many such works celebrate not only Christ's suffering and death but also his resurrection: Grünewald's famous *Crucifixion* is only one part of his altarpiece at Colmar; another panel depicts the Resurrection [Plate 1]. Eastern representations of the Resurrection, e.g. the mural in St Saviour in Chora in Istanbul [Plate 2] and many icons, depict the risen Christ as harrowing Hell (he is leading up Adam and Eve, surrounded by Abel, St John the Baptist, kings and patriarchs) – the beginning of the New Heaven and New Earth that are promised. Likewise Eastern icons of Pentecost, by depicting in the foreground a king being unbound, suggest the freeing of the world – again conveying the idea that the Redemption embraces the transfiguration of all things as well as the forgiveness of individual sinners.

The theme of the passion and death of Christ was also the subject of many medieval Mystery Plays. But 'plays of redemption' would also include any ones that deal with responses like guilt, repentance, atonement, and forgiveness, e.g. Shakespeare's *Measure for Measure*, or *The Winter's Tale*. Some of these responses are found too in Classical Greek drama – we should not, I think, restrict our consideration here to explicitly Christian examples. The Greek tragedians dealt with the great themes of guilt and atonement, especially Aeschylus in the *Oresteia* trilogy, and also with that of dying for others. The figure of Alcestis, who offered up her life to save her husband, Admetus, from death, and who was the subject of a play by Euripides, was regarded by some early Christian writers as prefiguring Christ, both in her self-giving and in her being raised from the dead by Hercules' overcoming Death (and Hercules, in turn, was also regarded as a precursor of Christ, in his harrowing of Hell).[27] Greek tragedy also offers us examples of suffering victims who heal and purge others: writing of Sophocles' *Antigone*, F.W. Dillistone says, 'In and through the suffering of Haemon and Antigone the curse is annulled, corruption removed, the total situation is repaired and restored.'[28]

More recently, there is the genre of the novel to consider: both Dostoevsky and Tolstoy, for example, were concerned in different ways with guilt and redemption, especially in *Crime and Punishment* and *Resurrection*. A particular theme found in other writers (especially some twentieth-century Roman Catholic novelists) and worth noting now is that of vicarious suffering, conveyed for instance in François Mauriac's *The Knot of Vipers,* in which the central figure, Louis, is, it seems finally redeemed through the death some years ago of his little daughter, and in his *The Woman of the Pharisees*, in which the Abbé Calou (the real saint in the book, who is the pendant of the pseudo-saint, the pharisaical Brigitte Pian) suffers for the unhappy boy committed to his charge, Jean de Mirbel; and also, I think, in Georges Bernanos' *The Diary of a Country Priest,* in which the unnamed young priest is represented as a sacrificial victim, dying for his village.

We find the idea of redemption through suffering in a much weaker sense in those who succeed in expressing something of what they have learnt from their own suffering, and of the serenity they have achieved, in their later works, illustrating the common claim that good may be brought out of evil: one thinks of some of Rembrandt's late self-portraits, or of Beethoven's conveying his

---

[27] Martin Hengel, *The Atonement: The Origins of the Doctrine in the New Testament*, tr. J. Bowden (London, 1980), pp. 9,20; Hamish Swanston, *Handel* (London, 1990), pp. 49–52. The latter discusses Handel's use of these stories in his operas, as Christian parallels.

[28] F.W. Dillistone, *The Christian Understanding of Atonement* (London, 1968), p. 127.

spiritual strength and resignation in his late quartets or in the 'Agnus Dei' of the *Missa Solemnis*. Aldous Huxley suggested that these two 'came through' their suffering in a way that Goya did not.[29]

Already, I think, it is apparent that there are different ideas of redemption implicit in these examples, like atonement through suffering (both for oneself and for others), reconciliation, and transfiguration through the living Christ, as well as more general ideas like repentance and forgiveness. It is also apparent that different arts have their own strengths and weaknesses, fitting different aspects or phases of redemption. I have already suggested that, if redemption is a process which is worked out over a period of time, then narrative arts like novels and biographies will be particularly appropriate, and to some extent plays and films.

Films are an interesting and difficult case: as 'moving images' they have some of the virtues of both narratives and visual arts, though their brevity imposes limitations (a film might give some sense of Jesus' personality, but could it convey his saving work?). There are of course many religious films, ranging from Cecil B. de Mille's Biblical spectaculars like *The Ten Commandments* to Martin Scorsese's *The Last Temptation of Christ*.[30] In Andrei Tarkovsky's *Sacrifice* a man seemingly averts a nuclear crisis through an act of renunciation. Tim Robbins' *Dead Man Walking* confronts us with the issue of salvation: whereas the prison chaplain thinks that the important thing is to ensure that the

---

[29] See Aldous Huxley, 'Variations on Goya', in his *On Art and Artists* (London, 1960), pp. 214–25. With regard to Rembrandt's late self-portraits, John Hospers rightly remarked that although a painting cannot be 'true-to' a series of events like those in a play, or to anything requiring a temporal sequence of presentations, it can present powerful and convincing characterizations, somewhat in the way that a character in a drama or a novel can. See his *Meaning and Truth in the Arts* (Hamden, CT, 1964), p. 173.

[30] See Alan Pavelin, *Fifty Religious Films* (Chislehurst, 1990), and Clive Marsh and Gaye Ortiz (eds.), *Explorations in Theology and Film: Movies and Meaning* (Oxford, 1997).

condemned murderer, Matthew Poncelet, receives the sacraments before he dies, Sister Helen Prejean realizes that his salvation will depend in the first instance on honesty and taking responsibility for what he has done.

Many films that do not set out to be overtly religious often draw on religious themes: *Close Encounters of a Third Kind* is reminiscent of the visions of Ezekiel, *ET* reflects the story of the Incarnation, and *One Flew Over the Cuckoo's Nest* embodies Isaiah's model of the Suffering Servant. They may also convey hopes of liberation, e.g. from physical slavery, emotional bondage, or lack of opportunity; and they may likewise suggest hopes of a better world, as *Gold Diggers of 1933* did at the time of the American Depression; or they may depict a dark world, in which people experience alienation, paranoia and despair, as is seen in many of the Hollywood films noir of the 1940s, e.g. *Double Indemnity* or *The Postman Always Rings Twice*, or later films like *Taxi Driver* and *Apocalypse Now* (based remotely on Conrad's *The Heart of Darkness*). They may show a hero who carries out a redemptive task by defeating evil powers that threaten a community; or a more ordinary person who sacrifices himself or herself for others; or an averagely sinful man changed by events, as is Thornhill (played by Cary Grant) in Alfred Hitchcock's *North by Northwest*.[31]

At first sight, architecture would seem to be the most unpromising medium, if not wholly irrelevant to our subject (apart from the sculpture and stained glass that may be in a building). Yet many people have written of the bleakness and sense of anonymity of modern cities. With reference to the ideas of alienation and reconciliation in his study of four modern writers, Kafka, Silone, Lawrence, and Eliot, Nathan Scott says that they all define 'the man of their time in terms of isolation and

[31] See Christopher Deacy, 'An application of the religious concept of redemption in *film noir*', in *Scottish Journal of Religious Studies* xviii (1997), pp. 197–212; idem, 'Screen Christologies: An Evaluation of the Role of Christ-Figures in Film', in *Journal of Contemporary Religion* xiv (1999), pp. 325–37; and John R. May (ed.), *Image and Likeness: Religious Visions in American Film Classics* (New York, 1992).

estrangement, and the world in which he lives as a "waste land" awaiting redemption'. This is not strange, says Scott, given 'those icily nonchalant monuments of Le Corbusier and Mies van der Rohe ... '[32] If indeed some architecture can contribute to this sense of a wasteland, then presumably other architecture can lift the heart and spirits, for instance the lightness and delicacy of some South German baroque churches? Whilst it seems strange to speak of such architecture having a redeeming function, I do not see why one should not describe it as a channel of grace.[33]

A more central and perhaps also more difficult case is that of music. Beethoven's *Fidelio* might be described as an opera of liberation, and Wagner's *Parsifal* one of redemption. Bach's *Passions* are based on Gospel narratives; similarly, Handel's *Messiah* draws on texts from the Old and New Testaments. It is tempting to say, of the religious examples, that their redemptive significance depends, as with hymns, on the texts. But this is to ignore the effect which music itself may have, regardless of a libretto or text. The remark of Mendelssohn's which I quoted, about the impact on him of Bach's chorale *"Schmücke dich, o liebe Seele"*, suggests that we need to look at such effects, as does another remark that Mendelssohn made, that the thoughts which music expresses are not too indefinite to be put into words, but too definite. If music can express emotions, can it express ones as specific as repentance, the desire to expiate one's sins, or a wish to forgive or to be forgiven? Can the aria 'And He shall feed His Flock' in Handel's *Messiah* convey something of 'the tenderness of God' even to someone who does not hear or understand the words?

In his study *Atonement: From Holocaust to Paradise* Ulrich Simon points to the ways in which music involves time and dynamics,

---

[32] Nathan A. Scott, *Rehearsals of Discomposure*, p. 258.

[33] Robin Gibbons writes of the 'sacrament of building', of any place which 'engaged and still engages people with a transformative presence', in his article 'Celebration and Sacrament: Holy Place and Holy People', *New Blackfriars* vol.77, no.904 (May 1996), p. 234. See also John W. de Gruchy, *Christianity, Art and Transformation: Theological Aesthetics in the Struggle for Justice* (Cambridge, 2000), ch.5, on the transformative potential of architecture.

and hymns can arouse contrition and reconciliation; he uses the puzzling phrase 'the atoning effect of music'.[34] A few pages later, he asks 'Who but the most unmusical and insensitive can fail to be "atoned" by being attuned to the great masses of Haydn';[35] and he has also earlier said that 'the music of Monteverdi, Bach, Handel, Haydn, Mozart and Beethoven undoubtedly resolves and takes away sin and guilt. The creation becomes redemptive in the listener.'[36] At first reading this sounds like the kind of idolatry which Dixon, Scott, and Wolterstorff were attacking. If the Cross is believed to atone for our sins, is it not blasphemous to speak of music in a similar way? And is not Simon in danger of confusing evanescent moods or emotions with something much greater? But the use of inverted commas round the word 'atoned' in my second quotation should alert us to what Simon means here. In English the word 'atonement' means 'at-one-ment', i.e. reconciliation, and the verb 'to atone' is originally derived from the noun. Simon is concerned with how we may become 'at one' with God, and how this may be communicated. Hence he says, 'Bach's music . . . directly communicates penitence, forgiveness, union with and in Christ, praise and consummation'.[37] This remark disposes of the suspicion of idolatry, I think. Nevertheless, we are left with other difficult questions: whether music can convey such specific emotions, if so how, and whether someone from a non-Western culture could understand Bach and the other composers mentioned in the way that Simon claims.

Simon's comments about music seem more appropriate to poetry, in which very personal and specific emotions are conveyed to the reader or listener. In T.S. Eliot's work written after his religious conversion of 1927, especially the *Four Quartets* for example, we find the theme of redemption in time very strongly

[34] Ulrich Simon, *Atonement*, p. 121.
[35] Ibid., p. 124.
[36] Ibid., pp. 62–3.
[37] Ibid., p. 125. See also again Peter Taylor Forsyth, *Christ on Parnassus*, pp. 224–5, on this point.

expressed. In the last of the four, 'Little Gidding', Eliot sees Christianity as offering a shape and a meaning to time. Michael Edwards relates Eliot's later work to his earlier *The Waste Land*:

> His poetic activity after his conversion is more specifically a determined attempt to 'redeem' his earlier verse, by discovering redeemed experience to the side of the fallen experience which that verse knew so well.[38]

This comment raises some interesting questions: what changes occurred in Eliot's experience or understanding, and could they have occurred in the reverse direction? And is there also non-redemptive or anti-redemptive art?

Rival Accounts and Understandings

One could give many more examples of the arts and literature of redemption, and others will come up in later chapters; but my purpose in this chapter is primarily to sketch out the issues of religious understanding that they raise. Why look to art and literature for illumination on questions about redemption? This purpose requires, however, that we address briefly the questions suggested by Edwards' quotation, because they impinge on our main concern.

Non-redemptive and anti-redemptive art might include several things: work still reflecting a Christian belief rejected by the artist or writer, perhaps offering a secularized version of Christianity; work ignoring or rejecting Christianity; and work reflecting a non-Christian alternative. More radically, an artist or writer may completely reject *any* conception of redemption, salvation,

---

[38] Michael Edwards, 'Rewriting *The Waste Land*', in David Jasper and Colin Crowder (eds.), *European Literature and Theology in the Twentieth Century: The Ends of Time* (London, 1990), p. 74.

liberation, and so forth. There are examples of all these kinds of art and literature.

Many nineteenth-century and early twentieth-century writers and artists still reflected a view of life heavily influenced by Christian belief, even if they had rejected the latter. George Eliot rejected the religious background in which she had grown up, but she still presented a sympathetic account of Christianity in some of her novels, especially *Adam Bede*. And even where the Christian background is not in evidence, one might say that she is often still concerned with ideas of salvation. In *Middlemarch,* for example, Dorothea learns from the suffering caused by her ill-advised marriage to Casaubon, so that good comes out of evil; and in *Daniel Deronda* Daniel can be described as in some sense trying to redeem the unhappy Gwendolen Harleth, and perhaps also his fellow Jews. D.H. Lawrence might also be seen as a writer in search of salvation, but he, I think, had travelled further down the road away from Christianity than had George Eliot.

Some writers present a 'flat' account of the world, or perhaps describe unhappiness without allowing for any way out of it other than death. Philip Larkin described A.E. Housman as the poet of unhappiness, while Thomas Hardy in some of his novels, especially *Jude the Obscure* and *Tess of the D'Urbervilles*, presented seemingly irredeemable situations. More recently, Louis Begley's semi-autobiographical novel, *Wartime Lies*, about a Jewish child in Poland during the Second World War, suggests that wisdom does *not* grow out of suffering, and that pain is not redemptive; all one can learn from the scenes depicted in the novel is how to survive by wariness and adaptability.[39]

There are, however, also *religious* alternatives to Christian ideas of redemption: all the major religions of the world have their soteriologies. In his *The Varieties of Religious Experience* William James said that at the core of all religions there lies an uneasiness, a feeling that 'there is *something wrong about us* as we naturally

---

[39] Louis Begley, *Wartime Lies* (New York, 1991). Jerzy Kosinski's *The Painted Bird* (Boston, 1965) conveys a similar message, against a similar background.

stand', and a solution, 'a sense that *we are saved from the wrongness* by making proper connection with the higher powers'.[40] More dramatically, Ludwig Wittgenstein wrote:

> People are religious to the extent that they believe themselves to be not so much *imperfect*, as *ill*. Any man who is half-way decent will think himself extremely imperfect, but a religious man thinks himself *wretched*.[41]

Different soteriologies, however, give varying accounts of what people are saved *from*, what they are saved *for*, and the means or mediators of salvation. There are striking differences, for example, between what Buddhism and Christianity teach on 'liberation', 'salvation', and 'release'. A Buddhist might well accept Wittgenstein's remark, but say that Western religions tend to misdiagnose the illness and wretchedness in question or to offer inadequate remedies.

It would take us too far afield to consider examples of non-Christian soteriologies expressed in art and literature. Statues of the Buddha as Saviour are the most familiar ones known in the West, apart from ancient Greek and Roman examples and modern revivals of pagan religious themes (e.g. in Wagner's *The Ring* as compared with his – idiosyncratic – use of Christian ideas of redemption in *Parsifal*). But there are many other examples of such arts, e.g. the dances of liberation performed by monks in some schools of Buddhism.

Despite the differences between them, religious soteriologies do not usually accept either cosmic pessimism or the optimistic progressivism of many secular movements. More sceptical stances are, however, also found. In Albert Camus' *The Plague*, when Fr Paneloux says to Dr Rieux, after they have both attended a child dying in hospital, 'You, too, are working for man's salvation', the

---

[40] William James, *The Varieties of Religious Experience* (Fontana edn., London, 1960), Lecture 20, p. 484.
[41] Ludwig Wittgenstein, *Culture and Value*, tr. P. Winch (Oxford, 1980), p. 45e.

doctor replies, 'salvation's much too big a word for me. I don't aim so high. I'm concerned with man's health; and for me his health comes first.'[42] Writing of Samuel Beckett's *Molloy*, Martha Nussbaum remarks that its ending (in a garden) suggests the philosophy of Epicurus or the final pages of Voltaire's *Candide*: 'We can be redeemed only by ending the demand for redemption, by ceasing to use the concepts of redemption.' Beckett, she says, is attacking religious desire, like Epicurus and Nietzsche, who 'believed that a religious view of the world had deeply poisoned human desires in their time, constructing deformed patterns of fear and longing'.[43]

Thus sceptics may attack not only the ethics and eschatology of a religion, but also its analysis of the human predicament and the remedies it offers. Moreover, we cannot assume that Christian concepts like atonement and redemption are universal: we shall need to take account of cultural diversity.

Of course, many of the artists and writers whom I have mentioned so far would vehemently reject the view summarized by Nussbaum. Dostoevsky and Mauriac, for instance, would see the 'demand for redemption' and its possible fulfilment as an inescapable fact of human life and experience, which they depict in some of their works. The question, then, with which the examples that I have discussed confront us is: who has seen life most profoundly and portrayed it most cogently?

---

[42] Albert Camus, *The Plague*, tr. S. Gilbert (London, 1973), p. 203. Compare Friedrich Engels' assertion, in his 'On the History of Early Christianity', that both Christianity and socialism preach forthcoming salvation from bondage and misery; but Christianity places this salvation in a life beyond death, whereas socialism looks for it in this world, in a transformation of society. See K. Marx and F. Engels, *On Religion* (Moscow, 1955), p. 316.

[43] Martha Nussbaum, *Love's Knowledge: Essays on Philosophy and Literature* (New York, 1990), pp. 305, 306. Similarly, in an essay on Beckett's *Endgame*, Stanley Cavell compares Beckett with Nietzsche, who claimed that Hamlet's apparent indecisiveness stemmed really from his seeing 'the cost of action, the hardest of all truths, that redemption is impossible, that nothing makes up for anything'. (*Must we Mean what we Say?*, p. 154.)

This study will address that question by examining the contribution made by some art and literature to our understanding of soteriology. After suggesting a framework for the study in terms of what I shall call the three 'Acts' of the Drama of Redemption, I shall look at significant examples of how these Acts are treated by artists and writers, and assess how they contribute to our understanding of Christian redemption.

This study will also, I hope, contribute to the more general topic of the relation between art, literature, and theology. To some extent, the distinction that I made earlier, between primary expressions and illustrations, suggests that the main contribution that this study will make will be through leading the reader to ask what is actually *shown* (e.g. God's redeeming actions) through the primary expressions. If indeed art and literature increase people's religious understanding, this will be mainly through what they show, as compared with the more discursive understanding offered by theology. It is unlikely that they will prove theological opinions and theories; but they may well help us to understand the circumstances in which the latter arise, and also, perhaps, make certain views of life more attractive or plausible.

I shall also argue, however, that the process is two-way: for although art and literature may contribute towards religious understanding, and sometimes pass judgement on theology, theology may in turn criticize them as inadequate in some respect. Thus the relation between them may be reciprocal. If theology's weakness here tends to be to regard art and literature mainly as illustrations, that of the artist and writer may be a failure to bring art and literature into dialogue with other expressions of religion.

So far, however, I have not said what 'redemption' means; for I have been looking in this chapter more at what the 'arts of redemption' include, and introducing the issues of religious understanding that they raise. Before proceeding further, therefore, I need to say a little more about the theological background and about the problems that it raises for people today.

CHAPTER TWO

What is Redemption?

Soteriological Concepts

If, as I suggested at the beginning of the last chapter, a lot of traditional soteriological language fails to 'touch down' in people's experience today and to address their deepest concerns, then we have a serious problem of religious understanding. But there is also another deep issue at stake here, that of theodicy: for the claim that suffering (whether that of Christ or that of ourselves) redeems has been one common response to the problem of evil. Thus soteriology and theodicy are close neighbours.

In practice, religions rarely attempt to offer worked out theodicies, for the latter may seem to belittle suffering, or turn out to be misguided efforts to construct explanations where we lack the knowledge to do so. More often, religions concentrate rather on showing solidarity with sufferers, attempting to mitigate the effects of suffering, and helping people to bring fruit out of it. The problem then becomes not so much one of answering those who charge that the existence of evil proves atheism or provides evidence against the existence of God, as of showing that we can make some religious sense out of pain and suffering. In practice, too, suffering may sometimes draw people towards religion, because it offers hope and possible ways of dealing with their problems, and perhaps because they think that they have felt God's presence and effective power in their suffering. Thomas V. Morris notes the latter point when he says,

> surely it is a deep religious insight that the goodness of God
> is at times manifested in the suffering we are allowed to

endure as well as in the more immediately pleasant of his gifts to us.[1]

The connection between soteriology and theodicy, and the problem of making religious sense out of pain and suffering, have been perceived not only by theologians, but by novelists and dramatists. Thus Shusaku Endo, for example, expresses the connection in a striking scene in his novel *The Samurai* (about a late sixteenth-century samurai, Hasekura Rokuemon, who travels from Japan to Europe to help to open up his country to the West, and who gets himself baptized, with the encouragement of a Franciscan missionary, Velasco, in order to assist his endeavour). The samurai is looking at the crucifix on the wall of his cabin on the ship, and is puzzled:

> 'I ... have no desire to worship you', he murmured almost apologetically. 'I can't even understand why the foreigners respect you. They say you died bearing the sins of mankind, but I can't see that our lives have become any easier as a result. I know what wretched lives the peasants lead in the marshland. Nothing has changed just because you died.'
> Velasco claimed that this beggarly man would save all mankind, but the samurai could not understand what that salvation meant.[2]

Later on, the samurai finds his own solution to the problem, in terms of a version of Liberation Theology: on his return to Japan, he is put under house-arrest, and then taken away to prison (and to likely execution); and he finds consolation in the Christ of the poor and oppressed who will accompany him on his last journey. But in the passage quoted Endo expresses the feeling of puzzlement which he himself experienced in much Christian

---

[1] See Thomas V. Morris, 'A Response to the Problem of Evil', *Philosophia* xiv (1984), pp. 173–85.
[2] Shusaku Endo, *The Samurai*, tr. Van C. Gessel (London, 1982), p.173.

teaching.[3] Before, however, I say more about such puzzlement and lack of understanding, I need to say more about the terminology being used.

We have, it seems, three central concepts: 'salvation', 'redemption', and 'atonement', surrounded by an array of other concepts like 'sacrifice', 'healing', 'liberation', 'deliverance', 'forgiveness', 'reconciliation', and 'sanctification'. This language can be used on many different levels. One can literally be 'saved' from drowning or 'redeemed' from slavery, and the religious use of these terms is related to such literal uses. In many cases the religious uses are metaphorical: 'redemption' is a metaphor deriving from, for example, ancient slave-markets.[4] As time went on, the terms became almost technical theological ones: people came to speak of *the* Redemption (often regarded as including the Incarnation, Cross, and Resurrection), or *our* salvation; and 'Redeemer' and 'Saviour' became titles of Christ, closely related to claims for his divinity (of which his saving power was taken as evidence). Also, later, wider uses arose, in ordinary language, poetry, and various specialized fields of discourse. Thus we can 'redeem' debentures on the stock market; and we say things like 'the candidate redeemed her earlier poor performance in the examination by her good answer to the last question', or 'going

[3] See Jean Higgins, 'The Inner Agon of Shusaku Endo', *Cross Currents* xxxiv (Winter 1984–85), pp. 414–26.

[4] Such a metaphor is what Trevor Hart calls a 'metaphor of release'. He finds two other kinds of soteriological metaphor, those of transformation and of new access to God, and thinks that the multiplicity of such metaphors mirrors the different facets of God's saving action. See his 'Redemption and Fall', in Colin Gunton (ed.), *The Cambridge Companion to Christian Doctrine* (Cambridge, 1997), pp. 189–206.

Many other writers have pointed to the variety of soteriological models and metaphors, e.g. Karl Barth, who found four kinds of imagery in the New Testament: forensic, financial, cultic, and military. See his *Church Dogmatics* vol.iv, part 1 *The Doctrine of Reconciliation*, tr. G.W. Bromiley (Edinburgh, 1956), pp. 273–83. Ian Ramsey, in his *Christian Discourse* (London, 1965), pp. 28–60, argued that heresies arise when one model is 'ridden to death'. See also again Colin E. Gunton, *The Actuality of Atonement*.

abroad at that particular juncture of my life was my salvation'. The phrase 'redeeming the situation' has become a common way of describing the taking of vigorous measures to remedy a misfortune, thereby bringing good out of evil. These different kinds of language are often combined, especially in poetry. George Herbert's poem 'Redemption' starts off with a literal use, from renting houses:

> Having been tenant long to a rich Lord,
> Not thriving, I resolved to be bold,
> And make a suit unto him, to afford
> A new small-rented lease, and cancel th'old.

It then goes on to a figurative use, with reference to the Cross.

Salvation

I think that the three central concepts that I have singled out are like a series of Chinese boxes fitting into one another, with 'salvation', the most general concept, as the outermost box. This relationship is illustrated in the common claim, made by many Christians, that they are saved because Christ has redeemed them on the Cross, shedding his blood to atone for human sin.

Because of its generality, the notion of 'being saved' is often obscure, even to religious believers, and within Christianity it has varying connotations in different traditions. Writing in 1956, George Caird told the story of a former Bishop of Durham, who, when accosted by someone who asked him if he was saved, replied, 'That depends on whether you mean *sōtheis*, *sōzomenos*, or *sesōsmenos*. If you mean *sōtheis*, undoubtedly; if you mean *sōzomenos*, I trust so; if you mean *sesōsmenos*, certainly not.'[5] In his reply the bishop was contrasting a participle in the Greek aorist tense,

[5] George Caird, *Principalities and Powers: A Study in Pauline Theology* (Oxford, 1956), p. 80.

which denotes a single act in the past, with a present participle, denoting a ongoing process of salvation, and with a perfect participle, denoting a final consummation. Caird comments, 'Salvation in the New Testament is always a past fact, a present experience, and a future hope ...'[6]

One should also note that, as a matter of logic, if people are saved, they are saved *from* something, *for* or *to* something, usually *by* someone. This consideration also applies to concepts like 'redemption' and 'liberation' (but whereas Westerners, perhaps influenced by Liberation Theology, might construe the latter in terms of being freed from poverty, injustice, and oppression, Buddhists might be more concerned with liberation from illusion, craving, and suffering, to be brought about through spiritual discipline).

Often these relations are not made explicit, so that 'salvation' and so on are used as short-hand terms, both in the Bible and in later theology. When Peter exclaimed 'Lord, save me' (Matt. 14.31), he meant 'save me from drowning'; the modern reader, however, will probably read a deeper significance into his cry, in the light of later Biblical usage and Christian tradition, e.g. St Paul's claim that through Christ we are saved from God's anger, reconciled with Him, and thereby saved from sin, death, and the Law (Rom. 5.9–21). But, again, we must not forget that 'to save' and 'salvation' are ordinary words and that they are used widely in the New Testament, e.g. of being saved from captivity, death, disease, and possession by demons,[7] and used elsewhere of good health, well-being, and safety on journeys. Some of the Greek gods, including Asclepius, the god of medicine, were called 'saviour', as was the philosopher, Epicurus. Plato writes of the 'salvation' of a philosopher, if he remains free from the opinions of the mob (*Republic* 494a).

---

[6] Ibid., p. 81.
[7] See Gerhard Kittel, *Theological Dictionary of the New Testament*, vol.vii, tr. G.W. Bromiley (Grand Rapids, 1971), pp. 965–1024, on *sōzo, sōtēria*, and related terms.

Both the positive and the negative connotations of 'salvation' (as of cognate terms like 'redemption' and 'liberation') presuppose certain judgements about what one is saved *from* and *for*. The positive connotations have come to be narrowed down in much Christian theology, especially to obedience to God, forgiveness, new life through the Holy Spirit, and life everlasting.[8] Hence we have lost the connotations of good health and flourishing which the ancient terms often had. It is worth remembering that many of the early Christian Fathers referred to Christ as a 'physician',[9] a usage recalled by Newman in the passage quoted from *The Grammar of Assent* in Chapter 1. Similarly, St Ignatius of Antioch described the Eucharist as the 'medicine of immortality, the antidote against death'.[10] Yet if a church today were called 'Christ the Physician', it would be regarded as strange, despite our familiarity with the Gospel accounts of the miracles of healing.

In Eastern Orthodox theology the connection is also stressed between salvation and *theōsis* (divinization – a term derived, in Christian theology, from 2 Pet.1.4, which describes Christians as coming to share in the divine nature). John Meyendorff notes this connection when he says that, for patristic thought,

> salvation implies communion with God for the human nature, and its transfiguration, and exaltation at the level of

---

[8] John McIntyre, *The Shape of Soteriology,* pp. 33f. Dietrich Bonhoeffer noted the tendency to equate Christian salvation with release from this world, in his letter of 27th June, 1944: see his *Letters and Papers from Prison,* ed. E. Bethge (Fontana edn., London, 1959), p. 112.

[9] E.g. St Augustine, *Sermon* 87:13, in Migne, *Patrologia Latina* (abbreviated henceforth as *P. L.*), 38:537, and *Sermon* 88:1 (*P. L.* 38:539). Cf. also St John of Damascus, *De Imaginibus* iii.9, in Migne *Patrologia Graeca* (abbreviated henceforth as *P. G.*) 94:1332D, for the joining of human and divine in Christ as a 'medicine'.

[10] Ignatius, *Letter to the Ephesians* xx.2; earlier on he too had described Christ as 'physician' (vii.2). Cf. Exod. 15.26 for the idea of God healing the Israelites.

uncreated divine life ... by making divine his own human
nature, Christ opened salvation by deification to all ... [11]

Orthodox theologians sometimes accuse Western theologians,
both Catholic and Protestant, of having an impoverished soteriology, too much concerned with human guilt and atonement
(often expressed in juridical categories), and with personal
salvation through Christ's death (more than his life and
Resurrection), and too little concerned with the healing of human
nature, with cosmic regeneration or transfiguration, and with
the role of the Holy Spirit. They themselves emphasize
the destruction of death and the inauguration of a new creation,
with possibilities of transfiguration here and now. Thus
Meyendorff brings out the positive connotations of redemption
when he says, 'Redemption is not only a negative remission of sins
but also and primarily a new freedom for children of God in the
communion of the new Adam.'[12]

Some recent Western theologians have tried to offset the
tendency to stress the individual's guilt and final destiny, and to
restore the resonance of the term 'salvation' by emphasising its
positive aspect, of restoration to wholeness. Paul Tillich, for
example, said that 'it is the Christ who brings the New Being, who
saves men from the old being, that is from existential
estrangement and its self-destructive consequences'.[13] He also
alludes to a traditional image, of Christ as victorious over the
powers of evil: 'Without the experience of the conquest of
existential estrangement, the *Christus Victor* never could have

[11] John Meyendorff, *Christ in Eastern Christian Thought* (New York, 1975),
pp. 170–1. Cf. H.E.W. Turner, *The Patristic Doctrine of Redemption*, pp. 95, 121.

[12] John Meyendorff, 'New Life in Christ: Salvation in Orthodox Theology',
Theological Studies 1 (1989), pp. 481–99, at p. 499. Among Orthodox writers, see
also Georges Florovsky, *Creation and Redemption* (Belmont, MA, 1976), p. 103;
Vladimir Lossky, *In the Image and Likeness of God* (London, 1974), ch.5, esp. pp.
103–10 on the role of the Holy Spirit in *theōsis*; and Philip Sherrard, *The Sacred
in Life and Art* (Ipswich, 1990), ch.7, esp. pp. 104–6.

[13] Paul Tillich, *Systematic Theology*, vol.ii (London, 1957), p. 174.

arisen.'[14] Salvation, for Tillich, is to be understood in terms of the 'healing and saving power of the New Being in all history', and our participation in this power.[15]

Tillich's language is reminiscent of existential psychiatry. Other theologians, however, look more to politics. In Liberation Theology (which Gabriel Daly describes as having helped to produce a 'cultural rejuvenation of soteriology'[16] in our time) human wholeness and God's saving power are seen partly in terms of the overcoming of political and economic oppression, injustice, and poverty. Gustavo Gutiérrez, for instance, points to the ways in which terms like 'salvation' have been wrongly spiritualized, so that they are taken to refer only to an inner spiritual realm or to life after death.[17] He does not deny that Christian liberation must involve liberation from sin (which, for him, has a collective dimension), for he sees such liberation as at the root of political liberation,[18] and he sees political and economic liberation as only one aspect of Christian liberation (which is, in any case, as we shall see, a Biblical category). His attack on the spiritualizing of terms like 'salvation' was to some extent anticipated already by St Irenaeus, who argued that our bodies too must partake of salvation, for they are temples of the Holy Spirit and members of the Body of Christ.[19] Another, more recent, theological emphasis (consonant with the Orthodox stress on the regeneration

---

[14] Ibid., p. 198.

[15] Ibid., p. 193. 'New Being' is Tillich's term for the salvation revealed in Christ, overcoming the gap between essence and existence; cf. pp. 136–7.

[16] Gabriel Daly, *Creation and Redemption* (Delaware, 1989), p. 189.

[17] Gustavo Gutiérrez, *A Theology of Liberation*, 2nd edn., tr. C. Inda and J. Eagleson (London, 1988), pp. 83–91.

[18] Ibid., pp. 100–3, 149. See also Jon Sobrino, *Jesus the Liberator: A Historical-Theological Reading of Jesus of Nazareth*, tr. P. Burns and F. McDonagh (London, 1993), pp. 18, 222, for a similar critique of the narrowing of much Western soteriology. Sobrino argues that Jesus came to bring freedom from a variety of evils, moral, physical, and social.

[19] Irenaeus, *Adversus Haereses* (abbreviated henceforth as *Adv. Haer.*) v.6.2, alluding to 1 Cor. 3.16*f*, 6.13*ff*; cf. also *Adv. Haer.* v.2.2–3.

of the cosmos), which I shall discuss later, is the concern with ecology, with rescuing or saving our environment.

Redemption

The three-fold analysis which I have suggested as appropriate to 'salvation' also applies to 'redemption'. H.E.W. Turner says, 'We are not only redeemed *from* something, we are also redeemed *into* something ... we are also made "partakers of the Divine Nature".'[20] He might also have added '*by* someone' (perhaps at the cost of something.[21]) Sometimes some of these theological connections are made explicit, e.g. in Ps. 130.8, where God is said to redeem Israel from iniquity, and sometimes not; and different theologies often tend to emphasize one of the connections more than the others, e.g. the costliness of redemption.

The term 'redemption' embodies the metaphor of getting or buying back, and it is used to translate a number of different Hebrew and Greek terms in translations of the Bible.[22] One such term is *ga'al*, which denotes especially the duty of a kinsman to ransom his relatives from slavery or debt (e.g. in Ruth 4.1–11). The kinsman doing this would be a *go'el* (redeemer); hence the term had often a family connotation (cf. Lev. 25.48f.). It is used of God, in virtue of His covenant with Israel and his loving-kindness (e.g. in Isa. 43.14, 44.24). The verb *pada* also means to ransom or redeem: it is used of God's rescuing Israel from slavery in Egypt (Deut. 7.8) and later from exile (Jer. 31.11).

[20] H.E.W. Turner, *The Patristic Doctrine of Redemption*, p. 117.
[21] I think that it would be pushing the metaphor too far to ask who demands or receives the price. One might ask, however, what it is about the redeemer that enables him to perform the function – one slave cannot usually redeem another if they are both in chains.
[22] See H. Wheeler Robinson, *Redemption and Revelation: In the Actuality of History* (London, 1942), ch.xii; and Edward Schillebeeckx, *Christ: The Experience of Jesus as Lord*, tr. J. Bowden (London, 1980), pp. 477–514.

The idea of ransom from slavery would have been a familiar one in ancient Greece and Rome as well as in Israel, so it is not surprising that the metaphor of redemption was widely used in the New Testament (most commonly expressed by the Greek word *apolutrōsis*,[23] though other terms were also used). St Paul describes Jesus as having redeemed us by his death (e.g. in Rom. 3.24f., Eph. 1.7), and as having 'bought' us from the curse of the Law (Gal. 3.13; cf. 1 Cor. 6.20). More widely, he writes of our being 'freed', *from* e.g. the slavery of sin (Rom. 6.18), slavery to corruption (Rom. 8.21), and the law of sin and death (Rom. 8.2), *to* enjoy glory as the children of God (Rom. 8.21; cf. Gal. 4.5 for our being adopted as sons).

Unlike 'salvation', 'redemption' is a metaphor, potentially, I think, a very powerful one – which is why I have chosen it as the leading *motif* of this study. Unfortunately, it has become a dead metaphor for many people, one which fails to convey to them the ideas of freeing, reclaiming, restoring, or healing, largely perhaps because it has become almost a technical term in theology: a street evangelist who asked people whether they were redeemed would probably evoke the same puzzled response as one who asked about their salvation. The cognate English term 'ransom', however, usually used to translate *lutron* in Mark 10.45 ('to give his life as a ransom for many') has, I think, kept more of its resonance.

Atonement and Sacrifice

In Christian theology the Redemption is connected closely with the Incarnation, Cross, and Resurrection; but I think that there is an especially close relationship with our third central concept, that of 'atonement': for we are said to be redeemed from sin and

---

[23] See Gerhard Kittel, *Theological Dictionary of the New Testament*, vol.iv (Grand Rapids, 1967), pp. 328–56, on *luō* and related terms. *Apolutrōsis* came to be used to denote liberation in a more general sense.

death *by* Christ, *at the cost of* his suffering and death, which atoned for or expiated our sins.

In English the terms 'atone' and 'atonement' have a double meaning. As I remarked in the last chapter, the noun 'atonement' meant originally 'at-one-ment', i.e, being at one with or reconciled, and the verb 'to atone', a later formation than the noun, was originally used to mean 'to set at one', i.e. to reconcile (e.g. in Shakespeare, *Richard II*, I.i.202). As time went on, they took on the sense of expiation, because a reconciliation often requires one party to make up for an offence given to the other. Thus the terms are used often to translate words from the Hebrew root *kpr* (which means literally 'wiping away' or 'covering'), used of sacrifices and scapegoats which 'atone for' or 'expiate' sins and thereby bring forgiveness (see Leviticus, especially chapter 16); and also, in the New Testament, to translate *katallagē* (though modern translations prefer 'reconciliation' here, for the Greek term was used often of healing breaches between friends, and St Paul says Christ 'made peace' on the Cross, in Eph. 2.15*f* and Col. 1.20) and *hilaskesthai* and its related terms (used of Christ's death in Heb. 2.17 and Rom. 3.25). In other modern languages the equivalent terms do not always have quite the religious connotations that the English terms 'atone' and 'atonement' have acquired; for instance, the German *versöhnen* and *Versöhnung*, which have a more common meaning in ordinary language.

The idea of atoning for, in the sense of expiating, others' sins is not restricted to Christianity; for, originating in the cultic sacrifices instituted in Leviticus, it continued in later Judaism. The Suffering Servant of Isaiah expiates the sins of others (Isa. 53.4–12); and the Maccabean martyrs were regarded as having given their lives in atonement (2 Macc. 7.32, 37*f*; 4 Macc. 1.11, 6.28*f*., 17.21*f*., 18.4) – hence later on martyrdom came to be closely associated with sacrifice and atonement, both in Judaism and Christianity.[24]

---

[24] See Frances M.Young, *Sacrifice and the Death of Christ* (London, 1975), pp. 35–6, 56–7; and Martin Hengel, *The Atonement*, ch.1, supplemented by further evidence in John O'Neill's review of that book in *Theology*, lxxxiv (1981), pp. 464–5.

In later Judaism the testing and purifying nature of any
suffering was stressed, and also its atoning role for oneself and for
others. The Babylonian Talmud said, 'He who joyfully bears the
chastisements that befall him brings salvation to the world . . .',[25]
whilst in the *Zohar* we read the words of the rabbi Shim'on
(second century CE):

When the righteous are seized by disease or affliction, it is in
order to atone for the world. Thus all the sins of the generation are atoned for. When the Blessed Holy One wants to
bring healing to the world, he strikes one righteous human
among them with disease and affliction; through him He
brings healing to all.[26]

The idea of atonement is linked closely to those of expiation or
propitiation, and also, in both Jewish and Christian tradition, to
that of sacrifice (which of course is found in many other
traditions, often without the idea of atonement). The notion of
sacrifice involves renouncing or surrendering something, and
offering it up as a gift to a god or a spiritual power, to make it holy

---

Hengel also gives parallel examples from ancient Greece, while Young illustrates
the idea from Nikos Kazantzakis' novel *Christ Recrucified* (pp. 128–31; cf. pp.
13–15 for her analysis of ideas of sacrifice in two other modern novels, John
Steinbeck's *To a God Unknown* and William Golding's *Lord of the Flies*.

Jon Sobrino writes, with reference to Christians murdered in El Salvador, of
martyrs healing wounds, in his *The Spirituality of Liberation*, tr. R.R. Barr
(Maryknoll, NY, 1988), p. 155.

[25] Ta'anith 8a, in I. Epstein (ed.), *Babylonian Talmud*, vol.iv (London, 1938), pp.
33–4.

[26] *Zohar* 3: 218a, quoted in D.C. Matt (tr.), *Zohar: The Book of Enlightenment* (New
York, 1983), p. 19; cf. p. 196, n.50. Irving Greenberg notes (in the context of a
discussion of the use of the model of the Suffering Servant in post-Holocaust
Jewish theology) that the concept of vicarious suffering is one of the great
themes in the High Holy Day liturgy. See his 'Cloud of Smoke, Pillar of Fire:
Judaism, Christianity and Modernity after the Holocaust', in Eva Fleischner
(ed.), *Auschwitz: Beginning of a New Era? Reflections on the Holocaust* (New York, 1977),
p. 36.

(*sacrum facere*). The purpose of the offering (often of an animal, whose blood is shed) could include propitiating an angry god, off-loading the sins of a community onto a victim who somehow takes them away when put to death (as likewise a scapegoat might, when driven away), or offering praise and thanksgiving, e.g. at a harvest festival. In Judaism there were sacrifices confirming the covenant between God and Israel, commemorations of Passover, thanksgivings at harvest-time, individual sin-offerings, collective offerings at the Day of Atonement whereby the people's sins were 'covered over' or blotted out, and sacrifices of praise and thanks-giving. As time went on, there was a move away from ritual slaughter to a more 'interiorized' understanding, in terms of renunciation, asceticism, and acts of compassion and charity, in many of the prophets and in the Penitential Psalm:

> For thou hast no delight in sacrifice;
> were I to give a burnt offering, thou wouldst
> not be pleased.
> The sacrifice acceptable to God is a broken
> spirit. (Ps. 51.16*f*)[27]

In our culture the practice is unfamiliar, though we still use the term 'sacrifice' of people giving up their lives for their country in war (which is not wholly alien to the original meaning), or else metaphorically (for many people a dead metaphor); and we admire the voluntary self-giving of people like Martin Luther King and Gandhi. But the practice, or the recent memory of it, was familiar enough in a Jewish milieu when the New Testament was written, and it was against this background that some of it

---

[27] Cf. Frances M. Young, *Sacrifice and the Death of Christ*, pp. 25–9, 32-5, and Ian Bradley, *The Power of Sacrifice*, pp. 55, 86–98, 244–5. Bradley sees such a development as having occurred in some other religions. He calls for a restoration today of the wider idea of sacrifice (which he calls 'the grand law of the universe'), understood as a surrender and dedication to God and our neighbour, reflecting God's own sacrifice, not just in the Incarnation and on the Cross, but in His continuous activity in creation.

(though not the Gospels) interpreted Jesus' death as a Passover sacrifice (1 Cor. 5.7) or as a sacrifice for sin, e.g. Heb. 7.27, 9.14–28, 10.10–12, as one model among others; and this model assumed a central role in much of later Christian tradition.

The victim of an atoning sacrifice, or the scapegoat driven out into the wilderness, was regarded by the Jews as suffering its fate *for* the people, expiating their sins; and Christ is said by Christians to have died *for* all. Now the word '*for*' here can be construed as 'instead of', i.e. as a substitute for, rather in the way that Abraham sacrificed a ram in place of Isaac (Gen. 22.13), or that a *go'el* might make a compensatory payment for someone who had got into difficulties (Lev. 25.47–9). Here we have the root of the theory of penal substitution (found e.g. in Calvin), which interprets Christ's death in terms of his accepting vicarious punishment for us. But '*for*' can also be construed as 'representing': John McIntyre makes this distinction, giving the analogy of an international soccer-player, who represents his country but is very different from the substitute waiting by the pitch.[28] Many modern writers prefer to see Christ on the Cross as our representative. Walter Kasper, for example, writes of Christ dying for us, as representing us, and he relates the idea of representation to that of the solidarity of the whole human race. He explains the distinction in question thus:

> The substitute renders the person replaced superfluous, whereas the representative gives him scope, keeps his place open and vacates the place again. Representation therefore takes nothing away from the other: on the contrary, it alone makes possible the other's freedom.[29]

[28] John McIntyre, *The Shape of Soteriology*, pp. 99f.
[29] Walter Kasper, *Jesus the Christ*, tr. V. Green (London, 1976), p. 222. St Thomas Aquinas saw the Church, the Mystical Body of Christ, as *quasi* one person, which has been redeemed by its head, Christ (*Summa Theologiae*, Pt.3, q.49, art.1).

Kasper describes this freedom as 'liberating us for discipleship in the obedience of faith and for the service of love'.[30] He sees Christ as having established a new human solidarity, enabling us to restore a disfigured and out-of-joint world (this restoration is required of us, as a matter of justice, since it is we who have destroyed the order of the world). Such an account, however, still requires us to explain how Christ's death has benefited those for whom it was offered.

The idea of representing one's country, mentioned by McIntyre with reference to sport, has a more obvious context in the case of war: soldiers fight *for* their countries, and there is also the question of collective guilt and responsibility. The latter question troubled many members of the German opposition to Hitler, and they found some comfort in the idea that their work and their deaths might to some extent atone for or redeem their country's crimes. One of them, Major-General Henning von Tresckow, wrote in 1943,

> Just as God once promised Abraham he would not destroy Sodom if but ten righteous people could be found there, so I hope that God will not annihilate Germany for our sakes.[31]

The example of Abraham pleading with God (Gen. 18.23–32), to which von Tresckow alludes, was probably the source of the later Jewish tradition that there is a certain number of just people (*saddiqim*) in the human race (maybe unknown, and not necessarily Jews), whose merits keep the world from destruction. But by the time of the Babylonian Talmud the number was fixed at thirty-six, and later on they were known as 'hidden righteous'.[32]

---

[30] Ibid., p. 220. Kasper is much influenced here by the work of Dorothee Sölle.
[31] Anton Gill, *An Honorable Defeat: The Fight against National Socialism in Hitler's Germany* (London, 1994), pp. 254–5. For a discussion of the theological issues raised, see my 'Redemption, Atonement, and the German Opposition to Hitler', *Theology* xcviii (1995), pp. 431–40.
[32] '*Lamedvovniks*' in Yiddish. See Robert Murray, *The Cosmic Covenant* (London, 1992), pp. 139*ff.*

In the case of the death of Christ we are talking of one person representing all members of the human race throughout time. Here the notion of representation has travelled a long way from its more familiar contexts of sport, warfare, and parliamentary government. Hence some theologians bring in other, related, ideas, e.g. that of a corporate personality,[33] or they combine the ideas of substitution and representation, as I think Colin Gunton does when he says, 'Jesus is our substitute because he does for us what we cannot do for ourselves', and goes on, taking up the point made by Kasper and others, 'by the substitution he frees us to be ourselves'.[34]

There is also the question, which some of the literary examples that we shall look at raise, of whether later Christians can share in Christ's redemptive work: strictly speaking, Christians believe in only one mediator and redeemer, Christ, but St Paul writes of his 'making up what is lacking in the suffering of Christ' (Col. 1.24), and some later Christians, e.g. Newman,[35] have seen saints as having a representative role. Hence, as we shall see, novelists like Mauriac and Bernanos present some of their characters as 'Suffering Servants', taking on the sins of others.

Problems and Alternatives

There are other traditional concepts and images which a complete theological treatment would have to cover, for instance that of Christ as Illuminator (a neglected patristic theme revived

---

[33] H. Wheeler Robinson, *Redemption and Revelation*, pp. 257–61.

[34] Colin Gunton, *The Actuality of Atonement*, pp. 165–6. Cf. Karl Barth, *Church Dogmatics*, iv.1, pp. 230–1, 282. Barth says that Christ's sacrifice took place 'in our stead and for us' (p. 282).

[35] 'And all of us, the more keenly we feel our own distance from holy persons, the more we are drawn near to them, as if forgetting that distance, and proud of them because they are so unlike ourselves, as being specimens of what our nature may be ...' (J.H. Newman, *The Grammar of Assent*, pp. 407–8).

by Abelard), or as victorious, an idea which Tillich mentions,[36] and which was captured in much early Christian art, sometimes depicting Christ as a knight carrying the Cross as his standard and inflicting defeat on the enemy. Paul Fiddes points to the recurrence of the theme of victory over dark powers, e.g. in Tolkien's trilogy *The Lord of the Rings* and in the film *Star Wars*.[37] But it is already apparent that much of this traditional theology raises severe difficulties and problems of understanding, expressed graphically by Endo's samurai. Moreover, the examples from art and literature mentioned in the last chapter show that there are non-Christian alternatives.

If the world has indeed been saved or redeemed, why is this not more apparent (think again of Nietzsche's remark about Christians, 'they don't look redeemed')? How can one person's death have made such a supposed difference? Why should such historical particularities solve a universal human problem? If God was so offended by the sins of the human race, why would he be 'reconciled' by this single death? Did Jesus think or intend that it would do so, e.g. by acting as an atoning sacrifice? Why is Christianity the only major religion to have a developed theology of atonement? Does not our knowledge of other religions raise questions here? The notion of the sacrifice of a human being, or of an animal, as expiatory or propitiatory seems strange, if not absurd, to many people today. This is partly because the institution of sacrifice is alien to them; but also because the idea of an atoning sacrifice, at least as it was sometimes presented traditionally (e.g. in terms of propitiating an angry God) seems to be bad moral doctrine, if not sado-masochistic. Likewise with the

---

[36] The latter image is the main subject of Gustaf Aulén's, *Christus Victor: An Historical Study of the Three Main Types of the Idea of the Atonement,* tr. A.G. Herbert (London, 1931).

[37] Paul Fiddes, *Past Event and Present Salvation,* p. 112. F.W. Dillistone also mentions imaginative presentations of the idea in C.S. Lewis' and Charles Williams' work, in his *The Christian Idea of Atonement,* pp. 113–14.

philosophy of punishment implicit in some traditional treatments, such as Calvin's.[38]

One may avoid some of these difficulties by stressing rather Christ's obedience and heroism, his taking on our burdens and suffering, and his forgiveness, as many modern authors do. But this still leaves us with the problem of *how* one person can be said to have acted for the whole human race (whether as representative or as substitute), and whether and how it has become effective. Substituting talk of 'alienation', 'estrangement', 'oppression', 'wholeness', and so on for the more traditional religious language still leaves us with the question of Christ's representative role and its effectiveness. We are confronted with the problem which puzzles many Jews, of how Christians can believe that the world has indeed been redeemed. In his address 'The Two Foci of the Jewish Soul' Martin Buber said that 'to the Jew the Christian is the incomprehensibly daring man, who affirms in an unredeemed world that its redemption has been accomplished'.[39] Elsewhere he contrasted the individualism of Christian redemption, with the Jewish idea of the redemption of the nation (as a prelude to the redemption of the whole world). He saw Christianity as having forsaken the idea of the holiness of the nation and the absolute value of its task, in favour of the idea of the establishment of the kingdom of God over individual redeemed souls in the world.[40] (What Buber says represents much later Christian

---

[38] Some of these objections were already made in the nineteenth century, e.g. by John Stuart Mill. See his letter of 1840 to Robert Barclay Fox, in *Collected Works of John Stuart Mill*, vol.xiii (Toronto, 1963), pp. 452–3. For more recent criticisms of traditional theories, see Leonardo Boff, *Passion of Christ, Passion of the World*, tr. R.R. Barr (Maryknoll, NY, 1989), ch.7, and Rosemary R. Ruether, *Introducing Redemption in Christian Feminism* (Sheffield, 1998), pp. 99–105.

[39] Martin Buber, *Essays in Time of Crisis* (New York, 1963), p. 40.

[40] Martin Buber, *The Origin and Meaning of Hasidism*, tr. M. Friedman (New York, 1960), pp. 129*f*, 205*f*. For a study of three other twentieth-century Jewish thinkers, using redemption as its central theme, see Susan A. Handelman, *Fragments of Redemption: Jewish Thought and Literary Theory in Benjamin, Scholem, and Levinas* (Indiana, 1989).

teaching accurately enough, but it does not, I think, do justice to the early Christian idea that the Church is the new Israel, the new People of God – cf. 2 Pet. 2.9f.)

Faced with obvious and familiar difficulties like these, some theologians seek to restate and to defend traditional doctrines. Kasper, for example, uses modern ideas of representation and solidarity to defend an essentially Anselmian theology of the Cross and Redemption. On the other hand, his former colleague at Tübingen, Hans Küng, rejects explicitly both Anselm's account and the idea of sacrifice, and prefers to stress Christ's obedience and self-offering, his taking on the lot and curse of outcasts, his love for us, and his identifying with us, especially by standing alongside us in suffering.[41]

We find perhaps the most radical questioning by a theologian of traditional accounts of atonement and redemption in some of John Hick's work. His critique of such accounts is part of a wider attack on traditional Christology, particularly the doctrine of the Incarnation; that attack, in turn, is part of a view which seeks a 'Copernican Revolution' in the Christian understanding of other religions. For Hick, the major religions are all different perspectives on one ultimate reality, 'the Real', and the various forms of salvation, liberation, and so on that they preach are different ways of viewing the transformation of human existence from self-centredness to 'Reality-centredness'.[42] Life is 'fallen', lived in alienation from God, or caught in illusion (*maya*), or pervaded by suffering (*dukkha*); but the Ultimate, the Real, is good and gracious, and there is a way to it through faith, spiritual discipline, or submission to God: 'In each case, salvation/liberation consists in a new and limitlessly better quality of existence which comes about in the transition from self-centredness to Reality-centredness.'[43]

---

[41] Hans Küng, *On Being a Christian*, tr. E. Quinn (London, 1977), pp. 391, 419–36.

[42] John Hick, *An Interpretation of Religion* (London, 1989), p. 36.

[43] John Hick, 'On Grading Religions', *Religious Studies* xvii (1981), pp. 451–67, at p. 453. This essay is reprinted in Hick's *Problems of Religious Pluralism* (London and Basingstoke, 1985).

The substance of *Christian* salvation is constituted by our transformation 'from self-centredness to God-centredness', and its
experience is that of being 'an object of God's gratuitous
forgiveness and love, freeing the believer to love his and her
neighbour'.[44] Whether religions are 'soteriologically effective'
cannot be decided with any finality now – Hick has to appeal to
eschatological verification, i.e. to the ways in which we reach
fulfilment in a life after death – but he thinks that we have grounds
for 'cosmic optimism', and that we may see the fruits of religious
beliefs and practices here and now in the saintliness of their
adherents.[45]

Hick understands Christian atonement as 'at-one-ment' with
God now and in the life to come (he shows a lot of sympathy
with the Eastern Orthodox concept of *theōsis*), and rejects any
account of it in terms of satisfaction or expiation. In the parable
of the Prodigal Son the father forgives his son without demanding
any reparation. So all that we have to do to be forgiven is to ask
God, and to forgive others (though Hick admits that genuine
penitence requires that we make reparation to those we have
injured). We must understand the Cross in terms of Jesus' utter
self-giving, and perhaps as the martyrdom which religious leaders
and prophets risk; and for us, it may be the cause of repentance.
But Hick rejects any understanding of the Cross in terms of
sacrifice (natural though this was at the time), or of atonement in
the sense of expiating our sins.[46]

Most critics of Hick have concentrated on his view of the
relationship between world religions, and on his rejection of
the doctrine of the Incarnation. As regards soteriology, he has
been accused of glossing over differences. Paul Griffiths and
Delmas Lewis state that 'there are ... irreducible differences

---

[44] John Hick, *An Interpretation of Religion*, pp. 44, 47.
[45] John Hick, 'On Grading Religions', pp. 461*ff*; cf. his *An Interpretation of Religion*,
pp. 301, 356*ff*, 380.
[46] John Hick, 'Is the Doctrine of the Atonement a Mistake?', in Alan G. Padgett
(ed.), *Reason and the Christian Religion: Essays in Honour of Richard Swinburne* (Oxford,
1994), pp. 247–63.

between religions as to their soteriological goals'.[47] Similarly, Harold Netland says 'Hick has adopted a kind of "lowest common denominator" soteriology':[48] even if it is clear what moving from self-centredness to Reality-centredness means, surely Pauline 'justification', Hindu *moksha,* and Zen *satori* include much more than this. He asks whether Hick's soteriology is any more than common morality.[49]

I think that the answer to Netland's last question is in fact 'yes', in that Hick does have an eschatology, which he sees as closely linked with soteriology: he says that whether people are transformed to Reality-centredness is only finally verified eschatologically; he notes too that traditional Christianity presents transformation as a result of salvation rather than itself constituting salvation, for it distinguishes between Christ's atonement for our sin (or 'justification'), and our sanctification.[50] Hick himself regards the latter as the substance of salvation – hence, again, his attraction to the idea of *theōsis*.

Netland is, however, right, I think, in finding the concept of 'Reality-centredness' obscure, if not empty. Furthermore, in his Christology and in his anxiety to fit Christianity into his 'Copernican Revolution', Hick rides rough-shod over what some would regard as one of the strengths of Christianity: its concern with the historical particularity of Christ's life, work, death and

[47] Paul Griffiths and Delmas Lewis, 'On Grading Religions, Seeking Truth, and Being Nice to People: A Reply to Professor Hick', *Religious Studies* xix (1983), p. 79. R. Corliss likewise raises the question: if values differ, can they be the product of the same divine reality? Cf. his 'Redemption and Divine Realities: A Study of Hick and an Alternative', *Religious Studies* xxii (1986), pp. 235–48; see also Gavin D'Costa, 'John Hick and Religious Pluralism: Yet Another Revolution', in Harold Hewitt, Jr. (ed.), *Problems in the Philosophy of Religion* (London, 1991), pp. 3–18; and Hick's reply, ibid., pp. 24–7.

[48] Harold A. Netland, 'Professor Hick on Religious Pluralism', *Religious Studies* xxii (1986), pp. 248–61, at p. 256.

[49] Ibid., p. 257.

[50] John Hick, *An Interpretation of Religion*, p. 44.

resurrection[51] (a concern which can, and should lead people to new directions of reflection and action; writing of Liberation Theology, Paul Fiddes notes that 'a lack of interest in what Jesus was actually doing for the poor and oppressed around him leads to theories of salvation which make no contact with the real needs of those who suffer under the Pilates of today').[52]

Netland's charge of reducing soteriology to common morality, even if unfair to Hick, may be applicable elsewhere. If religious terms like 'redemption' and 'salvation' seem meaningless to people, one solution is to translate them into something else, e.g. psychological growth and healing, or political emancipation. But Gabriel Daly rightly warns against trading too much on the ambiguity of the term 'liberation', and of identifying any historical event or situation with salvation (which, he says, is eschatological[53]), and also of psychologizing concepts like 'reconciliation' and 'healing'. I would however observe that although Daly is right that 'Hope in resurrection is central to the notion of salvation',[54] the other things that he mentions may be part of a comprehensive concept of Christian salvation (as Liberation Theologians have often been careful to remark).

I think that we travel further down the road which Netland and Daly wish to avoid when we wholly secularize notions like redemption and salvation by identifying them with some worldly process. Such an identification is commonly called 'reductionism'. Few writers do in fact set out to be reductionists: the accusation is usually made by opposing thinkers who charge them with evacuating something of importance from the beliefs that they are interpreting, and the reply may always be made, 'How can you be

---

[51] Cf. Vernon White, *Atonement and Incarnation* (Cambridge, 1991), pp. 33–5; also Thomas Weinandy, 'Gnosticism and Contemporary Soteriology: Some Reflections', *New Blackfriars*, vol.76 (1995), pp. 546–54.

[52] Paul Fiddes, *Past Event and Present Salvation*, p. 38.

[53] Gabriel Daly, *Creation and Redemption*, pp. 198*ff.*

[54] Ibid., p. 203.

so certain that *you* have interpreted the belief in question correctly, and have the right to dismiss my interpretation?' But in Marxist-Leninism and Freudianism we have two examples of secular movements that have taken over some of the trappings of religious movements striving for salvation. In the former case, we have a this-worldly eschatology, involving the triumph of a favoured people (the proletariat) through certain historical movements and through the efforts of writers, revolutionaries, and other 'prophetic' figures. I recall seeing on television part of a Russian film of the silent era in which a young Communist engineer 'saves' his drought-stricken village by drilling a new well, whilst the local parish-priest is shown as praying ineffectually, surrounded by a cloud of incense. Similarly, Freudian and some other psychiatry can be seen as offering a secular version of salvation: we are saved *from* the burdens of the past and the evil powers within us, *for* a life of fulfilment, *at the cost of* self-knowledge, with the help of a therapist (who may take over some of the roles of a confessor or spiritual counsellor). Hence some of its critics warn against its quasi-religious pretensions: Ulrich Simon, for instance, says, 'Therapeutic action without the penitential basis cannot be liberating. Without a transcendent orientation it cannot succeed.'[55] But of course not all psychiatrists can be labelled as 'reductionists' or would regard themselves as rivalling religion. Jung is the most obvious counter-example, but James Hillman also dismisses the idea of a 'secularized salvation', of hoping merely for more physical life[56]; for him, patients who are seeking to solve the problems of their psyches are indeed seeking to save their souls – what tradition has called salvation or redemption.[57] Similarly, from the other side, some theologians

---

[55] Ulrich Simon, *A Theology of Auschwitz* (London, 1967), p. 148. Stanley Hauerwas alleges that 'health care has become the primary institution of salvation in liberal societies, with doctors like priests and hospitals like cathedrals'. Cf. his *Dispatches from the Front: Theological Engagements with the Secular* (Durham, NC, 1994), p. 27.

[56] James Hillman, *Suicide and the Soul* (Dallas, 1978), p. 156.

[57] Ibid., p. 170.

have, as I have suggested, regarded psychological healing as part of a wider salvation, or else they have seen it as a way of helping us to come to understand religious concepts, what Don Browning calls a 'clarifying analogy'.[58] In both cases there is often a desire, evident in much modern writing, to indicate the possibility of *experiences* of redemption here and now.

Universal Responses?

I shall not seek to respond directly now to any of the problems that I have raised, for one of the aims of this study is to see to what extent an approach through art and literature can throw light on them. Instead, I shall end this chapter by returning briefly to an issue raised in the last chapter, that of the primacy of certain human responses, and ask about the possible universality of those responses and their attendant concepts. It may be that a particular religion, or part of it (e.g. a system of sacraments) answers certain deep human needs: thus F.W. Dillistone claimed that,

> Deep human needs which had found a certain satisfaction within the experience either of Greek drama or Hebrew liturgical practice were to find an alternative opened to them through the possibility of participating in the Christian mysteries.[59]

Similarly, a concern with the theology of the Atonement may grow out of a desire to be free of evil, either within oneself or in the world around one. For theology too, I think, grows out of a certain kind of soil, i.e. particular ways of life and their conditions.

The question, however, arises now: *are there* certain deep human needs that transcend different cultures; and if so, are they

---

[58] Don Browning, *Atonement and Psychotherapy* (Philadelphia, 1966), ch.1.
[59] F.W. Dillistone, *The Christian Understanding of Atonement*, p. 141.

reflected in art and literature? Is the desire to expiate guilt universal? Or should we subsume it under some wider concept, e.g. purification or the restoration of a moral order? In *Crime and Punishment* Dostoevsky implicitly argues for a universal awareness that murder involves guilt and the need for expiation, and he perhaps sees Raskolnikov as unconsciously seeking his own arrest and trial. He was not seeking to illustrate a philosophical thesis, but to depict what is profound in human life (he described himself as 'a realist in the higher sense'[60]), including the responses of guilt, repentance, atonement and forgiveness. Perhaps these are part of what Wittgenstein meant by 'the natural history of human beings'.[61]

It is not difficult to find other, similar, expressions of such responses. In his *Life*, Boswell relates how Dr Johnson stood in the rain in Uttoxeter market-place, signifying his later repentance and desire to expiate his refusal, years before, of his father's request to take some books to sell at the market there[62]: a simple example of what Ulrich Simon calls (with reference to a discussion of the Yom Kippur legislation of Leviticus 16), 'the deep-seated desire of human beings to clear themselves of guilt'.[63] More profoundly, there is Orestes' need to atone for his blood-guilt and to find inner peace, as depicted in Aeschylus' *Oresteia* trilogy.

The themes of penitence and forgiveness, and their costliness, are ubiquitous in Western art and literature: one thinks, for example, of depictions of the Prodigal Son (e.g. Plate 3); and, again, of Shakespeare's *Measure for Measure*, or *The Tempest;* or, more recently, of William Golding's *Free Fall*. But is forgiving (or apologizing or requesting forgiveness) a universal human reaction? Likewise, recognizing a need to atone? If they are not so, how do people repent and discern others' repentance? In an

[60] Cf. Robert Louis Jackson, *Dialogues with Dostoevsky: The Overwhelming Questions* (Stanford, 1993), p. 14.
[61] Ludwig Wittgenstein, *Philosophical Investigations*, §§ 25, 415.
[62] *Boswell's Life of Johnson* (Oxford, 1927), ii, p. 612.
[63] Ulrich Simon, *Atonement*, p. 83.

earlier book Simon claimed that, 'The complicated ritual of
Leviticus xvi summarizes not only Jewish but the whole human
need to get rid of sin',[64] noting how the great Jewish themes of
atonement were adapted in the Epistle to the Hebrews. But what
if people do not *want* to be redeemed or forgiven, or to atone for
their misdeeds, or do not even understand what it is to want these
things; or if they look for some other form of 'liberation' or
'release'? Those who have been brought up in a Christian or a
Jewish tradition often tend to interpret another culture (e.g. that of
ancient Greece) in terms of certain concepts from their own
culture, or to find anticipations of their own religious ideas in that
culture, e.g. dying for another person out of love in Euripides'
Alcestis. They may then risk distorting certain classics if they find
them resistant to their own framework of interpretation. It is, for
instance, difficult to interpret Sophocles' *Oedipus Tyrannus* in terms
of a framework of sin, repentance, atonement, and reconciliation
(on the other hand, his later *Oedipus at Colonus* approaches closer to
this framework – hence Schiller classified it as a 'tragedy of
reconciliation', like Aeschylus' *Choephorae*).

There is, however, a difference between coming to understand
another culture, and distorting it by imposing our own ideas on it;
and, in practice, the degrees of mutual understanding may be
much greater than some people imagine. Martha Nussbaum said,
in dialogue with Richard Kearney,

> I find when I talk to people from Sri Lanka, from Africa,
> from Latin America, that the story of *Antigone* resonates
> powerfully and there is something of universal importance
> that elicits a strong response.[65]

---

[64] Ulrich Simon, *A Theology of Auschwitz*, p. 85; though compare what he says in
Atonement, p. 129, on Hinduism and Islam.
[65] Richard Kearney (ed.), *States of Mind: Dialogues with Contemporary Thinkers on the
European Mind* (Manchester, 1995), p. 124.

After all, she remarks, ancient Greek culture is as foreign to *us* as it is to these people! Yet we do not find Sophocles' play incomprehensible. Furthermore, to choose a different kind of example, we do not find Thucydides' account of the dialogue between the Athenians and the Melians, and of the subsequent massacre of the latter for failing to support the Athenian war-effort, so different from modern accounts of war-crimes.[66]

An increase in understanding may sometimes be brought about simply by the events of one's own life. Towards the end of his life, Wittgenstein wrote (with regard to religious belief):

> Life can educate one to a belief in God. And *experiences* too are what brings this about; but I don't mean visions and other forms of sense experience which show us the 'existence of this being', but, e.g., sufferings of various sorts . . . life can force this concept on us.[67]

But, more germanely to this study, an increase in understanding may be brought about through encounters with works of art, or through the reading and study of literature. Even if the responses that I have mentioned are not universal, an artist or writer may nevertheless convey some understanding of them. Thus, in another of his novels, *Wonderful Fool*, Shusaku Endo seeks to mediate the idea of a 'Suffering Servant' to contemporary Japan. We are not closed up in our own histories and cultures.

The issues of understanding that I have just raised will be with us in later chapters: for my main purpose in this study is to investigate the ways in which an understanding of soteriological ideas can be conveyed and fostered through art and literature. In particular, I shall consider the ways in which they *show* us things. My next immediate task is to outline briefly a suitable framework for our study, that of a drama.

---

[66] Thucydides, *History of the Peloponnesian War*, bk.v, chs. 84–116.
[67] Ludwig Wittgenstein, *Culture and Value*, tr. Peter Winch (Oxford, 1980), p. 86e.

CHAPTER THREE

A Drama with Three Acts

There are, I think, two natural frameworks for a discussion, from a theological perspective, of 'images of redemption'. One of them we have encountered already in the last chapter: we can consider *from what, to what,* and *by whom* we are redeemed (also, possibly, how and at what cost). The other framework, my preferred one, is that of a drama with three Acts, which are interlinked, namely salvation history, present human life, and the life to come.

The second framework is suggested especially by Hans Urs von Balthasar's analogy between God's plan of salvation and a drama, in his *Theodramatik*.[1] The central *motif* of this monumental work is the claim that the Christian revelation, like human existence, can only appear in its full stature 'if it is presented as being dramatic

---

[1] Hans Urs von Balthasar, *Theodramatik* (four volumes, Einsiedeln, 1973–83). I shall refer to the English translation, *Theo-Drama: Theological Dramatic Theory*, tr. G. Harrison (five volumes, San Francisco, 1988–98) henceforth, simply using the short title *Theo-Drama* and volume number.

At the beginning of this work, which is concerned with God's action in and upon the world, and with the world's response, von Balthasar explains that God has taken the drama of our existence, which he describes as 'the drama of salvation' (i, pp. 112, 114) and inserted it into His own quite different play, which, nonetheless, He wishes to play on our stage: 'It is a case of the play within the play: our play "plays" in his play' (i, p. 20). Thus God is the hidden director in the world's drama.

See also T.J. Gorringe, *God's Theatre* (London, 1991), esp. ch.5, 'Divine Direction', and Raymund Schwager, *Jesus in the Drama of Salvation*, tr. J.G. Williams and P. Haddon (New York, 1999), for other uses of the analogies of a drama or of God as a theatre director.

at its very core.[2] Von Balthasar understands the idea of a drama widely, for he remarks that the 'theodramatic dimension' does not have to be clothed in the form of a drama, but can as well be expressed in the form of an epic, e.g. Milton's *Paradise Lost*, or in that of a novel, e.g. Dostoevsky's *The Devils* (he also notes the similarity to 'pilgrimages' like Dante's *Divine Comedy* or Bunyan's *Pilgrim's Progress*).[3] This is a consequence of the fact that the term 'drama' can denote either a set of events and actions or a linguistic medium, like a play. (This is also true of the term 'history'.) Thus 'dramatic' events can be described in a narrative, as well as represented in a play.

I think that the latter framework, that of a drama, includes the former, hence I shall discuss it first and use it as my main framework for this study. It is also, of course, particularly germane to art and literature (and not just plays), as von Balthasar notes.[4]

The Drama of Redemption

Christianity is concerned with past, present, and future. It recounts and celebrates a sacred history (in the sense of a set of actions and events), culminating in the life, death, and resurrection of Jesus Christ; it seeks to draw out the significance of that history for the present, since its effects are still being worked out through subsequent history (for although redemption is believed to have been brought about through Christ, it has not yet been wholly manifested); and it is concerned with the life to come, which it sees as dependent on both Christ's redemptive work and

---

[2] *Theo-Drama*, i, p. 20.

[3] *Theo-Drama*, i, pp. 168–9. See Francesca Murphy, *The Comedy of Revelation: Paradise Lost and Regained in Biblical Narrative* (Edinburgh, 2000) for the dramatic character of the Bible.

[4] Strangely, the part of *Theo-Drama* which presents von Balthasar's soteriology (iv. pp. 205–423), a section of which is entitled 'Dramatic Soteriology', appeals to relatively few literary examples – those that there are are taken mostly from the works of Bernanos and Claudel.

people's present response to it. These three phases are regarded as closely connected with each other. Thus F.W. Dillistone wrote, with reference to the Fourth Gospel, that 'the drama of the ages is played out on the stage of a small province of the Roman Empire'.[5]

The three Acts are very different metaphysically: the first, salvation history, covers several past centuries, extending, traditionally, from the calling of Abraham to the coming of Christ, his death and resurrection, and the mission of the Apostles; the second includes the stories of countless individual men and women, each of whose lives constitute a drama, with, in turn, several Acts and Scenes of its own; the third transcends both the past history of the human race and our present lives. Nevertheless, again, all three Acts are seen as closely interrelated.

Judaism, too has its salvation history, and also construes human history in terms of three Acts: but the first Act centres on the Exodus from Egypt, whilst the second, our present human life, is to culminate in the coming of the Messiah. Despite their differences, however, both Judaism and Christianity are religions of redemption. Irving Greenberg remarks that both religions come to their affirmations about human fate because of certain central events in history – in one case the Exodus, in the other the life, death, and resurrection of Christ. Both religions, too, are tempted to cut loose from earthly time by relegating redemption to the realm of eternal life (my third 'Act'): 'Yet both religions ultimately have stood by the claim that redemption will be realized in actual human history.'[6] Medieval Judaism, for example, despite the temptation mentioned, 'insisted that the Messianic Kingdom of God in this world was not fulfilled by the salvation of the world to come ... Messianic expectation was not totally spiritualized.'[7]

---

[5] F.W. Dillistone, *The Christian Understanding of Atonement*, p. 138.
[6] Irving Greenberg, 'Cloud of Smoke', pp. 7–8. See George W. Stroup, *The Promise of Narrative Theology* (London, 1984), pp. 146, 234, for the same point.
[7] Greenberg, 'Cloud of Smoke', p. 24.

Greenberg suggests that, in their common stress on redemption in history, both religions have influenced the modern Western view that human liberation can and will be realized in the here and now.

Different Christian traditions tend to emphasize one Act of the drama more than the other two, and this fact is captured in the smart response of a former Bishop of Durham to the evangelist's question 'are you saved?', mentioned in the previous chapter.[8] Typically, an Evangelical Protestant might reply to the question, 'Yes, I am saved, because I believe that Jesus died for me.' On the other hand, an old-fashioned Roman Catholic might well be puzzled by it, because he or she might think of salvation in terms of going to Heaven. Others might be put out by the question for a different reason, because they are more concerned with the working out of salvation in our present history. I take it that Tillich, Liberation Theologians, and many others come into this category. (If they are concerned with *only* the present life, they may well be accused of 'reductionism'.) Pauline theology seeks to link all three Acts: because of what has happened in and through Christ, once and for all, we have a new life here and now in the Holy Spirit, different from the one we would have had otherwise, and also a new future. Paul uses metaphors like 'first fruits' and 'earnest' (*arrabōn*) to bring out the way in which the Resurrection and the coming of the Holy Spirit are a partial realization in the present of what is to come subsequently in its fullness.[9] Later, in chapter 5, I shall argue that the lines of continuity between the three Acts go backwards as well as forwards: because of what is happening now, we reassess the significance of the past, and we can envisage ways in which the full realization of what we hope for will put both the present and the past in a new perspective, enabling us to discern a new plot, as it were. This is because God's design and purposes are worked out only gradually, by stages

---

[8] George Caird, *Principalities and Powers*, pp. 80–1.
[9] E.g. in Rom. 8.23, 1 Cor.15.23, 2 Cor. 5.5, and Eph.1.13*f*.

(traditionally called, developing Paul's language in Eph.1.9*f*, the 'economy of salvation').

Like theologians, artists and writers too have their own particular interests and emphases. Handel's *Messiah* jumps from the first Act to the third: from the Jewish prophecies and their fulfilment in the birth and death of Christ, to our future glory. By contrast, what I shall call 'novels of redemption', e.g. some of the works of Dostoevsky and Mauriac, are concerned mainly with the second Act. Dante's *Divine Comedy* is in theory concerned only with the last Act; but it sees people's fates in the life to come as dependent on their lives on this earth and on their attitudes to Christ, so the poet refers back constantly to history and to individuals both of his own time and of the remote past. As Stephen Crites says,

> However deep into the bowels of hell Dante leads us, however high into heaven, it is remarkable how he and his sinners and saints keep our attention fixed on the little disk of earth, that stage on which the drama of men's struggles in time are enacted. Far from reducing the significance of this time-bound story in which we are embroiled, such visions of happiness and horror make it all the more portentous.[10]

With reference to such examples, it is worth noting that different genres are more suited to different Acts (though obviously a variety of factors influences the emergence and use of these genres, e.g. people's preference for words or visual images, both collectively in different eras and individually. Historically, people have tended to think of Catholicism as having a preference for images, and Protestantism for words.) Classical Italian and Flemish painters took their subjects, when dealing with Christian themes, mainly from the birth, life, death, and resurrection of Christ, though sometimes they took subjects from the Old

---

[10] Stephen Crites, 'The Narrative Quality of Experience', *Journal of the American Academy of Religion*, vol.39 (1971), pp. 291–311, at pp. 306–7.

Testament, ranging back as far as the Garden of Eden. Novelists and dramatists usually deal with the second Act of the drama, since they write about their own times or about some earlier historical period, more commonly about the former. (Thomas Mann's tetralogy, *Joseph and his Brethren*, and, more recently, Dan Jacobson's *The Rape of Tamar*, are unusual in being novels dealing with Biblical characters. In his *The Shadow of the Galilean*, the New Testament scholar Gerd Theissen uses the genre of the novel to trace Jesus' reasons for not being a Zealot.) Poets have more freedom: compare Milton's *Paradise Lost*, T.S. Eliot's *Four Quartets*, and John Henry Newman's *The Dream of Gerontius*. With regard to the last of these, however, it should be said that eschatology is, as we shall see, a difficult and dangerous area. Of course, the Last Judgement, Heaven, and Hell were common themes in medieval and Renaissance art, but artists and writers who attempt to depict such things will find it difficult to avoid the two extremes of fantasy and banality. Perhaps music is more successful here: I think that Elgar's oratorio *The Dream of Gerontius* is a great improvement on Newman's original poem, as an attempt to convey the significance of death and the ultimate fate of the soul.

Few artists and writers attempt to convey all three Acts of the drama of redemption – perhaps Dante does so implicitly. In this study I shall mainly discuss the work of those who deal with the second Act, the working out of redemption in the present, that is, artists and writers who are concerned with human lives and relationships, and with the possibilities of change in them. Plays and narratives like novels enable us to see the nature of choices and actions, and their consequences for good or evil. The former genre is ideally suited to showing us certain human actions, responses, and interactions, such as forgiveness and reconciliation. On the other hand, narratives like novels and biographies are better suited to capturing the lengthy working out of the process of redemption in a person's life: it takes a long time for people to be truly liberated and healed, and often, it seems, the process is merely begun here on earth. But narratives may capture something of the earthly phase of this process – and its cost.

The links between the three Acts are manifold, both in terms of what happens in reality, and in how people experience and reflect on events. Religious believers trust that God's action is working through all three Acts, as He achieves his purposes. More specifically, they see human life in terms of the workings of divine grace. In one of his essays, Mauriac wrote:

> If there is a reason for the existence of the novelist on earth it is this: to show the element which holds out against God in the highest and noblest characters – the innermost evils and dissimulations; and also to light up the secret sources of sanctity in creatures who seem to us fallen.[11]

More specifically still, there are the many ways in which God's grace is believed to be shown: for instance, in repentance, in the healing of broken lives and relationships, in the cleansing of hearts which leads people to see things aright, and in unexpected forbearance, forgiveness, or generosity.

Divine action may or may not be discerned by those involved: God can act in hidden ways. When people think that they have perceived God's purposes and His actions of grace or providence, they often, as it were, discern a new plot or story in their lives. St Augustine's *Confessions* is an obvious example of such a retro-spective interpretation of a life. Crites also instances the way in which early Christian preachers, in their *kerygma*, offered people a new story.[12] Historical understanding, in any case, often involves

[11] François Mauriac, *God and Mammon* (London, 1936), p. 79.

[12] Crites, 'The Narrative Quality of Experience', p. 307. He cites the Introduction to St Clement of Alexandria, *Protreptikos*, as an example.

Stanley Hauerwas argues, too, that 'the past, no less than the future, must remain open to renarration', in 'Murdochian Muddles', in Maria Antonaccio and William Schweiker (eds.), *Iris Murdoch and the Search for Human Goodness* (Chicago, 1996), pp. 205–6. He is contrasting Christian belief in God's continuous working out His purposes in the providential care of creation with Iris Murdoch's apparent acceptance of the pointlessness of things.

finding a new narrative, analogous to a story, into which events fit, embodying a pattern of understanding and explanation.

In the order of knowledge, memory and anticipation (through hope or expectation) are the main links between the three Acts of the drama, and also between events within them. Any intelligent conscious subject will have a sense of temporality: as Crites remarks, without memory, experience has no coherence,[13] the present is the critical point between a fixed past and a future still to be resolved. But besides individual memories, there are also the memories of a community, transmitted through its traditions. In Judaism the story of the liberation from Egypt (which many later Christian writers saw as prefiguring redemption through Christ) is re-enacted in the Passover liturgy each year. In general its liturgy is an important vehicle for a religious community to 'make present' its memories, and also to anticipate what is to come.[14] A particular recent manifestation of this 'making present' is seen in the way in which some Liberation Theologians appeal to the concept of a 'dangerous memory'. It was J.B. Metz who, I think, coined this phrase. Just as, at the individual level, there are memories in which earlier experiences break through to the centre-point of our lives, revealing new and dangerous insights for the present, so, says Metz, political theology expresses Christian tradition in the modern world as a 'dangerous memory'. Metz also writes of Christian faith as a 'subversive memory', from which the Church must draw strength to criticize all totalitarian systems of government and ideologies offering only a limited emancipation.[15] Some Liberation Theologians see similar dangerous and subversive memories as having been created by those who later emulate Christ's death in martyrdom, like Archbishop Oscar Romero of San Salvador, killed in 1980 while

[13] Crites, 'The Narrative Quality of Experience', p. 298; he emphasizes the importance of St Augustine's *Confessions* here, esp. Bks.x–xi.
[14] J.S. Whale, *Victor and Victim*, pp. 146–7. Obviously the symbolism expressed in much liturgy plays an important role here.
[15] Johann Baptist Metz, *Faith in History and Society: Toward a Practical Fundamental Theology*, tr. D. Smith (London, 1980), pp. 109, 89–90.

saying Mass, and others killed in El Salvador about the same time.[16] This assumption raises, in turn, the questions of whether such deaths can be regarded as in some sense redemptive, if they inspire people to resist oppression and injustice; and of whether there is something like the 'butterfly effect' (whereby events can have effects in remotely distant places, e.g. if the flap of a butterfly's wings in Beijing could have climatic effects in New York), in the moral realm.[17]

Redemption from, to, by

If we see the process of Redemption in terms of three Acts (of which the second one, present human life, can be seen in terms of several phases or Scenes), then this framework will include the idea that we are redeemed *from* what is past, either in our own lives or somewhere in the history of the human race, *for* a new present and future in this world, and *for* the life to come, *by* the work of Christ. Hence, as I have suggested, one framework includes the other.

In his *Two Concepts of Liberty* Sir Isaiah Berlin distinguished between 'negative' and 'positive' freedom, between thinkers who see freedom mainly in terms of freedom *from* something (e.g. coercion) and those who envisage it more in terms of choice, self-realization, and so on.[18] This thought might be applied to many soteriological concepts, and indeed has been. Thus, discussing the Eastern Christian concept of *theōsis*, H.E.W. Turner says, 'We are saved not merely from something but also into something; not

---

[16] See again Jon Sobrino, *The Spirituality of Liberation*, pp. 153–6.

[17] A thought suggested by von Balthasar, though without using the phrase 'butterfly effect', in *Theo-Drama* iv, pp. 413*ff*, with reference to Bloy, Bernanos, and Claudel, and the doctrine of the Communion of Saints.

[18] Isaiah Berlin, *Two Concepts of Liberty* (Oxford, 1958). Schubert Ogden finds both kinds of freedom mentioned by St Paul: he cites Gal. 5.1 and 2 Cor. 3.17, and also mentions Luther's treatise *The Freedom of a Christian*. See Ogden's *Faith and Reason: Towards a Theology of Liberation* (Belfast and Ottawa, 1979), pp. 57–8.

merely from defeat but into life abundant.'[19] In the case of soteriology, what we are saved or freed *to* includes eschatological considerations, which do not come up in Berlin's analysis. Also, there is a third term to consider in soteriology: *by* what or whom are we saved, how and at what cost?

I think that this threefold framework covers many of the traditional soteriological concepts, e.g. liberation, victory over evil powers, salvation, and redemption. The means or cost would include concepts like sacrifice, expiation, and satisfaction. It remains for me to say a little more about the variety of things from and to which one may be redeemed. Matthew Fox reports that someone remarked to him at a conference, 'I have always wondered what I was being redeemed from. But I was afraid to ask.'[20]

Obviously we must be redeemed from something which is viewed as evil. Now this presupposes that we regard certain things as such, and that we think that we can be freed from them; hence Kenneth Surin calls for a 'phenomenology' of evil as a prelude to soteriology.[21] Modern literature can provide such a phenomenology, from the atmosphere of alienation and isolation, caught by Kafka or T.S. Eliot, or the 'triple bondage' (to solitude, unfulfilled love, and fate) experienced by many of Mauriac's characters,[22] to the horrors of concentration camps, in William Styron's *Sophie's Choice* or Heinrich Böll's *And where were you, Adam?* Thereby it increases our sense of evil, and perhaps our understanding of it. As to whether it contributes also to our understanding of possibilities of redemption, well, that is the subject of this study.

Traditional soteriology has tended to stress our redemption from sin (John 8.34–6), death (cf. 1 Cor. 15.54*ff*, Rev. 20.14), and,

---

[19] H.E.W. Turner, *The Patristic Doctrine of Redemption*, p. 121.
[20] Matthew Fox, *Original Blessing*, p. 51.
[21] Kenneth Surin, *Turnings of Darkness and Light* (Cambridge, 1989), pp. 143–4.
[22] Philip Stratford, *Faith and Fiction: Creative Process in Greene and Mauriac* (Notre Dame, 1964), p. 153.

to a lesser extent, 'sovereignties and powers' (Col. 1.15), e.g. the evil powers symbolized by the dragon in Rev. 12, and the beast in the subsequent chapter.[23] More recent treatments have, as we saw in the last chapter, also emphasized isolation and alienation, and oppression and injustice. They have also emphasized what we are redeemed *to*, and, again, they have gone beyond the traditional list of forgiveness, new life in the Holy Spirit, and everlasting life. Thus Nathan Scott, after noting that Kafka, D.H. Lawrence, Silone, and T.S. Eliot all see modern man as isolated and estranged, and the modern world as a '"wasteland" awaiting redemption', praises the last two writers for discerning the possibilities, through Christianity, of 'restorative energies' and reconciliation.[24] (One might ask again here: reconciliation with whom or what?) Similarly, Matthew Fox says, 'where a religious tradition begins with sin and centers its energies almost exclusively around sin and redemption from sin, then sin gets distorted and indeed trivialized; salvation loses its meaning ...', and recommends creation spirituality both as a remedy for the First World's impoverishment of the soul and the Third World's impoverishment of the body.[25] Such a spirituality will, he says, correct the imbalance of what he calls 'fall/redemption spirituality', and do justice to St Paul's teaching on the New Creation.[26] Elsewhere, he says that salvation is not individualistic or private: it must be comprehensive, 'a healing of all the cosmos' pain'.[27]

A cynic might say that these recent treatments have to go in the direction that they do, because of a lack of a sense of sin in people today, and consequently a lack of penitence, and because of a

---

[23] See the whole of F.W. Dillistone, *The Christian Understanding of Atonement*, ch.III.

[24] Nathan A. Scott, *Rehearsals of Discomposure*, pp. 258, 261.

[25] Matthew Fox, *Original Blessing*, p. 118; idem, *Creation Spirituality: Liberating Gifts for the Peoples of the Earth* (San Francisco, 1991), pp. xiii–xiv. Fox also criticizes Liberation Theology for its neglect of feminist and ecological issues (*Creation Spirituality*, p. xi).

[26] Matthew Fox, *Original Blessing*, p. 255. He cites Rom. 8.29, 2 Cor. 5.17, Gal. 6.15*f*, Eph. 4.22–4, Col. 3.9–11, 2 Pet. 3.13.

[27] Matthew Fox, *The Coming of the Cosmic Christ: The Healing of Mother Earth and the Birth of a Global Renaissance* (San Francisco, 1988), p. 151.

widespread scepticism about life after death. It is true that these factors render much preaching of Pauline theology incomprehensible or unwelcome in some contemporary cultures, and that many people are often more troubled by illness, natural catastrophes, the carnage of modern warfare, genocide, and other such tragic events. Nevertheless, I do not think that the writers whom I have just mentioned are pandering to the spirit of the age by reinterpreting traditional concepts to suit modern problems. Their concern, like mine, is to restore something of the richness of Christian soteriology, and to correct the imbalance of some traditional treatments.[28]

It is now time, however, to draw out what I have said in this chapter about the Drama of Redemption, by looking at its individual Acts and at some examples of the art and literature associated with them. In the next chapter I shall look particularly at examples concerned with the climax of Act I, the life, death, and resurrection of Christ, and discuss how they can add to our religious understanding.

---

[28] Of course, there is the danger of producing a new imbalance. I think that Matthew Fox risks this in his polemics against St Augustine (his *bête noire*) and fall/redemption spirituality. I do not think that he has shown that the latter is *incompatible* with creation spirituality: it is a matter of emphasis.

CHAPTER FOUR

Act I: The Past

Salvation History

In this chapter I shall look at some works of art and literature concerned with what is often called salvation history, which for Christians covers the sequence of events starting with the call of Abraham and culminating in the life, death, and resurrection of Christ. I shall give special attention to paintings of the Cross and of the Resurrection, both because of the centrality of those events in salvation history and because of the outstanding treatment of them by painters, which probably surpasses representations in paint of the other Acts of the Drama of Redemption. I shall not seek to offer a survey of such works, but rather to discuss a few examples, to see what is implicit in them and how they further our religious understanding. The particular issues that will concern us are the moving and expressive character of such works, and the extent to which they can convey the soteriological significance of the Cross and the Resurrection.

Not surprisingly, much Christian art and literature concerned with salvation history is based on the Bible. Its first book, Genesis, provides many subjects, right from its beginning: Paradise and the Fall have been favourite subjects for artists and writers over many centuries. One thinks of numerous pictures of Adam and Eve in the Garden of Eden (and the opportunities which the subject offered for a portrayal of the nude!), and of their expulsion from the garden, e.g. Masaccio's fresco in the Brancacci Chapel in Florence; or of poems like Milton's *Paradise Lost*. Sometimes the subject is treated as the beginning of human history; at other times Adam and Eve are taken rather to represent human nature in general. The 'fallenness' of the human race is a perennial topic in literature: we are not as we could and should be, not as God intended us to be, and we constantly frustrate our best intentions and hopes, failing to realize our potentialities; yet, somehow, at the same time we belong to a better world.[1]

A related theme which has recurred in literature and theology is that of the appeal to Adam's 'happy fault' ('*O felix culpa*'). The phrase is used in the Roman liturgy for Holy Saturday, and is probably derived from an earlier Gallican liturgy (and perhaps ultimately from St Ambrose's statement that Adam's sin brought more benefit than harm for 'God knew that Adam would fall, in order that he might be redeemed by Christ. Happy ruin, which is mended so as to be better.')[2] The theme is found in Langland's *Piers Plowman*[3] and, most famously in English literature, in Milton's *Paradise Lost*, Book xii, where Adam replies to St Michael's prophecy of Christ's redemption by exclaiming at the infinite goodness of God that can turn evil to good:

> ... full of doubt I stand,
> Whether I should repent me now of sin
> By mee done and occasiond, or rejoice
> Much more, that much more good thereof shall spring,
> To God more glory, more good will to Men
> From God, and over wrauth grace shall abound.
>
>   (11.473–8)

In an interesting article Arthur Lovejoy traces the theme back both through early Christian sources and through Milton's literary

---

[1] The ancient Greek myth of the Golden Age served a similar function in some ways. Dante, however, regarded such myths as reflecting a kind of folk-memory of our original happiness and innocence in Eden (*Purgatorio* xxviii, 139–41). This view may be contrasted with the modern tendency to regard *all* such stories as myths which are true only in so far as they reveal facts about human nature (Freud regarded many of his discoveries as having been anticipated by poets).

[2] Ambrose, *In Psalm* 39.20 (Migne, *P. L.* 14:1065).

[3] B Text, *Passio* v, lines 481*ff* in A.V.C. Schmidt's edition (London, 1995).

predecessors, including the sixteenth-century French poet Du Bartas, who put quite categorically the point that but for the Fall there could have been no Incarnation and Redemption. Lovejoy finds a variation on the theme in an early fifteenth-century lyrical poem that adds the idea that without Adam's sin we would not have Mary as our heavenly queen.[4]

Such treatments raise many questions: about what the Fall was (and is), and about its effects; about whether something evil, from which good is produced, can be described as good; about God's foreknowledge and will; and about whether the Incarnation and Redemption are indeed necessarily dependent on the Fall – Duns Scotus denied that the Incarnation was so, for Christ might have come on earth anyway, as the utmost expression of God's love for the human race. There is also our particular question of how and to what extent artistic and literary treatments add to our understanding here. It would seem that they are usually more valuable in exploring and expressing aspects of the Christian mystery than in speculating about or arguing out a theological case.

Many contemporary theologians make the point that the *whole* of Christ's life should be seen as having a redemptive significance, and not just his passion and death,[5] so the Atonement should not

---

[4] Arthur O. Lovejoy, 'Milton and the Paradox of the Fortunate Fall', in his *Essays in the History of Ideas* (Baltimore, 1948), pp. 277–95. Josiah Royce explored the idea with reference to the story of Joseph and his brothers in Genesis, rather than the Cross. After laying down the principle that 'The deed of atonement shall be so wise and so rich in its efficacy, that the spiritual world, after the atoning deed, shall be better, richer, more triumphant amidst all its irrevocable tragedies, than it was before the traitor's deed was done', he claims that Joseph's atonement lay not in any 'penal satisfaction' nor just in his love and forgiveness, but in his creating good out of ill: 'Through Joseph's work all is made, in fact, better than it would have been had there been no treason at all.' See his *The Problem of Christianity* (Chicago, 1968), pp. 186, 204).

[5] Cf. Leonardo Boff, *Passion of Christ, Passion of the World*, pp. 78, 90; and Hans Urs von Balthasar, *Theo-Drama* iv, pp. 260–1, who points to St Anselm's inadequacy on this point. Of course, many of the early Christian Fathers, e.g. St Athanasius, saw the whole of Christ's life as salvific.

be separated from the sacrificial ethos of his whole life.[6] They draw our attention to things like his solidarity with the poor, the suffering, and outcasts, his miraculous healings, his forgiving sinners, and his opposition to those who laid burdens on or exploited people. This thesis seems to find some support if we look at the vast range of subjects in Christian art. I have already drawn attention to the way in which the representation of the Good Shepherd preceded that of the Cross in early Christian iconography, expressing the point made by St Irenaeus that,

> this hand of God which formed us at the beginning ... has in the last time sought us out who were lost, winning back His own, and taking up the lost sheep upon His shoulders, and with joy restoring it to the fold of life.[7]

The concern with soteriological themes extends even to representations of the birth of Christ in a stable. No doubt the popularity of this subject for painters in the Middle Ages and in the Renaissance was influenced by the promotion of the crib at Christmastide by St Francis of Assisi. But their work often still retained levels of symbolism that are unfamiliar to most people today, especially with regard to the cosmic aspects of the Gospel narratives. The presence of animals in the manger (like perhaps that of beasts at the Temptations in the desert – cf. Mark 1.12*f*) may express the Jewish belief that 'when the Messiah comes, all animals will once again be tame and live in harmony'.[8] The magi,

---

[6] Some writers read back, as it were, Christ's cross and sacrifice into the Incarnation, e.g. Ian Bradley (in *The Power of Sacrifice*, p. 134), who quotes Donne's sermon on Christmas Day: 'the whole life of Christ was a continual Passion ... His birth and death were but one continual act, and His Christmas Day and His Good Friday are but the evening and morning of one and the same day.'

[7] Irenaeus, *Adv. Haer.* v.15.2 (with reference to the healing of the blind man in John 5.14).

[8] Dennis Nineham, *The Gospel of St Mark* (Harmondsworth, 1963), p. 64. Compare Stanley Spencer's paintings, *Christ in the Wilderness: Foxes* and *Christ in the Wilderness: Scorpions*, reproduced in Eric Newton, *Stanley Spencer* (London,

who were regarded as representing the non-Christian world, are shown as following a star, usually depicted in paintings of this scene. The shepherds, representing ordinary people (though in later Judaism they were a despised group, because they were suspected of stealing sheep and because their occupation prevented their fulfilling many regulations of the Law) are depicted as guided by angels (who were believed to have a cosmic function).

Christ's miracles were a common subject for painters, e.g. his walking on the water, or his healings (signifying also the forgiveness and spiritual healing that he was believed to have brought to humanity). As early as the third century we find representations of the healing of the woman with a haemorrhage and of the paralytic man, in the catacombs of SS. Peter and Marcellinus in Rome and in the house-church at Dura Europos.

Less common, perhaps, was his solidarity with the poor and outcasts, a theme that particularly attracts Liberation Theologians today. But Rembrandt's etching *Christ Among the Poor* [Plate 4] is an outstanding example. Perhaps previous generations were more interested in his glory: if so, this may partly explain the attraction of the subject of the Transfiguration for so many painters, e.g. Fra Angelico and Giovanni Bellini. But the Transfiguration was regarded also, and is regarded now, especially in the Orthodox Church, as an anticipation of the resurrection of Christ, of his coming again in glory, and of the final transformation of all things – the New Creation. Moreover, it represents the way in which the divine light can shine through human flesh. Because of its location, and because on this occasion Christ was accompanied

1947), Plates 15, 17. See also David Brown, *Tradition and Imagination: Revelation and Change* (Oxford, 1999), pp. 98–102; and more generally Matthew Fox, *The Coming of the Cosmic Christ*, pp. 96*ff*, and Robert Murray, *The Cosmic Covenant*, pp. 145*ff*.

On the other hand, Neil MacGregor suggests that the presence of the animals in the manger reflects the belief (echoing Isa.1.3) that the ox and the ass, unlike the Jews, recognized the Messiah. See Neil McGregor, with Erika Langmuir, *Seeing Salvation: Images of Christ in Art* (London, 2000), p. 21; and pp. 48–59 on the influence of the crib.

by some of his disciples, it forms a natural contrast with the Agony in the Garden, also a popular subject for painters. The contrast between the humiliated and the glorified Christ was, however, more obvious in depictions of the Cross and Resurrection, especially when the two were combined in one work, as in Grünewald's Isenheim altar-piece. Let us look, therefore, at some examples of such depictions.

The Cross

The image of Christ on the Cross was a relative late-comer in Christian art. The earliest surviving examples date from the fifth century. The earlier image of the Good Shepherd, found in the catacombs and the subject of some early Christian sculpture,[9] represents Jesus' dedication and sacrifice throughout his whole life, and his willingness to die for his flock (John 10.11), but the image as such does not convey suffering. However, many of the earliest representations of the Cross do not show a crucified and suffering Christ, either: they show only his head, or they show him glorious and triumphant, rather than in agony, wearing the tunic of a Byzantine emperor, or a purple royal or priestly robe.[10] Early Christian artists tended to avoid depicting Christ as dead, on the Cross or elsewhere. Hence the Entombment, too, was a late-comer in Christian art.

As time went on, emotional and dramatic *motifs* emerged, in Byzantine art in the late eleventh century, and later in the West: the *Christus Triumphans* gives way to the *Christus Patiens*, the Man of Sorrows, who displays his humanity, and who, through his evident suffering, evokes the spectator's sympathy. Georges Florovsky sees

[9] And also found later on, e.g. in the aria 'And he shall feed his flock' in Handel's *Messiah* (note how often the theme of sheep and shepherds recurs in this work).
[10] E.g. in a wall-painting in S. Maria Antiqua, Rome. See further Gertrud Schiller, *Iconography of Christian Art*, vol.ii, tr. J. Seligman (London, 1972), pp. 89–99; Nigel Spivey, *Enduring Creation: Art, Pain and Fortitude* (London, 2001), pp. 46–8.

the Western developments as influenced by the introduction of the devotion of the Stations of the Cross in the early Middle Ages, a devotion that was promoted especially by the Franciscans; and Henk van Os sees the concern with the wounds of Christ and with the instruments of the Passion as evidence of how the subjective relationship between believers and their Saviour came to seem more important than the historical accounts of his death.[11] Certainly, many painters chose subjects from the Way of the Cross, including the wiping of Christ's face by Veronica (an event not recorded in any of the canonical Gospels); and some mystery plays were based on this Way.[12]

In Italian and Flemish painting the suffering and humiliation of Christ are depicted, not just for the sake of realism, but to emphasize his sharing in human suffering and to arouse appropriate feelings, of repentance, compassion, and gratitude, in the spectator. Roger Fry claimed, in his essay 'Giotto', that the painter was dealing with emotions that previous art had scarcely touched.[13] A little earlier, the hymn *Salve caput cruentatum,* ascribed to St Bernard, was written; and translated by Paul Gerhardt in the seventeenth century, it found its way into Lutheran devotion and into Bach's *St Matthew Passion ('O Haupt voll Blut und Wunden')*. Such paintings and hymns, and sculptures and plays too, encouraged an imaginative identification with Christ in his Passion, and a sympathetic response in sensibility and action to his sacrifice; thus

---

[11] Georges Florovsky, *Creation and Redemption*, p. 302; Henk van Os, *The Art of Devotion in the Late Middle Ages in Europe, 1300–1500* (London, 1994), pp. 104–29. On the influence of Franciscan piety more generally, see Anne Derbes, *Picturing the Passion in Late Mediaeval Italy: Narrative Painting, Franciscan Ideologies, and the Levant* (Cambridge, 1996).

[12] See Lynette R. Muir, *The Biblical Drama of Medieval Europe* (Cambridge, 1995), pp. 135–6.

[13] Roger Fry, *Vision and Design* (Harmondsworth, 1937), p. 148. But Anne Derbes, in her *Picturing the Passion*, traces back this tendency in Italian painting earlier, to the mid-thirteenth century: by the 1240s, she argues, the suffering Christ is depicted as faltering and vulnerable, to elicit our 'sympathetic and affective participation' (p. 11); similarly the sufferings of the Virgin Mary and Mary Magdalen at the foot of the Cross came to be represented more affectively.

'In a mysterious way the Man upon the Cross retains His place in the human imagination as the timeless symbol of reconciliation through sacrifice.'[14]

The spectator might also find himself or herself identifying in some way with those who put Christ to death. Hieronymus Bosch, like several artists of his time, depicts the malice of those who mocked and tormented Christ in his *Christ Carrying the Cross* (in Ghent) or in his *The Crowning with Thorns* (in the National Gallery, London). In the latter painting they are shown as representing different classes of people, socially and perhaps also medically (Bosch attempts to depict the four 'humours').[15] Again, in such cases, the paintings may evoke self-understanding, compassion and repentance in their viewers.

The representation of the suffering Christ on the Cross was paralleled by representations of the suffering of those at the foot of the Cross, especially his mother. This expressed the tradition honouring Mary as the *Mater Dolorosa*, sharing the suffering of her son, a tradition captured in the *Stabat Mater* (set to music by Pergolesi, Haydn, Penderecki, and many others), and able to comfort the sufferer now. This suffering of Mary was also represented in the tradition of the seven wounds of the Virgin, matching her son's physical wounds, a tradition deriving

---

[14] F.W. Dillistone, *The Christian Understanding of Atonement*, p. 399; cf. also pp. 233*ff*; 330–2.

Not every depiction of the Crucifixion conveys its religious significance: what of Picasso's *Crucifixion* of 1930 (in his own collection), which just jumbles together aspects of the scene as an exercise in Cubism? Or Francis Bacon's triptych of 1965 (in Munich), in which Christ on the Cross is depicted as wearing a Nazi armband, not to make a political or religious point, but supposedly for the sake of the composition?

[15] I am grateful to the Rev. John McDade, S.J., for pointing this out to me, and for suggesting some of the other examples mentioned in this section. On Bosch's symbolism, see further Richard Foster and Pamela Tudor-Craig, *The Secret Life of Paintings* (Woodbridge, 1986), pp. 59–73.

ultimately from Simeon's words in Luke 2.35. The wounds were depicted by artists as being made by darts or arrows in her heart.[16]

We go a step further when artists and writers seek to depict reduplications of Christ's Cross in the sufferings of others. Thus Patrik Reutersward describes a reredos from a church in Andenes in Norway, showing Christ's Passion on the inside, and (seemingly) that of St Olaf on the outer wings[17]; whilst Nikos Kazantzakis' novel *Christ Recrucified* re-presents the Passion story through the narrative of events surrounding a modern Passion play on a Greek island. Von Balthasar too writes of the way in which the Cross may be reduplicated in Christians, and later gives the example of the death of the old Prioress, in seeming abandonment by God, in Bernanos' *Dialogue des Carmelites* (*Theo-Drama* iv, pp. 421–2; v, p. 339).

It was relatively easy for painters to depict the suffering, cruelty, and degradation of the Cross, and so to evoke the appropriate feelings among viewers, but less easy for them to suggest Christ's willing acceptance of his death, or to represent its saving significance. In general, one would not expect painters to try to express soteriological theories. Neil MacGregor, however, provides an interesting contrast here. Rogier van der Weyden's *The Seven Sacraments* (in Antwerp) depicts the Crucifixion in a cathedral, in which priests and bishops are administering the sacraments, thus expressing the Catholic belief that the sacraments continue Christ's work of salvation and are channels of grace. Lucas Cranach the Younger, on the other hand, expresses a Lutheran

---

[16] Later on, the wounds were written about by poets identifying themselves with the sorrowing Virgin at the foot of the Cross, e.g. in stanza vii of Richard Crashaw's 'Sancta Maria Dolorum'. Cf. J.A.W. Bennett, *The Poetry of the Passion*, p. 173, who also mentions Donne and Herbert.

A consideration of Mary's role would also have to include the tradition that she was the second Eve, a tradition originating in some of the early Christian Fathers and expressed in e.g. Giovanni di Paolo's *The Annunciation* (National Gallery, Washington).

[17] Patrik Reutersward, 'The Mystery of the Double Passion', in his *The Visible and the Invisible in Art: Essays in the History of Art* (Vienna, 1991), pp. 170–3.

'salvation by faith alone' doctrine in his Weimar altar-piece, in which he depicts a thin stream of blood squirting from Christ's side onto the head of his father, who is standing by the Cross together with St John the Baptist and Martin Luther (who has his Bible open at certain texts regarded as supporting his doctrine).[18]

These two examples show that painters often have to rely on the ability of the viewer to make the appropriate theological connections, sometimes by picking up iconographic clues. The connection of the second Adam, Christ, with the first one was hinted at by depicting a skull, supposedly Adam's, at the foot of the Cross in many icons and paintings. The similar story, that the wood of the Cross, the 'Tree of Life', grew from a branch of the Tree of Knowledge, the source of death, is depicted in Piero della Francesca's fresco of the death of Adam (in Arezzo). Angels or people (representing the Church) were often depicted as holding a chalice by the wound in Christ's side, e.g. in Raphael's *Crucifixion* (in the National Gallery, London), an obvious reference to the Eucharist – as also was the lamb bleeding into a cup in Grünewald's *Crucifixion* in the Isenheim altar-piece. A similar idea, alluded to in *Piers Plowman*[19] and found in some medieval illuminations, envisaged the blood from the wound as penetrating through the ground to Limbo, for the release of the souls there – an unusual variant on the theme of the Harrowing of Hell. Artists, too, could capture some of the cosmic aspects of the Crucifixion, as of the birth of Christ, e.g. the darkness and the earthquake (Matt. 27.45, 51–3), depicted in El Greco's *Crucifixion* (in Cleveland). (In a different sort of way, Salvador Dali's well-known painting in Glasgow, *Christ of St John of the Cross* perhaps also conveys a cosmic significance, in that Christ is depicted from above, suspended in space, with the earth beneath him. Dali

---

[18] See Neil MacGregor, *Seeing Salvation*, pp. 198–204. Before the Reformation, and for later Catholic painters like Rubens, the stream of blood and water from Christ's side was linked rather with the sacraments, as we shall see; cf. John Drury, *Painting the Word: Christian Pictures and their Meanings* (New Haven, 1999), pp. 101–2.

[19] *Passio* v, B text, lines 493–4 (in Schmidt's edition).

wanted to convey beauty and joy in this painting, so that it would be the absolute opposite of Grünewald's).

For a fuller expression of the saving significance of the Cross and for an understanding of its paradoxical character, however, we must look elsewhere, to works in other media, for instance poetry. As early as the eighth century we find, in *The Dream of the Rood* (11.85*ff*) the theme of the healing power of the Cross; and in *Piers Plowman* the patristic idea that the Crucifixion was necessary not just to redeem mankind, but in order that God should know the extremities of human suffering and death – an idea exploited by many twentieth-century theologians.[20] Later on, we find more speculative treatments of the subject: e.g. in Canto vii of the *Paradiso* Dante expresses in verse an Anselmian theology of the Cross, and in Book iii of *Paradise Lost* Milton expresses an Arminian one.[21] Then there are poems which put a question-mark against traditional theological interpretations, like Thomas Hardy's 'Unkept Good Fridays', which begins:

There are many more Good Fridays
    Than this, if we but knew
The names, and could relate them,
    Of men whom rulers slew
For their goodwill, and date them
    As runs the twelvemonth through.

Usually, however, poets have stopped short of theological specu-lation, and preferred a more devotional approach, expres-sing repentance and love of Christ, and reflecting on the mystery of the Cross. There is a wealth of such poetry especially in seventeenth-century English literature (though not, strangely, in

---

[20] E.g. Jürgen Moltmann, in his *The Crucified God: The Cross of Christ as the Foundation and Criticism of Theology*, tr. R.A. Wilson and J. Bowden (London, 1974), esp. pp. 270–8.

[21] On the latter see the analysis by Stephen Sykes in his *The Story of the Atonement* (London, 1997), pp. 26–36; and Brian Horne, *Imagining Evil* (London, 1996), pp. 62–75.

Milton). Mostly, the poets address themselves to Christ on the Cross (e.g. in Donne's 'Good Friday, 1613. Riding Westward'). But in Herbert's 'The Sacrifice' it is Christ who addresses us, with the refrain 'Was ever grief like mine?' (echoing Lam. 1.12).[22]

Nearer to our own time there are 'novels of redemption', some of which depict a Christ-like figure who suffers for others and acts as an instrument of reconciliation. I shall defer consideration of such novels, however, until Chapter 7.

The Resurrection

The question of conveying soteriological significance through art, noted with regard to the Cross, is raised also in the case of what is naturally associated with it, the Resurrection, depictions of which are, like those of the Crucifixion, relative late-comers in Christian art. In general, just as depictions of the Cross arouse feelings of pity, remorse, and love, those of the Resurrection are expressions of faith in God's ability to break the powers of this world, of confidence in Christ's victory, and of hope in a future beyond death, of which Christ's rising is believed to be the first fruits.

In the catacombs artists preferred to hint at the Resurrection indirectly, by using Old Testament images like the three children in the fiery furnace, Jonah and the whale, and Daniel in the lions' den. Elsewhere, again, early Christian artists depicted it indirectly, e.g. by showing Christ raising Adam from the underworld, or by depicting secondary events that confirmed the reality of the Resurrection, e.g. the Marys at the tomb (the 'Myrrh-bearers'),[23]

---

[22] J.A.W. Bennett traces this poem back to the Responses sung on Good Friday, which were also used in the Towneley Crucifixion Play and set to music by many composers, in his *Poetry of the Passion*, p. 154. See chs. vi–vii of that book for a good discussion of such seventeenth-century poetry. More modern examples include Edwin Muir's 'The Killing'.

[23] Found possibly as early as the middle of the third century at the baptistery in Dura Europos, and popular until the late seventh century, e.g. at S. Apollinare

or Christ appearing to the women after the Resurrection. We do not find depictions of the risen Christ until the second half of the seventh century.

In later Western art we find depictions of Christ rising from the tomb, alone (that is, apart from the sleeping soldiers). In Piero della Francesca's *Resurrection* at Borgo San Sepolcro, for example, a realistic figure, with a deathly face, is climbing out of the tomb, holding a standard (symbolizing victory). Even more realistic are some of Michelangelo's drawings (in the British Museum) of a naked Christ, full of life and vigour, emphasizing the corporeality of the risen Son of God. Such realism is also conveyed in many representations of Christ at Emmaus, e.g. Caravaggio's (in the National Gallery, London).

Although the cosmic significance of the Resurrection is mentioned in Western theology as early as St Ambrose (who said, 'In Christ the world has risen, heaven has risen, the earth has risen'[24]), it was not developed much in later Western theology and art.[25] It is otherwise in the East, however, where the theme of the Resurrection was linked to our redemption and resurrection, and indeed to the regeneration and renewal of the whole cosmos. This was symbolized, above all, by combining the depiction of the Resurrection with that of the Harrowing of Hell, in icons and other paintings – an important example of the way in which art may reveal a difference of theological emphasis and under-standing. In a mural at St Saviour in Chora (Kariye Kami) in

---

Nuovo in Ravenna or in an early fifth-century plaque in the British Museum. See Anna Kartsonis, *Anastasis: The Making of an Image* (Princeton, 1986), pp. 19–21. This book gives a very useful history of representations of the Resurrection up until the eleventh century. See also Patrik Reutersward, 'The Resurrected Christ: Problems in Representation', in his *The Visible and the Invisible in Art*, pp. 157–69.

[24] Ambrose, *De Fide Resurrectionis*, ii.102 (*P. L.*16:1344).

[25] There are a few exceptions, however, e.g. St Bonaventure: see John Saward, 'The Flesh Flowers again: St Bonaventure and the Aesthetics of Resurrection', *Downside Review* cx (1992), pp. 1–29, esp. pp. 18–20. The theme of the restoration of the cosmos has found its way back into Western theology in recent years, as we shall see, through an interest among some theologians in ecological questions.

Istanbul [Plate 2], for instance, a vigorously moving Christ draws up Adam and Eve from the underworld (where Satan lies bound), surrounded by St John the Baptist, David, Solomon, Abel, and many other figures, symbolizing the redemption of the righteous from death. Thus in such depictions Christ is not alone in his resurrection.

The redemption of the whole cosmos is more difficult to depict: usually it is symbolized by light, signifying glory.[26] If the cosmos is redeemed, then it too is redeemed *from* something *to* something: from futility to freedom and glory, according to Rom. 8.18–21. Hence many Orthodox theologians regard the beautifying of the world here and now as having an eschatological significance.[27] The theme is, again, rare in Western art, but John W. Dixon draws attention to Grünewald's use of light in his depiction of the Resurrection in the Isenheim altar-piece [Plate 1]; he says,

> Grünewald is an expressionist often seemingly obsessed with the tragedy of man. Yet he has caught perhaps more precisely than any other artist the glory of creation in the

---

[26] Fr Stamatios Skliris refers to 'the ontological function of light' (as opposed to the merely aesthetic) in Byzantine painting, in his 'The Relationship of Humanity with the Natural Environment as Revealed in Byzantine Iconography', in *So that God's Creation Might Live: The Orthodox Church responds to the Ecological Crisis* (Proceedings of the Inter-Orthodox Conference on Environmental Protection, Nov. 1991, published by the Ecumenical Patriarchate of Constantinople, 1992), p. 59.

This function of light is seen most obviously in depictions of the Transfiguration, in which 'what the disciples saw was not simply an illumination of Christ's body from some external source; what they saw was the divine light itself ...' (George Pattison, *Art, Modernity and Faith* [2nd edn., London, 1998], p. 126).

[27] See, for example, Sergius Bulgakov, 'Religion and Art', in E.L. Mascall (ed.), *The Church of God: An Anglo-Russian Symposium* (London, 1934), pp. 75–91. I discuss other examples in my *Spirit and Beauty: An Introduction to Theological Aesthetics* (Oxford, 1992), ch.7.

light of the incarnate Christ and the transfiguration of matter in the light of the resurrected Christ.[28]

The Harrowing of Hell, which is traditionally associated with Holy Saturday and therefore regarded as intermediate between the Crucifixion and the Resurrection, was usually depicted separately in Western art, e.g. by showing Christ preaching to the dead in the underworld. The only Scriptural backing for the idea is 1 Pet. 3.18–19, a text first used in this connection by St Clement of Alexandria (in *Stromateis* vi.6.47), but it is also found in the apocryphal Gospel of Nicodemus. The theme was a popular one in later art and literature, e.g. medieval manuscripts, mystery plays, and a window in King's College Chapel, Cambridge. Theologically, it signifies the opening of the era of Redemption for the whole human race, achieved through the Incarnation, Passion, and death of Christ.[29] In more recent centuries, the idea has become less popular: it would be interesting to speculate why – presumably its lack of Scriptural backing, its mythical character, and the modern sympathy for Universalism with regard to salvation are some relevant considerations. Walter Kasper, however, still finds the idea valuable, as conveying that those who died before Christ are not simply to be regarded as what he calls, echoing Walter Benjamin, 'the waste-products of history'.[30] More widely, the 'theology of Holy Saturday' has been recovered and

[28] John W. Dixon, *Nature and Grace in Art*, p. 78. Tillich praised Grünewald's painting because it shows the Resurrection 'as a transformation of the finite into the infinite, symbolized by the sun in which the body of Christ disappears', as contrasted with some paintings in which Christ seems to just return to the world as if nothing has happened. See Paul Tillich, *On Art and Architecture*, ed. John and Jane Dillenberger (New York, 1987), p. 117.

Some other Western artists have depicted light shining from the body of the risen Christ, signifying its glorification, e.g. William Blake, in his watercolour, *The Resurrection* (in the Fogg Art Museum, Harvard).

[29] A. Kartsonis, *Anastasis*, p. 6. Cf. also F.W. Dillistone, *The Christian Understanding of Atonement*, pp. 98–102.

[30] Walter Kasper, *Jesus the Christ*, p. 224.

developed recently by von Balthasar, though his interest in it is mainly with regard to the desolation of Christ and his seeming abandonment by the Father, on both Good Friday and Holy Saturday, and his solidarity with the dead, rather than with regard to Christ's preaching to or leading the dead out of Hell.[31]

Consideration of the Resurrection, like that of the Crucifixion, should not be restricted to the plastic arts. There are also poems, like George Herbert's 'Easter'; and there is the music of the Resurrection. John Bowden instances settings of the words '*et resurrexit tertia die*' in Bach's *Mass in B Minor* and in several other Masses set to music by leading composers, works by Olivier Messiaen and Robert Saxton, and Gustav Mahler's Second ('Resurrection') Symphony.[32]

These works raise again a question about understanding, previously asked in Chapter 1: will such music stand on its own feet? That is to say, would people who did not know the context and purpose of the works, and relevant texts like the Creed, understand any of their religious meaning? A similar question could be asked about the 'music of Pentecost', e.g. Mahler's setting of the *Veni, Creator Spiritus* in his Eighth Symphony, or John Tavener's *Hymn to the Holy Spirit*. A full answer to these questions would require us to consider the difficult issue of whether music is a kind of language, a claim made in a strong form by Deryck Cooke.[33] This question is a much debated one; but of course

---

[31] Hans Urs von Balthasar, *Mysterium Paschale*, tr. A. Nichols (Edinburgh, 1990), ch.4; idem, 'Mysteries of the Life of Jesus (V): Jesus' Death on the Cross – Substitution and Descent into Hell', in Medard Kehl and Werner Loser (eds.), *The von Balthasar Reader*, tr. R.J. Daly and F. Lawrence (Edinburgh, 1982), pp. 150–3.

[32] John Bowden, 'Resurrection in Music', in Stephen Barton and Graham Stanton (eds.), *Resurrection: Essays in Honour of Leslie Houlden* (London, 1994), ch.17. See also Geoffrey Turner, 'The Music of Death and Resurrection', *The Month*, n.s.xxi (1988), pp. 589–95.

[33] Deryck Cooke, *The Language of Music* (Oxford, 1959). For later discussions, see e.g. Peter Kivy, *Philosophies of Art* (Cambridge, 1997), chs. 6–7; Roger Scruton, *The Aesthetics of Music* (Oxford, 1997), ch.7, esp. pp. 203–10; and Jeremy S. Begbie, *Theology, Music and Time* (Cambridge, 2000), pp. 15–30, 39.

music can have a 'meaning' without its being a language. So for our purposes now it is probably sufficient to claim that key, tempo, rhythm, and devices like the Picardy Third enable composers to express, in certain contexts, feelings like sadness, joy, peace, and fear; and that, similarly, the sequence of equilibrium-tension-resolution, which is the most pervasive temporal structure of tonal music, can communicate release (the expressive power of melody is more difficult to determine). Thus in the case of Bowden's example of the '*et resurrexit*' from the B Minor Mass, Bach returns to the key of D Major with a jubilant chorus, to express joyful triumph.[34] By contrast, a little earlier on he has used a *passacaglia* (originally a slow stately dance constructed on a ground bass) before the '*et crucifixus est*', to express grief.

There are also, I think, 'novels of resurrection', of which Tolstoy's *Resurrection* is the most well-known; in such works we are concerned not so much with Christ's resurrection as with our own, understood here, as Dennis Nineham says, as 'primarily . . . a "risen" way of living in the here and now'.[35] The novel also raises the issue of whether one can 'redeem' one's own past, i.e. change the significance of past actions and events, which I shall discuss in the next chapter.[36]

Art and Theological Understanding

The examples I have discussed so far in this chapter raise a more general issue: the occurrence of a particular theme (or the

[34] See Wilfrid Mellers, *Bach and the Dance of God* (London, 1980), pp. 225–6, for a musical analysis of this passage; also Wendy J. Porter, 'Bach, Beethoven and Stravinsky Masses: Images of Christ in the Credo', in Stanley Porter, Michael A. Hayes, and David Tombs (eds.), *Images of Christ Ancient and Modern* (Sheffield, 1997), pp. 375–98.

[35] Dennis Nineham, 'Tolstoy's *Resurrection* Revisited', in Stephen Barton and Graham Stanton (eds.), *Resurrection*, pp. 213–22, at p. 219. Such a new life might be regarded as a fruit of Christ's resurrection.

[36] This is not to say that Tolstoy did not believe also in a life after death.

absence of one) in art and literature usually has significant religious or theological implications, and sometimes the recurrence of a theme at a particular time or place indicates a change in emphasis or understanding. I have instanced such historical or geographical variations in the case of Eastern and Western treatments of the Resurrection, where the former stress the cosmic significance of the event more than the latter do. Likewise, Western art tends to express the authority of the risen and ascended Christ through representations of the Last Judgement, a theme especially popular in medieval and Renaissance art, whereas Eastern art does it more through representations of him as the *Pantocrator* (e.g. in the mosaic at Daphne). A further example is that of Pentecost. Again, Eastern paintings of this event seek to capture the cosmic significance of the coming of the Holy Spirit. Thus in icons the disciples are usually depicted sitting at a table, whilst in front of them is a bound king, lying on the ground and being freed of his bonds, signifying that the Spirit frees the cosmos, too.[37] In Western representations, only the Apostles are usually depicted, with tongues of fire resting above their heads (another variant is that of a large hand depicted above them, with light streaming down from its fingers onto their heads).

Thus art may convey a theological understanding. Sometimes, however, the latter has to be explained in words (especially in the case of unfamiliar iconography), because people are unable to make the necessary connections with their knowledge and experience. This, again, raises our general question of when and how art and literature are the primary vehicles of religious devotion and understanding. In cases where we need a commentary in order to understand a poem or some iconography, this suggests either that an understanding of images and symbols

---

[37] See Paul Evdokimov, *L'Art de L'Icône: théologie de la beauté* (Paris, 1970), pp. 287*ff* (the whole of Part iv of this book gives a very helpful account of the theology implicit in the most common types of icon). See also Matthew Fox, *The Coming of the Cosmic Christ*, pp. 106, 216, for some reflections on the cosmic significance of Pentecost.

has been lost by later generations, or that they were never meant to be primary vehicles in the first place. A further consideration, however, is that an image or a symbol often has an immediate power, touching a depth of feeling, and hinting at a wealth of meaning which is there to be discovered by further experience and reflection. Evdokimov may have had this in mind when he wrote, 'In the West the theologian instructs the artist, in the East an iconographer is a charismatic who contemplates the liturgical mysteries and instructs the theologian.'[38] The immediacy of images and symbols is also an important factor contributing to the power of the liturgy.

When, then, can art and literature, like liturgy, be primary expressions of religious ideas? When they convey these ideas immediately, I think, without need of paraphrase or explanation, especially through the use of powerful images and symbols; that is to say, when they show things or express them directly. This is not, however, to depreciate works of art and literature that depend on some prior understanding of a text – what I shall later call 'illustrations'. After all, etymologically, an illustration is something that throws light on something else. In the case of art and literature dealing with the first Act of the Drama of Redemption, that of sacred history, their dependence on Scripture and Church tradition means that their primary value will lie usually in their expressive quality, and also in their conveying the significance of that history more profoundly.

I shall return to these issues of showing, expressing, and understanding in Chapter 9. In the meantime, I want to look at art and literature that reflect the other two Acts of the Drama of Redemption, the present and the life to come. For Christians do not believe that Christ's redemptive work is simply a past event. As R.C. Moberly said,

---

[38] Paul Evdokimov, 'Nature', *Scottish Journal of Theology* xviii (1965), pp. 1–22, at p. 18.

... no theories of atonement which try to explain the whole meaning of it as a transaction completed, as transaction, outside the personalities of the redeemed can state with any adequacy that aspect of the truth to which the consciousness of the present day is most keenly – and rightly alive.[39]

In the next chapter, therefore, I shall begin to consider how the redemptive work of Christ is believed to be carried out in the lives of people in later centuries, and how the understanding of this belief too is conveyed in art and literature.

[39] R.C. Moberly, *Atonement and Personality* (London, 1901), p. 218.

CHAPTER FIVE

Act II: Present Redemption

Rumours of Redemption

Shortly before he died in 1994, the playwright Dennis Potter was interviewed on television. Asked about his religious beliefs, he replied that he believed 'God is a rumour'.[1] I would like to adapt his remark and say that for many people redemption seems like a rumour. We touched in the last chapter on some aspects of the history of redemption, and later on we shall look also at its cosmological and eschatological aspects. But what of the present life? How is redemption being manifested now? Supposedly it is being worked out by God's action in history, leading up to the Second Coming and the Last Judgement. But we need also some sense of present redemption in order to understand soteriological claims in terms of our own experience and to make them at all convincing. Otherwise we feel again the sharp force of Nietzsche's gibe that Christians do not look redeemed, something that raises questions about the meaning of redemption as much as about the qualities of believers.

If, however, there are rumours of redemption evident here and now, then there may be some plausibility in such claims. The artist's and writer's task may be to discern those rumours, for example in the ways in which good is brought out of evil, in

---

[1] In his *A Rumour of Angels: Modern Society and the Rediscovery of the Supernatural* (London, 1970), a study by a sociologist of the survival of 'intimations of transcendence' in a supposedly secularized society, Peter Berger quotes a priest working in a slum in a European city as saying that he did so 'so that the rumour of God may not disappear completely' (p. 119).

forgiveness and reconciliation, and in the redeeming power of love. Thus, for example, Peter Taylor Forsyth saw in Wagner's *Parsifal* 'not so much a message from the delivering God as a representation of deliverance in man's soul ... a real regeneration worked out through spiritual process within'.[2] If the expression of the 'rumours' carries conviction, the writer or the artist has succeeded in conveying a vision of what might be, of what, the religious believer hopes, will be. In this chapter I shall discuss such visions, and then consider the apparent stumbling-block of tragedy.

I have in effect just suggested that if indeed redemption is being worked out through history, one would expect it to make some difference here and now, and perhaps thereby to hint also at some anticipation of what is to come. Many Jews have seen the re-establishment of Israel in this way: Emil Fackenheim quotes a prayer by the Israeli Chief Rabbinate beginning 'Our Father in Heaven, Rock of Israel and her Redeemer, bless the State of Israel, the beginning of the dawn of our redemption ...'[3] Christianity looks rather to the Church and to the Holy Spirit. Thus many Christians regard the Church as the redeemed creation, or the beginning of it. J.S. Whale, for instance, describes it as 'redeemed humanity *in nucleo*'.[4] But to justify such an ambitious claim one needs to indicate how redemption is worked out in individual lives in history: again, within the grand cosmic narrative there are the narratives of individual persons. So one

---

[2] Peter Taylor Forsyth, *Religion in Recent Art*, pp. 254f.

[3] Emil Fackenheim, 'The Holocaust and the State of Israel', in Eva Fleischner (ed.), *Auschwitz: Beginning of a New Era?*, p. 205.

[4] J.S. Whale, *Victor and Victim*, p. 98. Earlier on he had said that Christians regard the world as 'penetrated by "the powers of the age to come" '(p. 17). The idea that what is happening here and now is, in some respects, an anticipation of what is to come is captured in many Biblical images, e.g. 'earnest' or 'first fruits'. St Paul uses these metaphors of the Holy Spirit (Rom. 8.23; 2 Cor. 5.5), whose fruit is love, joy, peace, and so on (Gal. 5.22). He also writes of 'newness of life' (Rom. 6.4), 'new creation' (2 Cor. 5.7; Gal. 6.15), and a 'new nature created after the likeness of God' (Eph. 4.24).

place to start looking might be amongst plausible examples of restored humanity, at those whose hearts have been healed, who seem to be reconciled and at peace with God and their neighbours, and who manifest the fruit of the Spirit.

Penitents, Saints, and Mediators

The theme of new life is found especially in narratives like John Bunyan's autobiographical *Grace Abounding*, some biographies, and many novels (often hinted at rather than depicted). Thus Dostoevsky suggests a new life for Raskolnikov with Sonya, at the end of *Crime and Punishment*, and Tolstoy for Nekhlyudov in *Resurrection*. Flannery O'Connor's short story 'Revelation' depicts a woman, Mrs Turpin, being jerked out of her complacency and self-deception by a chance encounter with someone in a doctor's waiting-room, and her ensuing illumination, humility, and repentance.[5] The contrast between sinfulness, repentance, and new life is obviously attractive to the creative writer, and for a religious one it may also convey something of the power of God's grace over time (one common analogy for the individual's progress in life towards redemption is that of a pilgrimage, an analogy expressed classically by Bunyan in *The Pilgrim's Progress*). The related themes of forgiveness and reconciliation between people are often found in plays, e.g. Shakespeare's *King Lear*, *Measure for Measure*, and *A Winter's Tale*. Lastly, and most importantly I think, there is also the idea of saintliness; but this is notoriously difficult to convey convincingly and interestingly, for it is very hard to depict a fully integrated, whole, Christ-like person, who seems to be inspired or guided by the Holy Spirit.

[5] See L. Gregory Jones, *Embodying Forgiveness* (Grand Rapids, 1995), pp. 53–8, and D.Z. Phillips, 'Mystery and Mediation: Reflections on Flannery O'Connor and Joan Didion', in David Jasper (ed.), *Images of Belief in Literature* (London and Basingstoke, 1984), pp. 24–41, for analyses of O'Connor's story.

Perhaps one reason for the difficulty of depicting the transformation to saintliness is that artists or writers may fail to bring
out the humanity of their subjects. As François Mauriac said,

> The saints form material for novelists as much as any other
> living people ... The reason why most novelists have failed in
> their portrayal of saints may be due to the fact that they have
> drawn creatures who are sublime and angelic but not
> human, whereas their sole chance of success would have lain
> in concentrating on the wretched and human elements in
> their characters that sanctity allows to subsist. And this is the
> special realm of the novelist.[6]

One remembers here that 'hagiography' is usually a pejorative
term: there are few lives of the saints, or other depictions of
sanctity, that are great literature or do justice to the personality
and influence of their subjects. Yet Mauriac himself certainly
attempted the task that he delineated, e.g. with the Abbé Calou in
his *The Woman of the Pharisees*, as also did Dostoevsky with Fr
Zossima in *The Brothers Karamazov*.

I shall leave further comment on Mauriac's point about the
novelist's role until Chapter 7: what he says also raises questions
about what criteria for sanctity are being used, and whether there
may be a number of models of saintliness even within
Christianity (not to mention other religions). There are other
genres besides the novel to be considered now.

Numerous Italian Renaissance painters and others have
painted pictures of saints, such as St Mary Magdalen (taken as
representing redeemed sinners), early Christian martyrs like St
Catherine of Alexandria and St Sebastian, or later saints like
St Francis of Assisi and St Dominic. In Orthodox churches icons
of the saints are always to be found: one of their most obvious

---

[6] François Mauriac, *God and Mammon*, pp. 79–80; cf. his *Journal* III, in *Oeuvres
Complètes* vol.iii (Paris, 1963), pp. 262–4, for a similar point.

functions is to remind people of models of holiness. Thus Leonid Ouspensky says,

> The saints are few in number, but holiness is a task assigned to all men, and icons are placed everywhere to serve as examples of holiness, as a revelation of the holiness of the world to come, a plan and a project of the cosmic transfiguration.[7]

Many Western theologians would agree with at least the first part of this, as an account of the value of pictures of saints. Yet earlier in the chapter Ouspensky is anxious to differentiate between Eastern and Western sacred art, and to trace the differences back to a different anthropology, especially with regard to 'deification'. The latter point is part of an anti-Western polemic by Ouspensky, which I shall not pursue; but anyone can agree with him that Eastern icons and later Western art certainly differ greatly in appearance, and that the former have a different role.

Earlier in his book Ouspensky says that 'true beauty is the radiance of the Holy Spirit, the holiness of and the participation in the life of the world to come'.[8] He sees an icon as participating in the holiness of its prototype, for the grace of the Holy Spirit sustains the holiness both of the represented person and of the icon; hence there is a link between venerating saints and venerating icons. He quotes St John of Damascus, who said that the grace of God rests on the image because 'the saints were filled with the Holy Spirit during their lives'.[9] His remarks explain why icons are 'sacramentals' and objects of veneration in Orthodox churches (one sees people bowing before them and kissing them, for example). They also remind us of the role of the Holy Spirit

---

[7] Leonid Ouspensky, *Theology of Icons* (Crestwood, NY, 1978), p. 228.

[8] Ibid., p. 190.

[9] Ibid., p. 201, quoting St John of Damascus, *First Treatise on Images*, ch.19 (Migne, *P. G.* 94. 1249c). See also Paul Evdokimov, *L'Art de l'Icône: théologie de la beauté*, pp. 176–7.

in Redemption, for the Spirit has been associated traditionally with sanctification (following Gal. 5.22*f* and 1 Pet. 1.2), as well as with some of the other ideas that I have discussed already, e.g. enlightenment and healing of the heart. The hymn '*Veni Sancte Spiritus*' describes the Spirit as 'light of our hearts'.[10]

Pictures and icons, however, are arts of space rather than of time, so they cannot give us a *narrative* of a saint's life, showing us the transforming action of God's grace over time (the nearest that we can get to this is in cycles of paintings about a single saint's life, e.g. the frescoes by Giotto and others in Assisi illustrating scenes from the life of St Francis); hence, again, the importance of narrative and drama.

A saint, and indeed any person, may play certain roles in his or her life as an instrument of God's redemptive power. In his *Nouveaux mémoires intérieurs* Mauriac wrote, 'The Redemption concerns us not only in that we are redeemed, but because we redeem.'[11] Hence we find in literature depictions of the various roles which people can play in the salvation of others. They may, for example be intermediaries, a role most famously played by Beatrice for Dante: T.S. Eliot pointed out, rightly, that to fully understand Beatrice's role as Dante's guide in Paradise, culminating in Canto xxx of the *Paradiso*, in which Dante sees her transfigured in beauty and then has a vision of the highest Heavens, we must know about her role in Dante's earlier work, the *Vita Nuova*, where she is depicted as having inspired his attraction towards God.[12] As a very different kind of example of intermediaries, one might also mention several of Wagner's music-dramas, in which, as Michael Tanner points out,[13] there are characters who are burdened with a past from which they can be

---

[10] Commenting on this in his last papers written in prison in 1944–45, before his execution by the Nazis, Fr Alfred Delp noted that 'we are here concerned with the Spirit of God in the very centre of life, bringing healing to its roots and its source'. See his *Facing Death* (London, 1962), p. 143.

[11] François Mauriac, *Nouveaux mémoires intérieurs* (Paris, 1965), p. 70.

[12] T.S. Eliot, 'Dante', in his *Selected Essays* (3rd edn., London, 1969), pp. 263, 274.

[13] Michael Tanner, *Wagner* (London, 1996), p. 186.

released only through a prodigious act, e.g. the Flying Dutchman, Tannhauser, Tristan, Wotan, and, above all, Amfortas in *Parsifal*, who, together with the Knights of the Grail, is saved by Parsifal, the innocent who does not know whence he comes.

Another common role is that of the Christ-like figure, who suffers and perhaps dies on behalf of others, a Suffering Servant or scapegoat. Randal Stewart sees something of this in the depiction of Billy's death and its aftermath in Herman Melville's *Billy Budd*, which, he suggests, carries overtones of Christ's death and ascension. In chapter 11 of his work Melville quotes 2 Thess. 2.7 on 'the mystery of iniquity', with reference to Claggart's depravity (possibly, Stewart says, Claggart felt shamed by Billy's innocence and beauty, and might have said of him, as Iago says of Cassio in *Othello* V.i.19–20, 'He hath a daily beauty in his life which makes me ugly'). After Billy's noble death, the sailors revere his memory: to them a chip of the spar from which he was hanged was 'as a piece of the Cross'. Stewart ends his essay by referring to 'the "victory" (through "defeat") of the Christlike Billy'.[14]

I agree that Melville was probably inspired by the Passion story, and that in Claggart we have an outstanding portrait of villainous evil. Yet I am not sure that Billy is exactly 'Christlike': I think that F.W. Dillistone is nearer the mark when he suggests that at first sight Billy is more akin to the unconsciously innocent Adam before the Fall (a comparison made by Melville himself in Chapter 2) than to Christ, at least until he strikes and accidentally kills Claggart; thereafter he seems to become a Christ-figure, in whom the 'central paradox of redemption appears: the champion who destroys sin must himself be destroyed that a full expiation may be made and a new order of life established'.[15]

---

[14] Randal Stewart, 'The Vision of Evil in Hawthorne and Melville', in Nathan A. Scott (ed.), *The Tragic Vision and the Christian Faith* (New York, 1957), pp. 238–63, at p. 262.

[15] F.W. Dillistone, *The Novelist and the Passion Story*, pp. 64–5.

In an earlier chapter (entitled 'A Lamb to the Slaughter') of the same book Dillistone gives further examples of such Christ-like figures, drawn from Mauriac's novels. He instances Xavier, in *The Lamb*, who is sacrificed to reconcile Jean de Mirbel and his wife Michèle; and the Abbé Forcas in *The Dark Angels*, a saintly priest who sees himself as carrying the load of people's secret evil actions, laid upon him. (He might also have instanced, I think, the Abbé Calou in *The Woman of the Pharisees*, whose vocation is to suffer for others.) Such examples show that,

> ... in Mauriac's view ... it is possible for a saintly Christ-figure at any point of time so to be identified with Christ in character and suffering and sacrifice that he can mediate healing and redemption to the generality of mankind.[16]

Again, I agree with what has been said so far. But it raises at least two major questions: *how* does the Christ-like figure mediate healing and redemption to others? And, are figures like Billy Budd to be regarded as tragic, and, if so, what is the Christian's attitude to tragic literature? Many critics have argued that there cannot be a Christian tragedy. The first question is more one for theologians, though I shall argue in Chapter 7 that the creative artist's and writer's task here is to depict convincingly a Christ-like figure who is regarded as mediating redemption. So let us now look briefly at the second question.

Christianity and Tragedy[17]

Writing in general terms of 'art of redemption', John W. Dixon said, 'Tragedy here has been redeemed and transformed, not

---

[16] Ibid., p. 40.

[17] It should be noted that there are 'plays of redemption' that are *not* tragedies, e.g. Shakespeare's *Measure for Measure* and T.S. Eliot's *The Cocktail Party*. In the latter, the redeemer figure, Sir Henry Harcourt-Reilly, is a psychiatrist; it is another character, Celia, who is crucified.

obliterated and forgotten, but caught up in a new meaning and a new life . . .'[18] Reinhold Niebuhr, too, said that Christianity stands beyond tragedy, both in general, because for it existence is ultimately under the dominion of a good God, and also with regard to tragic drama, because Christianity does not regard sin and guilt as inevitable – sin is freely chosen. Niebuhr admits, however, that there are indeed genuinely tragic elements in the human enterprise, simply because nobility and strength, dignity and creative ambition are mixed with our sin, and frequently make it more destructive. Thus Ibsen's Brand suffers for his idealism, but 'this idealism is a screen for unconscious impulses of power'.[19]

The obvious conclusion to draw from such treatments is that there can be no Christian tragedy; and indeed Dixon says later on the same page, 'No purely tragic work can be in the order of redemption, for it is only tragedy transfigured that can be fully loyal to the redeeming Lord.' From a very different point of view, George Orwell claimed in a famous essay, 'Lear, Tolstoy and the Fool', that 'It is doubtful whether the sense of tragedy is compatible with belief in God . . .'; for, he said, tragedy is incompatible with the kind of moral demand which feels cheated when virtue fails to triumph: 'A tragic situation exists precisely when virtue does *not* triumph but when it is still felt that man is nobler than the forces which destroy him.'[20] But Christianity, it seems, preaches that nothing good is finally lost, because there is always a wider picture, with the possibility of an ultimate resolution. Aldous Huxley, too, without appealing to religious considerations, argued that writing a tragedy involves isolating a single element from the totality of human experience: 'Tragedy is something that is separated out from the Whole Truth, distilled

[18] J.W. Dixon, *Nature and Grace in Art*, p. 78.
[19] Reinhold Niebuhr, 'Christianity and Tragedy', in his (ed.) *Beyond Tragedy: Essays on the Christian Interpretation of History* (London, 1938), pp. 153–69, at p. 157.
[20] George Orwell, 'Lear, Tolstoy and the Fool', in his *Collected Essays* (London, 1961), pp. 415–34, at p. 422.

from it, so to speak, as an essence is distilled from the living flower.'[21]

Many literary critics have agreed with Orwell in the years since he wrote his essay. For instance, George Steiner claims in his book *The Death of Tragedy* that tragedy is distinctive of the Western Hellenic tradition – the Jews had no theatre – and that Christianity ultimately has an anti-tragic vision of the world (Dante titled his poem a 'comedy'), for God's forgiveness is *always* possible (pp. 331–2). He does recognize what Schiller called 'tragedies of reconciliation', e.g. Sophocles' *Oedipus at Colonus* and the end of Aeschylus' *Oresteia* (p. 174), and acknowledges that there can be partial or episodic Christian tragedies where people are deflected from God's purposes, or 'tragedies of waste' (pp. 335, 342). Similarly, Steiner argues that although Marxism has provided new myths, images, and world-orders, its metaphysics, like those of Christianity, are anti-tragic, for they express a cosmic optimism (pp. 323–4).[22]

Still, despite such comments, some theologians (above all, Donald MacKinnon[23]) have wrestled with the question of the relationship between Christianity and tragedy – surely Gethsemane and the Cross are in some sense tragic? Of course, Christianity preaches ultimate reconciliation and redemption; but we should not look for too easy a resolution, or ignore the

---

[21] Aldous Huxley, 'Tragedy and the Whole Truth', in his *On Art and Artists*, pp. 60–8, at p. 65.

[22] George Steiner, *The Death of Tragedy* (London, 1961). Yet Steiner also argues that in our modern urban, bourgeois culture the loss of the currency of concepts like grace, damnation, purgation, and blasphemy has led to a 'death of tragedy' (pp. 197, 319–20), for tragedy presupposes a religious or quasi-religious sense: 'tragedy is that form of art which requires the intolerable burden of God's presence. It is now dead because His shadow no longer falls upon us as it fell on Agamemnon or Macbeth or Athalie' (p. 353).

[23] Donald MacKinnon, 'Atonement and Tragedy', in his *Borderlands of Theology and Other Essays* (London, 1968), pp. 97–104; 'Theology and Tragedy', in his *The Stripping of the Altars* (London, 1969), pp. 41–51; *The Problem of Metaphysics* (Cambridge, 1974), pp. 122–45; 'Ethics and Tragedy', in his *Explorations in Theology* (London, 1979), pp. 182–95.

appalling cost of Christ's victory. As Stewart Sutherland says, 'the point of the reconciliation, the redemption, the re-connection, can only be grasped following the depths of the experience of disconnection and discontinuity'.[24]

The issue depends partly on what is meant by 'tragedy'. The term is used in common speech of a sad and seemingly hopeless situation; and also of a kind of drama in which the characters move ineluctably to a catastrophic dénouement, partly through events or fate, and partly through their own folly and weakness. But the term has travelled a long way from its roots in the Greek word *tragoedia*, the original etymology of which may be 'goat-song'. Even among Classical Greek tragedies, there are a variety of outlooks. Sophocles' *Oedipus Tyrannus* does indeed present us with an irredeemable situation, in which Oedipus' terrible fate is worked out gradually. But in Aeschylus' *Oresteia* trilogy, the curse of the house of Atreus is eventually laid to rest and Orestes is freed from his blood-guilt in the final play, the *Eumenides*. Modern plays like Ibsen's *Brand* and Arthur Miller's *Death of a Salesman* follow the pattern of *Oedipus Tyrannus*.[25] But other plays allow for some resolution or possibility of redemption, often through the self-knowledge that some of the characters have acquired, e.g. *Measure for Measure* (though one should distinguish here, I think, between the self-knowledge of the main participants, that of peripheral characters, and that of the spectator or reader). Although Lear is still, at least in his own estimation, 'a very foolish fond old man' (*King Lear*, IV.vii.60) and dies a bleak death, he does

---

[24] Stewart Sutherland, 'Christianity and Tragedy', in *Literature and Theology* iv (1990), pp. 157–68, at p. 164.

[25] In a more recent article, Steiner has used the phrase 'absolute tragedy' of works that 'express the conception of human life as lawless chastisement, as some hideous practical joke visited upon man', e.g. Sophocles' *Oedipus Tyrannus*, Euripides' *Medea* and *Bacchae*, Marlowe's *Dr Faustus*, Racine's *Phèdre*, Berg's *Lulu*, and Goya's last paintings. See his 'A Note on Absolute Tragedy', *Literature and Theology* iv (1990), pp. 147–56.

For Steiner's later views, see also Graham Ward, 'Tragedy as Subclause: Steiner and MacKinnon', *Heythrop Journal* xxxiv (1993), pp. 274–87.

learn from his suffering, and comes to love Cordelia and to be reconciled with her. Even *Tess of the D'Urbervilles* is not an entirely bleak novel, for Angel Clare learns something from his final reconciliation with his wife.

A Christian author, however, is not in the same situation as a pre-Christian one like Sophocles, or a modern sceptic or agnostic. I think that Nathan Scott is right in saying, in the foreword to *The Tragic Vision and the Christian Faith*, that, since the advent of Christianity, one rarely encounters in the literature of tragedy 'a presentiment of existence as utterly unredeemable or of the human enterprise as fated ultimately to career into a meaningless void', for the tragedian's attention seems always to some extent to be engaged 'by at least the dream of a brave new world or country of the spirit wherein the brokenness of man may be repaired or healed'.[26] Another contributor to the same volume, Edmond La B. Cherbonnier, says that the tragedian sees the conflicts and calamities of existence as the inevitable consequence of the clash of equal and opposite forces, but the Bible 'regards neither the conflict as inevitable nor the forces as neutral', for the conflict is caused by human sin. Nor does the Bible regard high aspirations as *hubris*, for we are enjoined, 'Be ye holy even as your father in heaven . . .'; rather, it regards not aspiring high enough, that is infidelity to a spiritual calling, as the fundamental danger for us.[27]

---

[26] Nathan A. Scott, Jr. (ed.), *The Tragic Vision and the Christian Faith*, p. xi. For an illuminating discussion of the differences between Greek and Christian tragedy, see David H. Hesla, 'Greek and Christian Tragedy: Notes Toward a Theology of Literary History', in Robert Detweiler (ed.), *Art / Literature / Religion: Life on the Borders* (Chico, CA, 1983), pp. 71–87. He argues, for instance, that in the latter kind of tragedy people more often go wrong through their own fault, whether it be weakness or defiance, and not through fate, ancestral curses, and so on, hence there is more room for the notions of grace, repentance, forgiveness, and reconciliation. It should be said, however, that flaws of character often play a major role in both types.

[27] Edmond La B. Cherbonnier, 'Biblical Faith and the Idea of Tragedy', in Nathan A. Scott (ed.), *The Tragic Vision and the Christian Faith*, pp. 23–55, at pp. 42, 52.

But if we have done wicked or foolish actions, with 'tragic' consequences, in what sense are they redeemable? Surely, what is past is past, and 'it is no use crying over spilt milk'? I believe that there is a possible response to these obvious questions, and that it raises some important considerations for us now. This response consists in seeing that although we cannot indeed change the past, we can retrospectively change its effects and its significance – what I shall call 'redeeming the past', using a phrase from Christina Rossetti's prayer 'Redeem me from the irrevocable past' in her poem 'After this the Judgment'.

Redeeming the Past

In his *De Profundis* Oscar Wilde wrote that, without repentance, we do not truly realize what we have done; hence, he said,

> The moment of repentance is the moment of initiation. More than that: it is the means by which one alters one's past. The Greeks thought that impossible. They often say in their Gnomic aphorisms, 'Even the Gods cannot alter the past.' Christ showed that the commonest sinner could do it, that it was the one thing he could do.[28]

Wilde may be contrasted here with Harry in T.S. Eliot's *The Family Reunion*, for whom 'everything is irrevocable, the past unredeemable'.[29] A similar point has been made also by many philosophers and theologians, who have argued that, although the

---

[28] Oscar Wilde, 'De Profundis', in his *De Profundis and Other Essays* (Harmondsworth, 1973), pp. 97–211, at p. 179.

[29] T.S. Eliot, *The Family Reunion*, I.iii, in *Complete Poems and Plays of T.S. Eliot* (London, 1969), p. 315. C.A. Dinsmore regards the irrevocableness of the past as one of George Eliot's fundamental teachings, quoting Adam Bede's remark that 'There's a sort o' damage, sir, that can't be made up for' (*Atonement in Literature and Life* (Boston, 1906), p. 121). I am not sure, however, that this does full justice to *Middlemarch* or *Daniel Deronda*.

past is indeed unchangeable in itself, we can nevertheless seek to change the effects of past happenings, including our own actions, through repentance, and thereby we can change the significance of the past.[30]

I think that we are dealing here with two related ideas: (i) something can be salvaged from the past, in that the evil effects of what has been done are removed or mitigated, and possibly some good is brought out of it – we do not need to be prisoners of our pasts; (ii) the evil done is put into a wider context, so that our view of it changes, and perhaps painful memories are healed: for although we cannot alter past facts, we *can* change their meaning. These two ideas are linked, in that it is we who can to some extent construct the new context: our actions now and in future change the significance of past facts, so that we as it were, cast a good light on the past, or repaint the picture.[31]

The first of the two ideas just mentioned, that of remedying past ills, extends to a lot of human life, in virtue of our ability to alter the effects of the past to some extent. We devote much effort to discerning the evil effects of past happenings and actions, to preventing or mitigating them as far as we can now, and to initiating other causal chains which may offset them in future. Doctors, mechanics, agronomists, mountain rescue teams, and those who have to anticipate (if possible) and deal with the conse-

---

[30] E.g. Diogenes Allen, 'Acting Redemptively', *Theology Today*, vol.41 (1984–85), pp. 267–70. Mark T. Nelson applies a similar argument to theodicy: using an idea of C.S. Lewis, he argues that human lives are 'diachronic wholes', so that the verdict of good or evil on any past lives depends on their final outcome. See his 'Temporal Wholes and the Problem of Evil', *Religious Studies* xxix (1993), pp. 313–24. See also Richard Creel, *Divine Impassibility: An Essay in Philosophical Theology* (Cambridge, 1986), pp. 151*ff.*

[31] Timothy Garton Ash points out, with reference to the re-assessment of Eastern European history and of the legacy of Communism that have taken place since the fall of the Berlin Wall in 1989, that German has two words, *Geschichtsaufarbeitung* (reappraising history) and *Vergangensheitbewaltigung* (overcoming the past), where English has none. See his *The File: A Personal History* (London, 1997), p. 194; and *History of the Present: Essays, Sketches and Despatches from Europe in the 1990s* (London, 1999), p. 294.

quences of floods, fires, and earthquakes, to mention only a few examples, do this in different ways; and indeed, anyone who has performed a harmful action may feel obliged to do so. When the action has been done deliberately, we feel that the wrongdoer should repent of it, apologize, and make some reparation. In the case of particularly heinous actions, we may feel that wrongdoers should try to achieve a deeper repentance and reconciliation with their victims by learning from their actions and by attempting to bring good out of evil, e.g. by dedicating themselves to other victims of similar crimes. Slave-owners, for instance, realizing their injustice and inhumanity, might not only free their own slaves and offer them compensation, but also devote efforts to anti-slavery campaigns for the rest of their lives; or torturers might not only renounce their trade and try to atone for what they have done to their victims, but might also campaign for the abolition of torture everywhere and for the alleviation of the suffering of all its victims. These examples envisage forms of penance and expiation which go a long way beyond wrongdoers merely doing justice to those directly affected by their actions, for they indicate a real 'cleansing of the heart', and a thorough change of attitudes and relationships.

The second idea involved in what I have called 'redeeming the past' is that of changing the significance of the past. A lot of familiar practices like apologizing and making reparation attempt to do this, as does forgiving, of which John McIntyre writes, 'In a way ... one of the prime characteristics of forgiveness is that it can remake the past, in the present and *for* the future.'[32] At an everyday level, trivial offences like carelessness and tactlessness may be forgotten or ignored by their victims if the perpetrator offers an apology. In other cases, e.g. damage to property, we look for restitution, as a sign of genuine repentance.[33] In the case of the most serious wrongs like adultery or betrayal, however, it is

---

[32] J. McIntyre, *The Shape of Soteriology*, p. 128.
[33] See Richard Swinburne's discussion in his *Responsibility and Atonement* (Oxford, 1989), ch.5, esp. pp. 81–7.

difficult to see how a genuine relationship could survive them, for what compensation could ever be given for such disruptions of a relationship? The common occurrence of people taking revenge through maiming or murder in such cases might suggest that this is so, and that punishment or retribution are the only possible human reponses. Yet sometimes reconciliations are achieved: an unfaithful lover may repent and succeed in restoring a relationship through a new and richer kind of love. But such reconciliations are rare and very costly, in terms of both repentance and forgiveness. The past evil cannot, I think, simply be 'disowned' (as Swinburne puts it), for the realization of what has happened must become part of the reconciliation and of the ensuing development of a deeper relationship; the good must relate to the evil, at least in that the partners have learned from it and thereby matured. So the picture of the past must be, as it were, repainted, by changing the significance of what has happened; which, in turn, is done by reconstructing its context by developing a different kind of present and future.

In the case of adultery and betrayal we are dealing with the seeming breakdown of an existing relationship, and the possibility of restoring it. Here there is already some basis for a reconciliation. But let us consider offences which seem so bad that not only can no compensation be given but we cannot conceive how those concerned could ever achieve reconciliation and forgiveness after coming to terms with the past. Dostoevsky's famous example in *The Brothers Karamazov*, Bk.5, ch.4, based on an actual event, of the landowner who set his pack of dogs on a child who had injured one of them slightly, so that the child was torn to pieces in front of his mother, is a case in point. Among other things, Ivan Karamazov asserts that even if 'eternal harmony' can be brought about only through human suffering, the tears of the child would remain unexpiated; hence the mother would still have no right to forgive her child's torturer. This is surely so. But what of the landowner? 'Disowning' his action or giving adequate recompense seem to be out of the question here. If, however, he were to change his life completely by freeing his serfs, giving away all his wealth, and devoting the rest of his life to the loving service of the poor, we might say that he had done something (though perhaps very little) to redeem his action. Again, it would be a matter of viewing his crime in the context of his whole life, seeing what he had learned from it, how deep his repentance was, and how he had sought to atone for it, and judging whether there had indeed been a real change of heart.[34]

The topic that I have discussed has, I think, a deeper significance than I have conveyed so far, for it is not only with regard to atonement that the issue of 'revisioning' the past arises. Later events, not just our own and other people's actions, often seem to show up the past in a different light and lead us to re-assess what has happened. At a trivial level, people may speak of good fortune redeeming past misfortunes, meaning merely that one compensates for the other. But more seriously, we often re-assess our education, relationships, and career-patterns, as well as mishaps and other seemingly fortuitous events. This is because the longer we live, the more things we have to relate to each other in our personal histories, and therefore the more possibilities of discerning new patterns; or, to use an analogy less passive in its connotations, the more strands we have to weave into the pattern.

The analogy I have just mentioned, like that of a picture used earlier, is one sometimes used in theological contexts. J.R. Lucas gives the analogy of Persian rug-makers who let their children help them and who can incorporate the children's mistakes into a revised design, to make the point that God, although (according to Lucas) He does not foreknow our free actions, can weave our sins and errors into His plan.[35] And of course theodicists often say that we do not see the whole picture in this life, or, more boldly, they appeal to the '*O felix culpa*' claim – that the misfortune of

[34] Richard Creel remarks, more generally, that Ivan's position presupposes that one could not 'make sense' eschatologically of the sufferings of the innocent; but what if Ivan could, after all, praise God on the day of resurrection, because then 'he will understand the why of it all'? (*Divine Impassibility*, p. 151). I shall raise some further questions about this line of argument later in this chapter.

[35] J.R. Lucas, *Freedom and Grace* (London, 1976), p. 39.

Adam's sin led to the unsurpassable expression of love seen in the Incarnation and Redemption; or that the evils suffered now may be 'defeated' (Roderick Chisholm's term, which he distinguishes from 'balancing off', i.e. merely compensating for [36]), in this life or eschatologically. Theology also raises the question of whether a third party can atone for the sins of others, even those of the whole human race (a question raised by Dostoevsky, for he depicts Alyosha Karamazov as appealing to the Cross in his reply to Ivan).

An obvious example of a very different kind of re-assessment of the past, with a practical purpose, is to be found in the practice of psychoanalysis[37]: the person being analysed seeks to relive the past, with a view to achieving a deeper understanding of it and thereby shaking off some of its burdens, so as to be able to fashion a more open and creative future. This practice finds an analogue in some works of literature in which writers re-evaluate their past lives: most obviously in autobiographies like St Augustine's *Confessions*, but also in works like Proust's *A la recherche du temps perdu* or D.H. Lawrence's *Sons and Lovers*. Such writers have different ends in view in their recovery and analysis of their past. Proust found his vocation as a writer in recovering the past from his unconscious, and thereby overcoming the disintegrative and transformative action of time; whilst St Augustine sought, among other things, to discern and to convey how God's grace and providence had worked through his life, especially during the years preceding his conversion.

The recalling and re-assessment of the past found both in writers like St Augustine and in psychoanalysis is not simply a matter of coming to a new perception of the past. Some historians may do this, as an end in itself; but our concern now is with the ways in which people learn from their own past, perhaps

---

[36] Roderick Chisholm, 'The Defeat of Good and Evil', *Proceedings of the American Philosophical Association*, vol.42 (1968–69), pp. 21–38.

[37] An example given by Elizabeth Templeton in 'On Undoing the Past', in her *The Strangeness of God* (London, 1993), pp. 43–60.

coming to a deeper understanding through this, and then fashion, as far as they can, a new kind of future. And, in turn, the nature of this future may occasion a further re-evaluation of the past – both the remote and the more recent past. We seem to be confronted with the possibility of a kind of continuous sequence of: living – evaluating and restructuring our lives – living – re-evaluating and restructuring, and so on, with an interplay between events, our actions, and the ways in which we reinterpret the past. As Kierkegaard said, we live life forward, but understand it backwards.

Such a sequence, as I have delineated it so far, is progressive: it seems, therefore, like my earlier discussion, with its talk of possibilities of reconciliation, to reflect an optimistic view of life. But of course we must also reckon with the possibility that the significance of the past can be changed for the worse. An adultery or a betrayal may cast a sulphurous light on the years preceding it, revealing the shallowness or the fragility of a relationship, either because people find anticipations in the past of what happened later, or because their whole retrospective judgement of events changes, or for both these reasons. In Hilary Mantel's novel *A Change of Climate* a wife reflects, after having learned of her husband's infidelity, 'it is in the nature of betrayal, she thought that it not only changes the present, but that it reaches back with its dirty hands and changes the past'.[38] Thus things can go the other way, and so our later re-evaluations too can go in diverse directions. Augustine did not seriously revise the perspective on his own life that he expressed in his *Confessions* (which he wrote about half-way through his life, in his early forties). But a disappointed subject of psychoanalysis might lose his or her initial optimism and decide that, after all the burdens of the past cannot really be shifted and that all one can do is to make the best of a bad job.

Now so far I have not made any grand claims about the direction of human life. Christianity, however, seems to envisage

---

[38] Hilary Mantel, *A Change of Climate* (Harmondsworth, 1995), p. 304.

that all situations are redeemable; and if we entertain the suppo-
sition of an afterlife, the range of possibilities is increased greatly.
In *In Memoriam* liv Tennyson wrote:

> Oh yet we trust that somehow good
>   Will be the final goal of ill, . . .
> That nothing walks with aimless feet;
>   That not one life will be destroy'd,
>   Or cast as rubbish to the void,
> When God hath made the pile complete;

Later on, in his short poem 'The Play', he used the analogy of a
play:

> Act first, this Earth, a stage so gloom'd with woe
> You all but sicken at the shifting scenes.
> And yet, be patient. Our Playwright may show
> In some fifth Act what this wild Drama means.

The analogy of a play of which the meaning is not apparent until
the last act is over, was also used by William Temple, from which
he drew the general principle, already noted by us earlier on, that
'The value . . . of any event in time is not fixed until the series of
which it is a member is over, perhaps, therefore, not to all
eternity.'[39]

Another analogy is offered by Elizabeth Templeton, from
music: the second playing of a theme exerts a kind of retro-
spective pull on the listener, so that: 'Hearing the recapitulation,
you hear what you heard before, but your before-hearing is
modified by your after-hearing.'[40] (Actually, I think that she should
have said that our *memory* of the before-hearing is modified: this
would still preserve her insight that the significance of the first
part depends partly on the latter.) She notes, interestingly, that the

[39] William Temple, *Mens Creatrix* (London, 1917), p. 173.
[40] Elizabeth Templeton, *The Strangeness of God*, p. 47.

term 'recapitulation' played an important role in St Irenaeus' theology of redemption, though of course without its musical connotations. For Irenaeus time is redeemed because the history of Adam is repeated or recapitulated in Christ, the second Adam, but with a very different outcome. More generally, she goes on to say that 'the past is therefore for God never fixed, since it is always liable to reopening in the new context of the eschatological future which he offers the world . . .'[41]

If that eschatological future involves a life after death for us, then what some of these writers (especially Temple) seem to be envisaging is that in eternity there is a refocusing or 'revisioning' of the past whereby we shall see our lives in a new light – see them, perhaps, as God perceives them, through participating in His wisdom. In the *Showings* of the medieval mystic Julian of Norwich we are told that part of the bliss and fulfilment of those who are saved will be that, at the Last Day, they will see the true reason why God has done all the things He has, and the reason, too, for all those things which He has permitted.[42] Such a revisioning seems to be depicted by Dante at the close of *The Divine Comedy*, where he sees everything held in the light of God, whose love binds all things together in one volume (*Paradiso* xxxiii.83–7); the healing of memories in the rivers Lethe and Eunoe has occurred already (*Purgatorio* xxvii.127–32). This new seeing presumably involves perceiving a relationship between the whole series of events, and thereby being led to change our views of the significance of the past. Templeton uses the phrase 'undoing the past'; I prefer my phrase 'redeeming the past', to describe this possibility.[43]

[41] Ibid., p. 55.

[42] Julian of Norwich, *Showings*, longer text, ch.75. This is an example of a very common line of thought (*'then'* we'll see), which Gabriel Daly calls 'meaning deferred', in his *Creation and Redemption*, p. 152.

[43] See further my 'Redeeming the Past', *Religious Studies* xxxxiv (1998), pp. 165–75. Paul Fiddes writes, with reference to T.S. Eliot and Karl Barth, of the 'healing' of time through God's action, in his *The Promised End: Eschatology in Theology and Literature* (Oxford, 2000), pp. 135–40.

I shall return to this issue, and more broadly to questions of eschatology, in Chapter 8. In the meantime, however, I want to look at an issue that has, once again, been suggested by the discussion of redeeming the past, that of narrative. Part of what is involved in 'revisioning' the past is that we come to some new understanding of it so that we re-narrate it, finding, as it were, a new plot. But the consideration of such a practice requires us to give a little attention to the nature and role of narrative in the literature of redemption.

CHAPTER SIX

Act II: The Role of Narrative

The question of the role of narrative has come up, in different ways, in both of the previous two chapters. The last chapter has confronted us with the issue of how we can re-conceptualize and re-narrate our own histories in the light of a new understanding brought about by later events; and Chapter 4 touched on the 'salvation history', especially that of Christ's death and resurrection, which plays a foundational role in Christianity. That history is conveyed in a classical form in the Bible, many parts of which are narratives of different kinds, e.g. the Books of Joshua and Jonah, or the Gospels. If redemption is believed to occur in time, through historical events (rather than through some ideology or general philosophy), it is not surprising that both its foundational events and its working out through particular actions and events in later generations should be expressed, at least partly, through narratives. Paul Ricoeur argues that there is a natural 'fit' between sequences of events and narratives, for the world unfolded by narratives is always a temporal world: time becomes human time in so far as it is organized as a narrative, and narrative in turn is meaningful to the extent that it portrays the features of temporal experience. Thus there is a correlation between the temporal character of human experience and the narrating of a story.[1]

---

[1] Paul Ricoeur, *Time and Narrative*, vol.i, tr. K. McLaughlin and D. Pellauer (Chicago, 1984), pp. 3, 52.

Of course, narrative is not the only way of dealing with time; and the natural correlation which Ricoeur discusses may take many forms, for there are, he says,

If Ricoeur is right, it is natural and fitting that, given the temporal character of redemption, there should be 'narratives of redemption', both of individuals and communities, in many religions. Before looking at the nature and role of such narratives in Christianity, however, I want first to consider briefly the variety of narratives and their function more generally.

The Varieties of Narrative

Some narratives are mere chronicles or *reportage*, where there is little scope for selection and interpretation, e.g. records of business meetings and descriptions of traffic accidents. At the opposite extreme come myths, which often represent some very general feature of human life. Somewhere between these two extremes comes the novel, which Sir Walter Scott defined as 'a fictitious narrative ... accommodated to the ordinary train of human events'. There are also dramatized narratives: at Passiontide most Christian churches have readings of the narratives of Christ's Passion in the Gospels, with different readers taking the parts of Christ, Peter, Pilate, and the crowd. In the *Passions* of Bach and of other composers these dramatized readings have been set to music and interspersed with arias and choruses that meditate and comment on the action (somewhat as in a Greek tragedy).

---

manifold ways of 'refiguring' time. Much of the rest of *Time and Narrative* explores this variety. For instance, Ricoeur contrasts the ways in which three novels, Virginia Woolf's *Mrs Dalloway*, Thomas Mann's *The Magic Mountain*, and Marcel Proust's *A la recherche du temps perdu* handle the time covered in the narrative (in the first of these works only a single day, in the other two several years). Lived time, the 'time of consciousness', differs from cosmic time, the 'time of the world'. See *Time and Narrative*, vol.ii, tr. K. McLaughlin and D. Pellauer (Chicago, 1985), pp. 100–52, and vol.iii, tr. K. Blamey and D. Pellauer (Chicago, 1988), pp. 127–41.

Walter Benjamin pointed to the importance of our modern sense of time for the rise of the novel as the crucial modern genre. See 'The Storyteller', in his *Illuminations*, tr. H. Zohn (Fontana edn., London, 1973), esp. pp. 87–8, 97–100.

Of the kinds of narrative mentioned so far, myths perhaps have the widest role in literature and art. In his dialogues Plato often interposes stories at certain points in the argument, for instance at the end of the *Republic* (the 'Myth of Er'). The role of these stories has been much discussed, but it would seem that Plato thought that certain topics, e.g. immortality, could not be dealt with adequately in a philosophical argument (*logos*) alone, but required a story (*muthos*) as well, for myths are rich in symbolism and appeal to the imagination. They can, as Mieke Bal notes (following Susanne Langer) be painted, acted, and danced, as well as told.[2] They often, too, seem to have a universal reference. The neo-Platonist Sallustius wrote of the myth of Attis and the Mother of the Gods, 'All this did not happen at any one time, but always is so',[3] indicating that, while myths may be regarded as true, this truth is not that of, say, history. A myth may be true-to-life somewhat in the way that a character like Thackeray's Becky Sharp is so, because, as John Hospers suggests, she is 'more revealing of human nature than any individual person we have met' (he goes on to argue that a work of fiction, through its insights into people and their behaviour, may convey 'truth-to human nature').[4] Thus both myths and novels can be, in a sense, true to life.

The term 'myth' is widely misunderstood today, largely because in everyday language it is often used as a synonym for falsehood.

---

[2] Mieke Bal, *Reading Rembrandt: Beyond the Word-Image Opposition* (Cambridge, 1991), p. 98. This work argues, more generally, that pictures may be 'visual narratives' – and here she is not thinking merely of story-pictures or comic strips. She discusses, for instance one of Rembrandt's most elusive works, *The Polish Rider* (in the Frick Collection, New York), pointing to the rider's sexual ambiguity and the strangeness of his gaze, seemingly directed at an unattainable object. Her analysis suggests, she says, 'a narrativization of this portraitlike painting' (p. 352).

[3] Sallustius, *Concerning the Gods and the Universe* iv, tr. A.D. Nock (Hildesheim, 1966), p. 9.

[4] John Hospers, *Meaning and Truth in the Arts*, pp. 163, 173. Cf. also Hugh Mellor, 'On Literary Truth', *Ratio* x (1968), pp. 150–68; and Colin McGinn, *Ethics, Evil, and Fiction* (Oxford, 1997), esp. ch.7 and Conclusion.

If, however, it is taken in the sense of a narrative which expresses certain truths and which has a guiding function in people's lives, then it would seem that many different kinds of narrative still fulfil that role, e.g. the story of the Battle of Britain in 1940, Aesop's *Fables*, or the Parable of the Good Samaritan. F.W. Dillistone, at the end of his *The Novelist and the Passion Story*, bemoans the lack in the West today of a 'central and controlling myth around which the lives of individuals and societies can be refashioned', and claims that, for Christians the record of the Passion, death, and resurrection of Christ constitutes such a story.[5]

Because of the dangers of misunderstanding involved in the use of the term 'myth' today (dangers which surfaced in 1977 with the publication of the collection of essays, edited by John Hick, *The Myth of God Incarnate*), I would prefer to use the phrases 'salvation history' and 'sacred history' of the Passion narratives. But I think that Dillistone is right in pointing to the function of those narratives: as J.B. Metz puts it, Christian soteriology is 'fundamentally memorative and narrative'[6]; hence, again, the Passion narratives transmit what he calls 'dangerous memories'. Dillistone is also right in pointing to the possible role of novels here (his book is a study of the way in which four modern novelists have used the pattern of the Passion narrative as a framework). More recently, narratives have also been used as a framework by some writers concerned with ethics, especially with the role of virtues in people's lives.

In his influential book *After Virtue* Alasdair MacIntyre called for a recovery of the concept of virtue in philosophical ethics. Now, since the virtues equip us for our journey through the harms and dangers of life, and since personal identity is bound up with the continuity of character in time, there is a close connection between the virtues, the practices in which they are embedded, and the narrative structure of human life (both of individuals and

[5] F.W. Dillistone, *The Novelist and the Passion Story*, p. 128.
[6] J.B. Metz, *Faith in History and Society*, p. 133.

of the communities to which they belong).[7] Thus narratives may give a coherence to human lives.

MacIntyre's thought here, along with that of Stanley Hauerwas, has given rise to the phrase 'narrative ethics'. The latter writer has also specifically connected virtue ethics and novels, e.g. those of Anthony Trollope. In an essay entitled 'Constancy and Forgiveness; the Novel as a School for Virtue',[8] Hauerwas claims that novels are 'epistemologically crucial', for without them we cannot understand a morality which regards virtues like constancy as primary. Through his characterization and narrative in *The Vicar of Bullhampton*, Hauerwas argues, Trollope enables us to see that true constancy cannot be built on pride, for that would make us subject to the judgement of others; rather, humility is crucial, if constancy is to derive from a stead-fastness that is not determined by the judgements of others. In another essay, 'On Honor: by Way of a Comparison of Karl Barth and Anthony Trollope',[9] Hauerwas contrasts the abstractness of Barth's discussion of honour, in his *Church Dogmatics* iii.4, with the concreteness of Trollope's understanding in his *Dr Wortle's School*, to the former's disadvantage (Hauerwas says 'Karl Barth's main problem is that he did not read enough Trollope'[10]). Through his narrative Trollope manages to explore why honour may require us to act against our society's moral conventions, as Dr Wortle does in defending the apparent

[7] Alasdair MacIntyre, *After Virtue* (2nd edn., London, 1984), esp. pp. 204ff. On the role of narrative in constituting our personal identity, see also Paul Ricoeur's essay 'Narrative Identity' in David Wood (ed.), *On Paul Ricoeur: Narrative and Interpretation* , pp. 188–99.

[8] In Hauerwas' *Dispatches from the Front: Theological Engagements with the Secular*, ch.1. See also Robert C. Roberts, 'Narrative Ethics', in Philip L. Quinn and Charles Taliaferro (eds.), *A Companion to Philosophy of Religion* (Oxford, 1998), pp. 473–80, esp. p. 476, for the point that great narrativists like George Eliot are often outstanding moral psychologists too.

[9] Stanley Hauerwas, *Dispatches from the Front*, ch.2.

[10] Ibid., p. 58. Later on he says, again of *Dr Wortle's School*, 'I hope that Barth has read it by now, for what good is heaven if it does not give us time to read all of Trollope's novels?' (p. 76).

bigamist Peacocke; but at the same time he conveys the societal ethos that produces someone like Wortle.

Perhaps, then, novels may fulfil for us some of the functions that lives of the saints performed traditionally. People used to read, and some still do read, such lives in order to understand the nature of virtues like constancy and fidelity (to God as well as to others) and their role in human lives, and to discern, in the way people change over time, the redemptive power of grace in those lives. Biographies and autobiographies may also perform a similar function today. But novels are particularly suitable for moral discernment and education, because, as Colin McGinn says, their authors can 'artfully fashion their characters and the events in which they participate with specific themes in mind'.[11]

Just as philosophical and religious ethicists have come up with the concept of 'narrative ethics', so some theologians have developed in recent decades what has come to be called 'narrative theology', i.e. a theology that starts from the 'story' of Christ and Christians. Such a theology emphasizes that Christian faith, like Judaism, has constant reference to events that have taken place in history, events that continue to unfold in the present and the future: they are remembered by a community as helping to constitute its identity, and regarded by it as continuing to imbue the present with meaning and to evoke hope in what is to come.[12]

---

[11] Colin McGinn, *Evil, Ethics, and Fiction*, p. 177. McGinn suggests that, somewhat as the theory is the unit of 'persuasive discourse' in science, so the story is such in ethics.

See also Edith Wyschogrod, *Saints and Postmodernism* (Chicago, 1990), esp. pp. 3–19, 25–9, for a very different account of ethical narratives, discussing the role of saints' lives in articulating moral practice, and the peculiarities of such narratives – which include, for her, 'hagiographic fictions' like Henry James' *The Wings of a Dove* (pp. 42–8). She also says 'Saints' lives are not only communicated *in* texts but *as* texts . . .' (p. 36), thus enlarging the notion of text, somewhat as Mieke Bal has done by treating Rembrandt's paintings as texts.

[12] See, for example, George W. Stroup, *The Promise of Narrative Theology.* Gerard Loughlin offers a useful survey and a judicious assessment of such theology in his *Telling God's Story: Bible, Church, and Narrative Theology* (Cambridge, 1996); and Paul Lauritzen raises doubts about some recent narrative theology in his article 'Is "Narrative" Really a Panacea? The Use of "Narrative" in the Work of Metz and

I shall shortly go on to discuss a particular type of narrative theology, that of narratives of redemption; but let me first mention briefly another use of narrative: its use in some psychotherapy as part of what is sometimes referred to as a 'talking cure'.

In his *Healing Fiction* James Hillman brings out the importance of psychotherapists helping to give patients some sense of a narrative in their lives through their case-histories or 'soul stories'. He says:

> Perhaps our age has gone to analysis not to be loved or get cured, or even to Know Thyself. Perhaps we go to be given a case history, to be told into a soul story and given a plot to live by. This is the gift of case history, the gift of finding oneself in myth.[13]

Of course, people may latch onto the wrong story: some 'therapeutic fictions' may mislead (as journalists' 'stories' may distort or over-simplify). Hillman quotes Patricia Berry, 'The most important difficulty with narrative: it tends to become the ego's trip.'[14] There are always the dangers of over-dramatizing our lives

---

Hauerwas', *Journal of Religion* lxvii (1987), pp. 322–39. Lauritzen also argues that Christianity insists that there is a 'master narrative': I take it that he is questioning the common postmodernist claim that there are no meta-narratives, made classically by Jean-François Lyotard in his *La Condition Postmoderne: Rapport sur le savoir* (Paris, 1979), pp. 7–8. For a critique of Lyotard and a defence of 'grand narratives' from a different angle, drawing on Ricoeur's work, see J.M. Bernstein, 'Grand Narratives', in David Wood (ed.), *On Paul Ricoeur*, pp. 102–23.

[13] James Hillman, *Healing Fiction* (Woodstock, CT, 1983), p. 49. Ricoeur, too, makes much of the ideas of plot and 'emplotment', both with regard to the individual's life and to history, in his *Time and Narrative*.

[14] Ibid., p. 21. Similarly, Ricoeur warns that 'the connection between self-constancy and narrative identity confirms ... that the self of self-knowledge is not the egotistical and narcissistic ego whose hypocrisy and naïveté the hermeneutics of suspicion have denounced ... The self of self-knowledge is the fruit of an examined life ...' (*Time and Narrative*, vol.iii, p. 247). Ricoeur goes on immediately to discuss the use of case-histories in psychoanalysis; he also warns against the risk of the analyst's abuse here of 'strategies of persuasion'.

and of being satisfied with fantasy or self-deception, so we need to get the story right (in the sense of excluding things which prevent us from attending to what is actually there in our lives). In another book, *Suicide and the Soul*, Hillman relates the idea of narrative to suicide, by discussing how the latter may seem to many people to be a need of the soul. Those who see suicide simply as a 'mistake' and therefore as something to be prevented, e.g. representatives of law, medicine, theology, and sociology, tend to look at the matter from the outside, and so fail to understand what is really going on. To truly understand, however, therapists should look for meanings; and this requires that they be drawn into the patients' experiences, particularly their sufferings.[15]

In both these books Hillman points to something of central relevance to the subject of this chapter: the importance of narrative for getting a sense of one's identity and for understanding the course of one's life. A 'soul story' is something like a plot in a novel: it tells us why things happened as they did. (Opinions differ as to whether such a story may appeal to unconscious motives or reasons, or not.[16])

[15] James Hillman, *Suicide and the Soul*, pp. 24–37, 41–4.
   What if the subject of psychoanalysis cannot discern any narrative? Or what if a narrative just exposes a 'man without qualities', or the disconnectedness and incoherence of someone's life? Nathan A. Scott quotes Joan Didion as comparing a bad phase of five years in her life with a 'cutting room experience', in his 'The Rediscovery of Story in Recent Theology', in Robert Detweiler (ed.), *Art/Literature/Religion: Life on the Borders*, p. 145. More generally, Scott points to the suspicion of narrative in postmodernism and in recent 'metafiction', but comments that one still has to ask whether life is being represented as an 'affair of fate and doom, and as something dark and irremediable and futile', or as a matter of Providence and redemption (p. 152).
[16] In his discussion of Adler's psychology Hillman argues that Adler saw his role as being to bring out the significance of what we have not yet fully understood about our lives, but without appealing to the unconscious: 'Adler was a *phenomenologist* ... Adler gives a *hermeneutic* explanation remaining wholly within the realm of consciousness and how it intends the world ...' (*Healing Fiction*, pp. 110–11).

Now such an understanding is not a matter of providing general explanations of things, as in the natural sciences. Those who look only for general explanations of suicides will fail to understand why *this* person saw it as the only possible solution to *these* problems. Since human beings have an 'inside', therapists, like historians, should look for explanations of conduct in terms of the patient's feelings, experiences, and purposes; and the analytical process is one of intensifying consciousness, which goes on as long as life itself (even though the subject may no longer need the analyst's help).[17]

The kind of explanation that is in question here is much more like that used by historians than that used by natural scientists, because, although the former may succeed in finding some generalizations or 'covering laws' when dealing with matters like climate or economics, history's primary mode of explanation is in terms of people's purposes in their actions; and this, again requires historians to construct narratives in terms of actions and purposes (as to whether all such narratives are part of a single grand narrative, whether it be 'God's novel' or a Hegelian 'Universal History', that is another question). To understand such human narratives, we must understand the actions and the purposes of the agents described in them. Louis O. Mink contrasts the two kinds of understanding and explanation, of history and the natural sciences, when he says 'An historical narrative does not demonstrate the necessity of events but makes them intelligible by unfolding the story which connects their significance.'[18] Holding in mind a sequence already passed through is also necessary, he remarks, for understanding a symphony or a novel. In the case of historical understanding, our

---

[17] James Hillman, *Suicide and the Soul*, pp. 41*ff*, 58, 143.
[18] Louis O. Mink, 'History and Fiction as Modes of Comprehension', *New Literary History* i (1969–70), pp. 541–58, at p. 545. See also idem, 'Narrative Form as a Cognitive Instrument', in R.H. Canary and H. Kozicki (eds.), *The Writing of History: Literary Form and Historical Understanding* (Madison, 1978), pp. 129–49; and, more generally, Patrick Gardiner (ed.), *The Philosophy of History* (Oxford, 1974), chs. iii–vi.

narrative descriptions and 'synoptic judgements' will convey how events are interrelated, and how actions are responses to events. Constructing such narrative descriptions will involve selectivity – it is only in art that stories have neat beginnings, middles, and endings. Hence, Mink says, narrative is 'a primary act of mind transferred from art to life'.[19]

Hillman seems to be more interested in the parallels between the therapist's task and that of the novelist than in those between the therapist's and the historian's tasks. Either way, however, we are concerned with narrative. The connection between the therapist's work and the theologian's (other than their concern with the cure of souls) is that Christian soteriology too is a matter of constructing a narrative. While such a narrative will include stories of many individual lives, it will also include a foundational salvation history or sacred history; and both of these narratives will look towards the life to come. Moreover, it will use over-arching concepts like redemption to link all the three things mentioned. Let us now look more closely at narratives of redemption.

Narratives of Redemption

If a writer wishes not only to depict an evil or disordered situation, but also to hint at the possibility of its redemption, it is likely that temporal genres like plays, epic poems, novels, and biographies may be the most appropriate vehicles for conveying how this possibility may be worked out through human lives. We are concerned with particular human lives, with the emotions, choices, and actions which are woven into them, and with the ways in which events can either frustrate these or provide new avenues of hope.

In the case of drama we are concerned with human choices and actions, in relation to circumstances and to other people's lives, and with their consequences. Usually, however, the span of

[19] Louis O. Mink, 'History and Fiction as Modes of Comprehension', p. 557.

time represented in plays is relatively brief, and there is no narrator to reflect upon the action (though in Greek tragedy the chorus performs an analogous function). Hence for a fuller and longer working out of many aspects of human life, a narrative genre is often more appropriate: thus, for example, in an essay on Samuel Beckett Martha Nussbaum claims that narrative is a particularly appropriate way of expressing the nature of human emotions and choices. She argues that emotions have a cognitive content, because they are related to our beliefs and judgements about the world, especially beliefs about what is important and valuable; so they are part of people's 'stories'. Hence to understand emotions and choices, we need to see something of the fabric of the life of which they are a part; and expressing this understanding is best done through a narrative showing sympathy and imagination – an example of what Nussbaum calls 'love's knowledge'.[20]

What Nussbaum says about ordinary emotions and choices is even more applicable to the long-term policies and decisions that are part of the stuff of soteriology: narratives, of different kinds, are particularly appropriate for conveying them. If redemption is being worked out through historical events, as Christians believe, then the expression of this belief will include narratives of various kinds, e.g. the Gospels and biographies, within the framework of the 'grand narrative' of Fall, redemption, grace, and glory. In an article 'The Narrative Structure of Soteriology' Michael Root argues that Christian soteriology is a matter of constructing a narrative that links together the story of what Christ did, in his life, death, and resurrection, and the 'stories' of our lives, using some overriding structure, like that found in Anselm's *Cur Deus Homo*. Such a linking together will, Root suggests, produce a new kind of understanding, which, following Ricoeur, he calls a

---

[20] Martha Nussbaum, *Love's Knowledge*, ch.12, esp. pp. 290*f.*

'configurational understanding', involving a redescription of the facts.[21]

It will be seen that the two things which Root wishes to link together correspond to the first two Acts of what I have called the Drama of Redemption. He does not mention Act III, the life to come, presumably because we cannot provide or envisage a narrative of this Act: although in a sense all three Acts can be seen as part of a single continuum, there is the question of how, temporally, the third Act relates to the single sweep of time of the first two Acts.

The narratives of the first Act, salvation history, cover various things: traditionally, the story of Eden and the Fall; the calling of Abraham; the history of Israel; the life, death, and resurrection of Christ; and the first decades of the Church's history. The relevant Biblical genres are of many kinds – it is worth noting that in the *Messiah* Handel, or rather his librettist, Charles Jennens, uses narratives only in the case of the birth of Christ (from Luke 2); his texts from the Old Testament are drawn from the prophets, especially Deutero-Isaiah, and those from the New Testament are mainly from 1 Cor. 15, Rom. 8, and Rev. 5. But obviously narratives usually play an important role in salvation history, e.g. much of Exodus, the Gospels, and the Acts of the Apostles.

The second Act, human life, can be related in many kinds of narrative, as I have suggested already. But those narratives can in

[21] Michael Root, 'The Narrative Structure of Soteriology', *Modern Theology* ii (1986), pp. 145–58. See also, again, J.B. Metz, 'Redemption and Emancipation' and 'Narrative', in his *Faith in History and Society*, pp. 119–35, 205–18.

Commenting on Root's article, Gerard Loughlin says 'A narrative soteriology suggests that salvation is not simply illustrated but constituted by the story of Jesus.' For there is a *storied* relationship between Jesus and those who are saved: the latter are 'enfolded' in the story. Thus Christian salvation is to be understood as 'the reordering of the subject's story by, and finally within, the story of Jesus Christ.' (*Telling God's Story*, pp. 211, 214).

All these works remind us of a question suggested by St Augustine and so many later writers, of whether Christianity revolutionized people's conception of time, by its proclaiming that the life, death, and resurrection of Christ are the climax of history.

turn be divided into three Acts, or perhaps, better, Scenes. For every human life has its past, its present, and its final outcome, whether the last be seen in terms of some decisive event, 'living happily ever after', or death (if the outcome is seen as a life after death, this takes us to Act III, which, as we have seen, cannot be narrated – Dante's narrative in the *Divine Comedy* is mainly that of his envisaged journey). Many 'novels of redemption' depict life in this way: for instance, François Mauriac's *The Knot of Vipers*, a novel of redemption *par excellence*, opens with the elderly Louis, expecting to die soon, writing to his wife Isa (to whom he has been unhappily married, largely through his misjudgement of her), to settle scores with her and his family. More about his past is thereby revealed, including the death many years earlier of their young child, Marie, who had offered up her suffering for her father; and the novel continues in the present, with the unexpected death of Isa. It ends with the death of Louis himself, seemingly converted to a love of God and of his family. Similarly, Dostoevsky's *Crime and Punishment* can be seen as having three Acts or phases within one narrative: Raskolnikov's murders, the time leading up to his confession and trial, and his later life with Sonya in Siberia, hinted at at the very end of the book.

Both these novels seek to depict a long process, involving change in human characters and lives. George Orwell commended Tolstoy too for his ability to give the reader a sense of characters who are growing: in his essay 'Charles Dickens' he says,

> His [Tolstoy's] characters are struggling to make their souls, whereas Dickens's are already finished and perfect. In my own mind Dickens's people are present far more vividly than Tolstoy's, but always in a single unchangeable attitude, like pictures or pieces of furniture. You cannot hold an imaginary conversation with a Dickens character as you can with, say, Peter Bezoukhov.[22]

---

[22] George Orwell, 'Charles Dickens', in his *Collected Essays*, pp. 31–87, at p. 82.

Mauriac is interpreting such growth in theological terms: he is clearly concerned to capture the working of grace in someone's life. Of course, he does not think that novelists should try to describe the essence of grace – that is not their function; but they can convey its action, for the narrative of human freedom may also be a narrative of grace and of its effect on people's lives. Many Christian novelists have seen part of their task as being to depict such grace-filled lives; their problem, as I have noted, is of how to do this in a convincing way.

Novels, of course, are only one kind of 'narratives of redemption', even of those relevant to Act II of the drama. I have mentioned others, like biographies and psychiatric case-histories. Novels, however, are among the most interesting and moving of such narratives; and they are perhaps the most widely read today. I shall, therefore, continue my discussion of narrative by concentrating on the special features of novels of redemption in the next chapter, and assessing how they contribute to religious understanding. Thereby, I shall be seeking to support the claims of narrative theology (albeit one greatly enlarged in its scope). For if Martha Nussbaum and others advise us to go to novelists like Tolstoy more than to philosophers in order to increase our understanding of love, why should we not also go to them, as well as to theologians, for an understanding of redemption and of our need for it?

CHAPTER SEVEN

Act II: Novels of Redemption

Lives and Narratives

I have already mentioned a few examples of novels which bring in ideas of redemption, atonement, or salvation, like Dostoevsky's *Crime and Punishment* and Mauriac's *The Knot of Vipers*. The former explores the themes of guilt, repentance, redemption through suffering, and new life; it also raises the questions of Sonya's role, and of whether Raskolnikov is unconsciously seeking his own arrest and trial. Of the latter novel, the author wrote in an essay that he found it easier to find the 'primitive flame' that still exists in the worst characters than to depict virtuous ones, and that in the main figure of the novel, Louis, he discovered a soul and the possibility of saving him without destroying him as a convincing character: 'the book ends when I have restored to my hero, to this son of darkness, his rights to light, to love and, in a word, to God.'[1]

Other obvious similar examples which spring to mind are Victor Hugo's *Les Misérables*, Graham Greene's *The Power and the Glory*, and much of the work of Flannery O'Connor, who, like Mauriac, wrote for people for whom 'redemption is meaningless' – she remarked of the modern reader, 'His sense of evil is diluted or lacking altogether, and so he has forgotten the price of restoration', whereas for her, 'the meaning of life is centred on our Redemption by Christ and what I see in the world I see in relation to that'.[2]

---

[1] François Mauriac, 'Le Romancier et ses personnages', in his *Oeuvres Complètes* viii (Paris, 1963), p. 299.

[2] Flannery O'Connor, *Mystery and Manners* (London, 1972), pp. 48, 32.

Then, more peripherally, there are novels which revolve around the ideas of moral redemption, redemption through love, or the recovery of one's honour, like Dickens' *A Christmas Carol* and *Our Mutual Friend*, or Conrad's *Lord Jim*, in which Jim thinks that he has to atone for his leap from the apparently sinking ship, of which he was the First Mate, and thus to redeem his honour. There are also works like Margaret Atwood's *Surfacing*, which use redemptive imagery to convey something other than conventional religious belief, such as the recovery of a sense of identity.[3] Then lastly, by way of contrast, there are novels which seem to deny the possibility of any redemption or which ignore the question. Thomas Hardy's concluding statement in *Tess of the D'Urbervilles* that ' "Justice" was done, and the President of the Immortals (in Aeschylean phrase) had finished his sport with Tess' reflects the author's loss of Christian faith and his cosmic pessimism, also seen in the ending of *Jude the Obscure*. In a less personal way, Emile Zola's naturalism concentrated on the scientific and documentary character of fiction, and left no room for ideas like divine grace, redemption, and providence. D.H. Lawrence saw himself as a religious writer, but the salvation that he envisaged was an alternative one to that of traditional Christianity; while, more radically, works like Samuel Beckett's *Molloy* seem to exclude from consideration even the desire for redemption.

Several of the works that I have mentioned were written by Roman Catholics, and it has been common practice in recent years for literary critics to refer to a tradition of 'the Catholic novel'.[4] I shall highlight such works in this chapter because I think that they particularly exemplify the 'novel of redemption'. In the case of French Catholic novels, Malcolm Scott has argued that this tradition can be traced back to the nineteenth century, and

[3] A point made by Mary Grey, in her *Redeeming the Dream*, p. 51.
[4] See, e.g., Bernard Bergonzi, 'The Decline and Fall of the Catholic Novel', in his *The Myth of Modernism and Twentieth-Century Literature* (Brighton, 1986), pp. 172–87; and my 'The End of the Catholic Novel?', *Literature and Theology* ix (1995), pp. 165–78.

that it arose as a conscious response to Realist and Naturalist writers, above all, Zola. The Catholic writers were trying to beat the latter at their own game, as it were, by presenting an 'alternative realism', that is, a very different but more 'realistic' account of human life.[5] In some cases, e.g. in many of the works of Mauriac and Bernanos, they give a very bleak picture, sometimes depicting extreme wickedness and suffering. But this is no mere fascination with evil: Mauriac, as we have seen, was concerned to penetrate below the surface and to discern the conflicts and the subtle movements of grace in the human soul, and thereby to understand the supernatural character of human actions, and this explains his apparent preoccupation with the abnormal, the diseased, and the monstrous (a tendency also seen in Bernanos and O'Connor), which shocked many of his *bien pensant* contemporaries. In his essay 'Le jeune homme' he writes 'There are no monsters. We are not so different from them',[6] and on occasion both he and Graham Greene quote Bossuet, 'One must go as far as horror to know oneself.'[7]

Thus Mauriac and writers like him would probably apply to themselves Dostoevsky's description of himself as a 'realist in the higher sense'.[8] Although they used their work to express their religious views, they were not propagandists or apologists. They

---

[5] Malcolm Scott, *The Struggle for the Soul of the French Novel: French Catholic and Realist Novels, 1850–1970* (London, 1989), pp. 5*ff*, 267–8. See also T.R. Wright, *Theology and Literature* (Oxford, 1988), pp. 110–28.

[6] François Mauriac, *Oeuvres Complètes* iv (Paris, 1963), p. 436.

[7] Philip Stratford, *Faith and Fiction*, p. 28.

[8] 'I am a realist in the higher sense, that is I depict all the depths of the human soul', quoted from the Russian edition of Dostoevsky's works by Robert Louis Jackson in his *Dialogues with Dostoevsky* (Stanford, 1993), p. 14. In a similar spirit, Dostoevsky wrote in a letter to Nikolai Strakhov in 1869:

> I have my own special view of reality (in art), and what the majority calls fantastic and exceptional sometimes constitutes the very essence of the real. The ordinariness of phenomena and a banal view of them are not yet realism, in my view, but even the contrary.

Cf. David A. Lowe (ed.), *Fyodor Dostoevski, Complete Letters*, vol.iii, 1868–71 (Ann Arbor, 1991), p. 137.

evidently felt that great issues may be decided here and now and that, as Wittgenstein put it,

> Christianity is ... a description of something that actually takes place in human life. For 'consciousness of sin' is a real event and so are despair and salvation through faith. Those who speak of such things (Bunyan for instance) are simply describing what has happened to them, whatever gloss anyone may want to put on it.[9]

But why did they regard novels as a suitable way of expressing their vision of life, rather than, say, philosophical or theological treatises? Why look to fiction for an understanding of redemption? I have already suggested one obvious answer to these questions, in terms of the appropriateness of a narrative or a drama for capturing the nature of actions and processes that are worked out in time (as Bunyan, whom Wittgenstein mentions, realized). But there are some other considerations worth mentioning, also related to the nature of narrative.

Martha Nussbaum, in an essay 'Fictions of the Soul', argues that the claim that only a novel can convey psychological truth is not just the claim that it can get around certain impediments more clearly than a philosophical text; rather,

> it is the claim that there is at least some knowledge, some important human knowledge, that it provides just in virtue of its being a novel ... that cannot even in principle be provided in another more intellectual way.[10]

---

[9] Ludwig Wittgenstein, *Culture and Value*, p. 28e.

[10] Martha Nussbaum, 'Fictions of the Soul', in her *Love's Knowledge*, ch.10; I quote from p. 256. See Cora Diamond, 'Martha Nussbaum and the Need for Novels', *Philosophical Investigations* xvi (1993), pp. 128–53, for a further exploration of Nussbaum's thesis.

Even when there are general truths at issue, she says, novels 'vigorously assert the importance and uniqueness of contingent particulars'. Moreover, the relevant truths may be subtle and elusive:

> not everything about the human soul *is* perspicuous ... the deepest depths are dark and shifting and elusive. A form of representation that implied otherwise would be artificial and untruthful.[11]

We saw in the last chapter how, in a later essay in the same book, Nussbaum claims also that the nature of human emotions and choices makes narrative a particularly appropriate mode of expression, arguing that emotions have a cognitive content, because they are related to our beliefs and judgements about the world, especially beliefs about what is valuable and important; hence they are part of people's 'stories'.

Nussbaum does not consider religious narrative here. She does not, therefore, discuss whether novels and religious narratives resemble each other in any way, or why this genre has attracted so many Christian writers. So we need to go on now to look at some of the distinctive features of novels of redemption. We are obviously concerned with human lives, through which redemption is being worked out; and, within these lives, with actions fraught with metaphysical depth, having certain consequences in this life, and perhaps beyond it. These actions may be good or evil: Raskolnikov thought at first that the killing of the old money-lender was of no more significance than killing a louse or a cockroach, and indeed was more justifiable, for she actually harmed people; but Dostoevsky persuades us otherwise, by setting forth the true nature of what Raskolnikov has done and its implications. The good actions may be regarded as 'graced', i.e. as *loci* of God's communication of Himself. Not that novelists should try

[11] Martha Nussbaum, *Love's Knowledge*, p. 258.

to describe the essence of grace – that is not their function; but they can seek to convey its action (or its seeming absence).

The novelist conveys something of the action of grace, and also of human emotions and responses, by showing forth rather than seeking to explain these things.[12] Flannery O'Connor wrote that 'Fiction writing is very seldom a matter of saying things; it is a matter of showing things.'[13] Such showings have many facets: symbolism is especially important, in helping to bring out the general significance of the particular, in conveying different levels of understanding, and in appealing to the imagination.

Sometimes the relevant actions may be long and complicated, but often they are fundamental human responses like repenting and forgiving (which may, nevertheless, be very costly). Sometimes the writer may analyse and moralize about them, but more frequently, as I have suggested, his or her task is just to present them to us: not as examples of general truths or as illustrations of theories, but as the very substance of life. Mauriac described himself as 'a metaphysician working in the concrete'[14]: he found the novel an ideal medium, because it can capture unseen movements and processes that are worked out only gradually in human lives, and because it can convey psychological truth. His description of himself reminds one of his older compatriot, the philosopher Maurice Blondel, who chose action as the subject of his first work, his doctoral dissertation *L'Action* of 1893, although this was regarded as an odd topic for philosophers at the time. Blondel described action as 'the point on which the powers of Nature, the light of the understanding, the strength of the will and even the benefits of grace converge'.[15] For Blondel action is primary; the intellectualizing, generalizing, and theorizing come later. And that is why I have insisted that the artistic and literary

---

[12] Later on, in Chapter 9, I shall discuss how liturgies too can 'show' things.

[13] Flannery O'Connor, *Mystery and Manners*, p. 93.

[14] François Mauriac, *Journal* II, in *Oeuvres Complètes* xi (Paris, 1963), p. 154.

[15] Quoted in Lester R. Kurtz, *The Politics of Heresy: The Modernist Crisis in Roman Catholicism* (Berkeley and Los Angeles, 1986), p. 76.

examples which I have mentioned and discussed should not be regarded merely as illustrations of soteriological themes. Rather, responses like wanting to be freed from the evil within oneself or surrounding one, desiring to be forgiven and to atone for one's wrongdoing, and realizing that one cannot do it alone, are the soil from which theology grows. The artist's and the writer's task here is to illuminate them, and thereby to help us increase our understanding.

Of course, artists and writers interpret their experience, and are selective in what they present to us. Dostoevsky, in *Crime and Punishment*, is concerned to present the moral order which he believed to be inherent in things, and the price of flouting it. So it is not surprising that in novels of redemption we notice a preference for certain themes.

Themes and Contrasts

Traditionally, at least in Western Christianity, redemption has been regarded, first of all, as redemption from sin. Writing of *Crime and Punishment* and its treatment of the theme of resurrection, Richard Harries says, 'Here the God who raised Christ Jesus from the dead, and who will raise us from death into immortal life, is experienced now raising us from the death of sin and despair.'[16] When reading many 'novelists of redemption' one is often struck by their sense of sin and the way in which they convey an atmosphere of evil. And they themselves are often quite candid about what they are doing. In his journal Mauriac writes, 'the sinner about whom the theologian gives us an abstract idea, I make incarnate'; and that the art of the imaginative writer is to make 'visible, tangible, odiferous a world full of wicked pleasures – and of sanctity, too'.[17]

---

[16] Richard Harries, 'The resurrection in some modern novels', in '*If Christ be not risen*': *Essays in resurrection and survival*, ed. E. Russell and J. Greenhalgh (London, 1986), pp. 40–55, at p. 53.
[17] François Mauriac, *Journal* II and III, in his *Oeuvres Complètes* xi, pp. 154, 262.

He portrays many memorable sinners: Thérèse Desqueyroux, who tried to murder her husband, in the novel named after her; Brigitte Pian, the self-deceived hypocrite and hounder of others, in *The Woman of the Pharisees* and *The Lamb*; the bitter and avaricious Louis, in *The Knot of Vipers*. In an essay on Mauriac (whom he admired greatly), Graham Greene commended his characters as having 'the solidity and importance of men with souls to save or lose',[18] and as manifesting the presence of forces of good and evil that penetrate them and give an extra dimension to character, a dimension which Greene found missing in many modern writers. Similarly, Greene wrote in another essay that his discovery of the work of Frederick Rolfe (Baron Corvo) made him aware of 'eternal issues, of the struggle between good and evil, between vice that really demands to be called satanic and virtue of a kind that can only be called heavenly'.[19]

Greene, too, created several memorable portraits of evil, like Pinkie in *Brighton Rock*, as well as more ambiguously sinful characters like Scobie in *The Heart of the Matter*. Yet he said 'Mauriac's characters sin against God, whereas mine, try as they may, never quite manage to'[20]; and the comforting words of priests to both Pinkie's and Scobie's widows after their deaths remind us of another remark of Greene:

> The novelist has this in common with the priest, that he studies mankind only after having plumbed the depths of his own heart and soul. If only to defend himself, he must defend others. He dare not over-simplify.[21]

---

[18] Graham Greene, 'François Mauriac', in his *Collected Essays* (Harmondsworth, 1970), p. 92.

[19] Idem, 'Frederick Rolfe: Edwardian Inferno', in *Collected Essays*, pp. 130–1.

[20] Idem, 'The Art of Fiction', in *The Paris Review* iii (1953), p. 34, quoted in Philip Stratford, *Faith and Fiction*, p. 237.

[21] Idem, in an essay on Fr Damien in *Essais Catholiques*, quoted in Philip Stratford, *Faith and Fiction*, pp. 29, 219.

But if Greene pulled his punches, Flannery O'Connor may be
seen as slapping modern agnostic readers in the face, in an
attempt to arouse in them a sense of evil and of the need for
redemption; and even more so Bernanos, who introduces Satan as
a character, in the guise of a horse-dealer, in a scene in his novel
Sous le Soleil de Satan, which Malcolm Scott describes as 'the most
radical gesture of defiance of the modern age that one is likely to
find in any twentieth-century writer'[22]; while Shusaku Endo wrote
for a culture, that of Japan, which, he thought, lacks the concept
of sin.

A preoccupation with sin naturally goes often with a concern
with repentance, exemplified in Louis in *The Knot of Vipers* or in
the nameless whisky-priest in Greene's *The Power and the Glory*, and
depicted as a change of heart which leads them to see things,
especially their own previous lives, differently; and also in the
countess in Bernanos' *The Diary of a Country Priest*. None of these
penitents live long after their repentance – perhaps because it is
easier and more interesting to depict a sinful rather than a
converted life![23]

In the case of works by Catholic writers repentance is linked to
the sacrament of Penance or Reconciliation, and to those who
administer it, priests. Hence the priest is a common figure in the
'Catholic novel', though not only there (think of the role of
clergymen in Anthony Trollope's Barsetshire novels or in Susan
Howatch's Starbridge cycle). There are several roles that they
play: the comic priest, e.g. Greene's Monsignor Quixote; the
detective, e.g. Chesterton's Fr Brown; the Liberationist ex-priest,
seen in Leon, in Greene's *The Honorary Consul*; or the saint. The
last of these roles, in turn, embraces several types: the suffering
reconciler, e.g. the Abbé Calou in Mauriac's *The Woman of the
Pharisees* or Bernanos' country priest; the whisky-priest in Greene's
The Power and the Glory, pursuing his vocation despite his own

---

[22] Malcolm Scott, *The Struggle for the Soul of the French Novel*, p. 242.
[23] Though, on the other side, one should mention e.g. Nekhlyudov in Tolstoy's
Resurrection and Raskolnikov in *Crime and Punishment*.

doubts and lapses; or the martyr (the same priest, at the end of the book).

Two things about the priesthood particularly interest the novelist of redemption: the priest's dedication to God and to his flock, and his sacramental role. The former finds a powerful symbolic expression in priestly celibacy, which makes the priest visibly a figure 'set apart'. Greene's priest in *The Power and the Glory* (who has an illegitimate child), reflects 'only the childless man has the right to call strangers his children'.[24] The Abbé Calou is depicted as the spiritual father of Jean de Mirbel in *The Woman of the Pharisees*; and Bernanos' country priest loves his parish like a father, and seems to be frustrated in his role until the scene with the countess, who despite being his superior in age, social status, and intelligence, leaves him with a sense of having achieved his vocation as a spiritual father.[25] Bernanos depicts him almost as a scapegoat in the original sense, i.e. an innocent driven out into the wilderness, having some physical peculiarity or deformity, and bearing the sins of others.

The priest is also 'set apart' because he has received the sacrament of Holy Orders, and because he is related to people in a special way through his sacramental role. The priest in *The Power and the Glory* journeys from place to place, baptizing children, hearing confessions, saying Mass, and giving the Last Sacraments to the dying. Many of the dramatic scenes in the novel, e.g. his attempts to buy wine, his stay in prison, and his final capture and interrogation (after being lured on and betrayed by an informer who pretends to bring news of a dying penitent) depend on his sacramental role. Greene describes the priest's realization that this role is not destroyed by his unworthiness[26] – a recognition of the Catholic principle that sacraments are valid *ex opere operato*, a principle also illustrated at the end of Bernanos' *The Diary of a Country Priest*, where the priest's last confession is heard by a

[24] Graham Greene, *The Power and the Glory* (Harmondsworth, 1971), p. 62.

[25] Georges Bernanos, *The Diary of a Country Priest*, tr. P. Morris (London, 1956), pp. 154–5. By contrast, however, the countess regards him as a child (p. 150).

[26] Graham Greene, *The Power and the Glory*, p. 195.

former priest living with his mistress. Chesterton's Fr Brown is depicted as gaining a lot of his intuitive understanding of people from his long hours in the confessional, and the connection is suggested by other Catholic writers. Hence Thomas Woodman writes of 'the privileged insight that the confessional is held to give into the hidden depths of evil in the human heart'.[27]

This interest in the priesthood can be contrasted with the relative lack of interest in successful marriages or happy long-term sexual relationships between people, seen in many Catholic novelists. One thinks of many examples of unhappy marriages in Greene and Mauriac (e.g. in the former's *The Heart of the Matter* and the latter's *The Desert of Love*) or of Bernanos' seeming lack of interest. This seems surprising, given Catholicism's 'high', sacramental view of marriage. But there are some general considerations to be taken into account, e.g. the traditional Catholic position, deriving from Luke 20.34–6 and 1 Cor. 7, that a celibacy dedicated to God is a higher calling than marriage, and many novelists' preference for depicting unhappiness and strain, for 'happiness is a blank sheet'; and also some more personal ones: Flannery O'Connor, following Elizabeth Sewell , accused Greene of having Catholic convictions but a Manichean sensibility,[28] while many critics have accused Mauriac of Jansenist tendencies (a criticism that he acknowledged[29]).

In Mauriac's case there was also perhaps the tendency to look rather at other forms of love: of parents and children, of priests for their flock, of God. Louis, in *The Knot of Vipers*, comes to a new love both of God and of his family, after his change of heart (similarly, the priest in Greene's *The Power and the Glory* comes to truly love his flock during and after his stay in prison – a crucial

---

[27] Thomas Woodman, *Faithful Fictions: The Catholic Novel in British Literature* (Milton Keynes, 1991), p. 135. A fuller discussion of the role of priests in novels would have to consider the changes in the Catholic priesthood and its social status since the Second Vatican Council.

[28] Flannery O'Connor, *The Habit of Being* (New York, 1979), p. 201.

[29] E.g. in *God and Mammon*, p. 103, and in *Writers at Work: The Paris Review Interviews, First Series* (London, 1958), p. 39.

scene in the book). Mauriac is often reluctant, it seems, to regard married love as a channel of grace and to see its fidelity as mirroring God's fidelity. And Greene's adulteries and unhappy marriages are what remain in the mind: Sarah Miles, in *The End of the Affair*, has to renounce her adulterous affair with Bendrix (whom she still loves) after her conversion; as Julia renounces Charles at the end of Evelyn Waugh's *Brideshead Revisited*. What seems to be lacking in the 'Catholic novel' are examples of couples who come to God *through* their love for each other, without losing the latter love. After all, the New Testament does not present love of God and love of neighbour as alternatives, one of which must be renounced for the other, as Greene well realizes, for he makes Querry say to the phoney Rycker in *A Burnt-Out Case* that he pretends to love a god because he loves no one else.[30] Walter Kasper writes, 'Human faithfulness is, as it were, the grammar by means of which God's faithfulness, definitively revealed in Jesus Christ, can be spelt out.'[31] But many novelists lack, it seems, a theology of marriage.

We find a faith in the redemptive power of romantic and married love elsewhere, e.g. in Dostoevsky, and, among twentieth-century Catholic novelists, in some of Heinrich Böll's work, e.g. his *The Bread of Those Early Years* and *And where were you, Adam?* Böll gives a theological justification of his position in an essay, 'Letter to a Young Catholic', in which he says that what is wrongly called 'physical love' is as much the substance of a sacrament as bread and wine: 'there is no such thing as purely physical love or purely spiritual love; both contain an element of the other even if only a tiny one. We are neither pure spirits nor pure bodies . . .'[32] Böll sees such love as redemptive, as having something of eternity in it, and in this essay and elsewhere,[33]

---

[30] Graham Greene, *A Burnt-Out Case* (Harmondsworth, 1975), p. 145.
[31] Walter Kasper, *Theology of Christian Marriage*, tr. D. Smith (London, 1980), p. 24.
[32] Heinrich Böll, *Brief an einen Jungen Katholiken* (Cologne and Berlin, 1961), p. 12.
[33] E.g. in his *Frankfurter Vorlesungen* (Munich, 1968), p. 110, and *The Clown*, tr. L. Vennewitz (London, 1968), p. 124. Another 'redemptive' theme that often crops up in Böll's work is his call for post-War Germany to repent and atone for the sins of the Hitler regime.

he attacks the Churches for their failure to understand it, despite the texts at their disposal. Thus Böll manifests what is commonly called a world-affirming spirituality, as contrasted with a world-denying one.[34]

Grace and Sanctification

Behind all the particular themes that I have just mentioned is a much larger one, that of the possibility of grace working within human lives to transform them. But there are different ways of depicting this, and often these differences reflect varying theologies of grace.

One way of portraying the action of grace is, as Flannery O'Connor notes, to imagine what a world *without* it would be like.[35] Thus in the Preface to *Trois récits* Mauriac admits to describing 'a miserable world emptied of grace'[36]; and in the Postscript to a late novel, *The Loved and the Unloved*, he writes

> The picture I have painted is indeed black. It shows mankind as warped, as showing to the world a mask fixed in a hard and hateful grimace. It shows humanity untouched by Grace.[37]

Some theologians might ask here: *is* there, in fact, any humanity untouched by grace? But Mauriac is trying to imagine what it would be like; and clearly he thinks that there is at least a seeming absence of grace for the normal modern man and woman. Sometimes, too, he seems to be describing *resistance* to grace, for instance in Brigitte Pian's self-deception, in *The Woman of the Pharisees*.

[34] See again Martin Green, *Yeats's Blessing on von Hügel*, pp. 65–96.
[35] Flannery O'Connor, *The Habit of Being*, p. 204.
[36] François Mauriac, *Oeuvres Complètes* vi (Paris, 1963), p. 122.
[37] Idem, *The Loved and the Unloved*, tr. G. Hopkins (London, 1953), p. 136.

Having shown the seeming absence of grace, a writer may then go on to point a contrast by trying to depict its presence and action, which may be as a slow change or as a sudden crisis or illumination. The latter is much easier to depict: one sees it in the priest's conversation with the countess in Bernanos' *The Diary of a Country Priest*, in the scene in the prison in Greene's *The Power and the Glory*, and in some of Flannery O'Connor's short stories, e.g. 'A Good Man is Hard to Find' and 'The Artificial Nigger'. Evelyn Waugh hints rather at a slow change in the heading of Part 3 of *Brideshead Revisited*, 'A Twitch upon the Thread', but it seems that it is the 'twitch' that shows the existence of the 'thread', in the melodramatic description of Lord Marchmain's death-bed conversion and its aftermath.

Many writers depict grace as working through sordidness, e.g. Dostoevsky in *Crime and Punishment*, Greene in *The Power and the Glory*, and Bernanos in most of his works. Such an approach, by establishing a contrast, brings out the transforming power of grace. But of course, transformation may be hard: in her letters Flannery O'Connor remarks that we resist grace because it changes us and change is painful; 'This notion that grace is healing omits the fact that before it heals, it cuts with the sword Christ said he came to bring.'[38] This pain is depicted in Francis Tarwater's career in O'Connor's *The Violent Bear it Away*, and also in Charles' and Julia's separation at the end of *Brideshead Revisited*.

But how is grace mediated? One way, as we have seen, is through the sacraments. A second way is through other people, often weak people, morally or physically (or both), e.g. the priest in Greene's *The Power and the Glory*, or the one in Bernanos' *The Diary of a Country Priest*, who is represented as a channel of God's mercy and love, and who reflects early on in the novel, 'Monks suffer for souls, *our* pain is on behalf of souls.'[39]

Bernanos is appealing here, I think, to the model of the Suffering Servant, interpreted as meaning that suffering can be

---

[38] Flannery O'Connor, *The Habit of Being*, pp. 307, 411.
[39] Georges Bernanos, *The Diary of a Country Priest*, p. 27.

redemptive, for oneself and, vicariously, for others, a model seen also perhaps in the character of Himmelfarb, who endures a mock crucifixion, in Patrick White's novel *Riders of the Chariot*. Some of Mauriac's characters spell out the theology implicit in this model: in his *Lines of Life*, Pierre Gornac imagines Christ on the Cross, motionless and 'incapable of doing anything for men save shed his blood', and concludes:

> Thus must his true disciple do: intervening only by way of sacrifice and blood-offering. One can change nothing in human beings, nor can human beings change themselves unless it be by the Creator's will operating in each one of them. They must be ransomed as they are, with all their load of propensities and vices ... All one can do is bleed and obliterate oneself for them.[40]

Mauriac describes another of his novels, *Dark Angels,* as a 'novel of the reversibility of merits and ... of vocation', in which the priest Alain Forcas, 'chosen, called from the midst of this fallen world, suffers and pays for all my wretched heroes'.[41]

Such an idea of making oneself a sacrificial victim derives from Isaiah, but probably also from St Paul's claim that through one's own suffering one may participate in the suffering of Christ's Passion, helping to complete the latter (Phil. 3.10; Col. 1.24). Mauriac believes that Christians who share in Christ's agony co-operate in the redemption of the world, and writes of the humblest suburban curate giving his

[40] François Mauriac, *Lines of Life*, tr. G. Hopkins (London, 1957), pp. 142–3.
[41] Idem, in the Preface to *Dark Angels* (not included in the English translation), in *Oeuvres Complètes* iii, p. ii; he goes on to say that the essential theme of all three novels *The Knot of Vipers, That which was Lost*, and *Dark Angels* is 'the redemption of the criminal mass by a small number of sacrificial victims' (p. iv). I have already mentioned in an earlier chapter the sacrificial theme in another of Mauriac's novels, *The Lamb*, in which Xavier is depicted 'in a passionate fervour of substitution', as praying: 'Always that – "take me in his stead", always that longing to assume the miseries of another's destiny' (p. 138).

life for sinners.[42] But he is also appealing, I think, to a particular interpretation of the doctrine of the Communion of Saints, involving the 'co-inherence of souls', i.e. the belief that all Christians, living and dead, are interdependent and can therefore assist each other. He writes in yet another of his novels of the 'discipline of exchange, of compensation, of transference which Grace imposes on the true believer ...'[43] This is in the context of describing the Abbé Calou's vocation to suffer for others. A few pages earlier, Calou himself has described the priest as, like the crucified Christ, a sign of contradiction to the world: 'The priest, fastened to the same instrument of torment and exposed to the same derision, confronts mankind with an enigma which it makes no effort to solve.'[44] Like Christ, he suffers for others:

> ... it is different for me, I can suffer: I know that. One can always suffer for others ... Do I really believe that? ... Yes, I do. What an appalling doctrine it is that acts count for nothing, that no man can gain merit for himself or for those whom he loves. All through the centuries Christians have believed that the humble crosses to which they were nailed on the right hand and left hand of our Lord meant something for their own redemption, and for the redemption of those they loved. And then Calvin came and took away that hope. But I have never lost it ...[45]

The latter quotation is in the context of Mauriac's describing Calou's sense of spiritual fatherhood for Jean de Mirbel: he is depicted as a suffering healer and reconciler.

---

[42] Idem, 'Souffrances et bonheur du Chrétien', *Oeuvres Complètes* vii (Paris, 1963), pp. 244, 259.
[43] Idem, *A Woman of the Pharisees*, p. 169. David Lodge uses the phrase 'mystical substitution' in his Introduction to the English translation of *The Knot of Vipers*, p. 7.
[44] Ibid., p. 163.
[45] Ibid., p. 142.

A similar example is that of the child Marie in *The Knot of Vipers*, who said 'for Papa' as she lay suffering and dying. Shortly before his own death, at the end of the book, her father, Louis, reflects,

> I had shut my ears so as not to hear Marie's words as she lay dying. Nevertheless, at her bedside the secret of death and of life had been revealed to me ... A little girl had been dying for me.[46]

Such examples perhaps illustrate Simone Weil's remark, 'The extreme greatness of Christianity lies in the fact that it does not seek a supernatural remedy for suffering but a supernatural use of it.'[47] One might also add, 'and does not offer a supernatural explanation of it, either'. For Mauriac's characters raise some obvious questions about the mechanics of the process of 'mystical substitution': why does one person's suffering benefit another? Is it that God accepts it, as He accepted the suffering of Christ on the Cross? If so, why? Mauriac does not feel that he is called on to answer such questions: Calou describes the Cross as an 'enigma', Louis has seen the 'secret of life and death'. The novelist's task is not theodicy or theological explanation: it is to *present* a convincing account of human life as he sees it. I shall return to this question in Chapter 9.

Besides looking at how people are represented as channels of grace for others, it is also illuminating sometimes to look at the analogies writers use when describing grace. Mauriac compares it to underground streams,[48] presumably there all the time, but erupting only occasionally. Waugh's 'twitch upon the thread' in *Brideshead Revisited* (the theme of which he describes as 'the

---

[46] François Mauriac, *The Knot of Vipers*, p. 198.
[47] Simone Weil, *Gravity and Grace*, tr. E. Craufurd (London, 1963), p. 73.
[48] François Mauriac, *Oeuvres Complètes* viii, p. 431, with reference to Greene's *The Power and the Glory*.

operation of divine grace on a group of diverse but closely related characters'[49]) conveys a similar idea.

These analogies suggest to some people that grace erupts or intervenes suddenly: Rayner Heppenstall wrote rather scathingly, 'In Greene's novels, the plumbing system of grace is in full flow ...'[50] Such an understanding has been attacked also by some modern theologians: for Karl Rahner, grace is abundant, not measured out meanly by God (this is partly a matter of his 'salvation optimism', and partly a matter of his theological anthropology: he thinks that there is a 'supernatural existential' in virtue of which all men and women are *a priori* open to grace, and grace is not a 'second storey' added on to an already complete first storey, i.e. 'nature'[51]). The analogies I have mentioned do not necessarily indicate that grace is a rare intervention, for underground streams and threads suggest something that is always there, even if apparent only on some occasions. Still Mauriac, at any rate, acknowledged that he often portrayed a grace-less world, and he describes grace as 'breaking in'.[52] An understanding of grace more like Rahner's is perhaps hinted at in the final scene of Bernanos' *The Diary of a Country Priest,* in which the dying priest, told that the priest who has been called to give him the *viaticum* has not arrived yet, says, 'Does it matter? Grace is ... everywhere.'[53] And Böll's view of life is often close to that of Rahner: for the former it is the ordinary, especially human love, that is a channel of grace.

Flannery O'Connor's remark, that grace, in order to heal, may be painful, perhaps suggests an Augustinian understanding of

---

[49] Evelyn Waugh, *Brideshead Revisited*, Preface to 2nd edn. (Harmondsworth, 1962), p. 7.

[50] Rayner Heppenstall, *The Double Image: Mutations of Christian Mythology in the Work of four French Catholic writers of today and yesterday* (London, 1947), p. 38.

[51] See especially Karl Rahner, 'Nature and Grace', in his *Theological Investigations* vol. iv, tr. K. Smyth (London, 1974), pp. 165–88.

[52] Again, see the Postscript to Mauriac's *The Loved and the Unloved*, esp. pp. 135–6.

[53] Georges Bernanos, *The Diary of a Country Priest*, p. 253. The words '*Tout est Grâce*' are quoted from St Thérèse of Lisieux.

grace, which makes a fairly sharp distinction between nature and grace, an understanding that may be contrasted with the Thomistic view, which Rahner is re-presenting, summed up in St Thomas Aquinas' saying 'grace perfects nature'. In her case, however, both theologies are present: often she presents the coming of grace as painful, as in the stories already mentioned, or in the story 'Revelation'; but sometimes the coming of grace is gentle and reconciling, as in the story 'The Artificial Nigger', in which Mr Head and his grandson are reconciled after the former has seemingly disowned the latter on a visit to the big city, when they see a grotesque plaster cast on their way back to the station.[54]

One of the main effects of grace is believed to be sanctification, so this consideration perhaps partly explains the concern of many novelists with saints as well as sinners (or, best of all, with sinners who become saints, like Fr Zossima in Dostoevsky's *The Brothers Karamazov!*). I have already mentioned some examples in the novels of Bernanos, Greene, and Mauriac, and quoted the last of these writers in his essay 'God and Mammon'. After saying that 'saints form material for novelists as much as any other living people', Mauriac warns that here the novelist is not dealing purely with humanity, but with the action of God on people, and on this point the novelist will always be beaten by reality, by the saints who have actually lived, and who are 'witnesses to a reality and an experience which is infinitely beyond the power of a novelist'.[55]

As far as saintly characters feature in novels, we need to consider the range of characters and the models of sanctity that they embody, what function they play in the narrative, and whether the authors are successful in whatever they are trying to do. Besides the many saintly priests already noted, there are lay-people like Gervase Crouchback in Waugh's *Men at Arms* trilogy, Ilona in Böll's *And where were you, Adam?*, and Alyosha in *The Brothers Karamazov*. Some of them, like Ilona and Alyosha, and Chantal in

[54] See further Lorine M. Getz, *Nature and Grace in Flannery O'Connor's Fiction* (Lewiston, 1982). Getz also discusses a third theology of grace, a Jansenistic one.
[55] François Mauriac, *God and Mammon*, p. 79.

Bernanos' *Joy*, might be described as 'innocents' (though a full decision on Alyosha would depend on the story of his subsequent life outside the monastery, which Dostoevsky promises us at the end of *The Brothers Karamazov*, as he promises us the story of Raskolnikov's and Sonya's later life at the end of *Crime and Punishment*). A closely related category is the 'holy fool', a traditional Russian type, seen in Prince Myshkin in Dostoevsky's *The Idiot*, and perhaps translated to the West in the character of Guy Crouchback (a gallant knight living in the wrong age) in the *Men at Arms* trilogy, and to Japan in that of Gaston in Endo's *The Wonderful Fool* or Otsu in his *Deep River*. There are also ambiguous saints, especially in Graham Greene's work, like Sarah Miles in *The End of the Affair* and Querry in *A Burnt-Out Case*. Many of these ambiguous figures would probably not be regarded as saints in the eyes of the world, or in the eyes of most Churches (which raises the question of what criteria of sanctity are being used by the authors). Then there are the pseudo-saints, above all Brigitte Pian in Mauriac's *A Woman of the Pharisees*, whose 'Frigid soul was led on to glory in its own lack of warmth', and who is balanced by the genuine saint, the Abbé Calou:

> Was she a saint? She was making great efforts to be one, and, at each step forward, fought hard to hold the ground she had gained. No one had ever told her that the closer a man gets to sanctity the more conscious does he become of his own worthlessness, his nothingness, and gives to God ... all the credit for the few good activities with which Grace has endowed him.[56]

Just as Brigitte Pian is deceived about herself, so Dr Courrèges, in Mauriac's *The Desert of Love*, is deceived in seeing the possibility of saintliness in Maria Cross.[57]

---

[56] Idem, *A Woman of the Pharisees*, p. 133.
[57] Idem, *The Desert of Love*, tr. G. Hopkins (Harmondsworth, 1989), p. 85.

The treatment of sanctity is very difficult, as Mauriac emphasized in his *God and Mammon*, and as Dostoevsky noted in a letter
in 1868, when he said about one of his characters, Prince
Myshkin in *The Idiot*, 'The main idea of the novel is to portray a
positively beautiful person. There's nothing more difficult than
that in the whole world, especially nowadays.'[58] Martin Turnell
points out that the difficulty is compounded when an author
attempts a depiction of sanctity in a first-person narrative, as
Bernanos does in *The Diary of a Country Priest*. Turnell compares
Bernanos' treatment with that of Dostoevsky in *The Brothers
Karamazov*, where he depicts Alyosha's sanctity by showing his
effect on other people.[59]

In assessing writers' depictions of sanctity we must also look at
what role saintly characters play within the novels and at what
their authors intend by their depictions. Most obviously, saintliness forms an extreme contrast with evil, hence many authors,
especially Greene and Mauriac, approach it through the idea of
sin. In *The Knot of Vipers* it is the evil Louis who points out that
sanctity consists in taking the gospel literally. Here the contrast is
between Louis' wickedness and the conventional but hypocritical
religious observance of his own family, who never let their
principles interfere with their lives, as one of them eventually
acknowledges.[60]

Often the idea is implicit that great saints could have been great
sinners, and perhaps were so in some cases (Mary Magdalen
again). Sinners may be sinners, but at least they are alive in the
spiritual sense, and know the power of love, even if they
sometimes misdirect their love. Sarah Miles' abandonment of
herself to her lover is what leads her, by a strange route, to

---

[58] David A. Lowe (ed.), *Fyodor Dostoevski, Complete Letters*, iii, p. 17.
[59] Martin Turnell, *Modern Literature and the Christian Faith* (London, 1961), pp.
66–7. It is worth noting that in *The Knot of Vipers* Mauriac attempts the opposite,
a first-person portrayal of a vicious character.
[60] François Mauriac, *The Knot of Vipers*, pp. 81, 208.

sanctity. Similarly, Mauriac wrote in the Preface to *The Dark Angels*, that this novel

> illustrates the idea that in the worst criminal there still subsists some of the element of the saint he could have become, while, on the contrary, the life of the purest being holds terrible potentialities ...

Later on a character in the book, the Abbé Forcas, reflects on those who seem dedicated to evil:

> ... the very depth of their fall gives a measure of the vocation they have betrayed. None would be blessed had they not been given power to damn themselves. Perhaps, only those are damned who might have become saints.[61]

The contrast between the two extremes is not merely an intellectual or a literary one: Greene spoke of the 'aura' of some saintly people, and of the way in which both extreme evil and extreme goodness have a similar power.[62]

The contrast with evil is also one way, again, of giving some content to concepts like 'grace' and 'sanctification'. In a memorandum prefacing a series of the lives of the English saints John Henry Newman wrote,

> As 'the heavens declare the glory of God' as Creator, so are the saints the proper and true evidence of the God of Christianity, and tell out into all lands the power and grace of him who made them ... They are the popular evidence of Christianity.[63]

---

[61] Idem, *Oeuvres Complètes* iii, pp. ii, 274.
[62] Marie-Françoise Allain, *The Other Man: Conversations with Graham Greene*, tr. G. Waldmann (London, 1983), pp. 156,162.
[63] Vincent F. Blehl (ed.), *The Essential Newman* (New York, 1963), p. 334.

One would not expect a novelist to be concerned with 'evidence' of Christianity, in the way that Newman was. But depicting a grace-filled character is, like showing a 'moment of grace', a way of presenting and illuminating an aspect of the Christian view of human life. The main pitfall for the novelist is that of forgetting Aquinas' maxim 'grace perfects nature', and thereby failing to depict a character who is attractive and convincing as a human being. A failure here may be part of a wider one, that of failing to provide a convincing picture of the world.

The novelist may also attempt to depict, specifically, a Christ-like figure, sometimes appealing to particular Christological models. Theologians would be interested in discerning such models; and, more generally, they might ask what models of redemption are implicit in the novels that we have been looking at. It is not always easy to say – is Sonya in *Crime and Punishment* an 'innocent' or a 'wounded healer'? But novelists are very different from theologians, and we should not regard their characters as illustrations of theories! Nor should we expect them to prove anything – Mauriac warns against this.[64] In fact, as we have seen, one model is recurrent in Mauriac's work, that of the Suffering Servant who takes on the sins of others and atones vicariously for them. But he does not seek to *explain* how the sufferings of the Abbé Calou or of the little Marie benefited others, but to convince the reader that they did so. Like Dostoevsky, he saw himself as a realist, though one who transposes reality rather than reproducing it, and he commends Christianity for its realism, which, he says, is betrayed by edificatory literature.[65] So the questions with which we are left are: have the novelists whom we have considered shown the world as it is, and are their depictions of the world convincing? Are Mauriac and Dostoevsky the true realists, rather than, say, Hardy and Zola? Who has best discerned

---

[64] In the Postscript to *The Loved and the Unloved*, p. 135.
[65] François Mauriac, 'La vie et mort d'un poête', *Oeuvres Complètes* iv, p. 393. Conversely, he criticizes Proust for contracting his universe by omitting grace (op. cit., viii, p. 281), and Zola for denying it (*Mémoires intérieurs*,[Paris, 1959], p. 244).

our deepest needs, and possibilities of fulfilling them? Who has led us to a better understanding of what is at stake here?

Novelists may also seek to portray saintly, Christ-like characters because Christian saints are supposed to be like Christ, being transformed into his image, as St Paul says (2 Cor. 3.18), and because this is also therefore a way of pointing up the connection between Act II in the 'drama of redemption' and the other two Acts. For if the saint is Christ-like, this is one way of suggesting how the effects of Act I are continually being manifested in the world. As to whether the writer or the artist can also make connections with Act III, the life to come, that is something which we shall consider in the next chapter.

CHAPTER EIGHT

Act III: The Life to Come

Christian tradition teaches that we are redeemed not only from sin, but also from death, through the Cross and Resurrection of Christ. Thus redemption will be perfected, as St Ambrose says, 'when all, who are graced to see the face of God, rise again in incorruptibility, honour, and glory'.[1] It would seem, however, that the task of representing the last Act of the 'drama of redemption' is the most difficult one: for how can an artist or a writer represent, in any medium or genre, what is 'beyond' this life? (I am assuming the traditional Christian position that hope in resurrection is central to the notion of salvation, hence, as people say, our 'stories' continue after our deaths; and that, consequently, talk of a life beyond death is not to be regarded merely as a metaphor for something in this life, a way of expressing hope in e.g. the power of love, liberation from one's worst self, political revolution, the future unity of the human race, and so on.)

There are, of course, many attempted depictions of 'the four last things', including pictures of the Last Judgement, e.g. Michelangelo's in the Sistine Chapel, of Hell, and, to a less extent, of Heaven. Likewise, there are many poetic portrayals of the beyond, both by Christian writers like Dante and Newman and by earlier writers like Homer and Virgil. Jean-Paul Sartre, in a very different way, depicts Hell in his play *Huis Clos*. But to what extent do such artists and writers add to our *understanding*? There is always the danger of portraying something fantastic, childish, or banal, without any depth; or of presenting a kind of Utopia that is a

[1] St Ambrose, *Letter* 35:13 (*P. L.*16: 1081).

projection of aspects of the present world, forgetting that religious beliefs in a life to come should be concerned more with salvation than with mere survival. Perhaps that is why the more 'indirect' media, especially music, are sometimes the most successful here.[2]

In this chapter I shall concentrate especially on the liberative and illuminative aspects of Christian eschatology (which, as many modern theologians point out, is not just a matter of personal survival, but also of the *telos* of history and indeed of the whole cosmos). I shall discuss first death: it is, traditionally, the first of the 'four last things', and in any case death terminates Act II of the 'drama of redemption' and so follows on naturally from our last subject, novels. Then I shall say something about how artists and writers have sought to depict individual survival and also return to a subject raised previously in connection with the Resurrection, that of cosmic transformation. Finally, I shall discuss how the last Act is related by artists and writers to the previous ones.

Death

Some people see death as, in Philip Larkin's words in his poem 'Aubade', the 'anaesthetic from which none come round',[3] and reject all speculation beyond this, or any 'immortal longings'; but, even so, many poets and musicians have sought at least to capture some sense of what they feel dying must be like, by suggesting a

---

[2] One reason for this may be that, as Jeremy Begbie says, music can give us a sense of time other than simple linear time, an 'interpenetrating' temporality. See his *Theology, Music and Time*, ch.4 *passim* and pp. 148–51.

[3] Seamus Heaney, noting that 'Aubade' was originally published two days before Christmas 1977, calls it the 'definitive post-Christian English poem', in a lecture 'Joy and Night' in his *The Redress of Poetry* (London, 1995), p. 156. He contrasts Larkin's 'metaphysically Arctic conditions' (p. 152) with W.B. Yeats' 'The cold Heaven', which, though not a theistic poem, still displays the poet's 'metaphysical need' (p. 147), and is an 'image of superabundant life' (p. 152); and also with Yeats' 'The Man and the Echo', which, says Heaney, 'manages to pronounce a final Yes' (p. 163).

certain atmosphere, e.g. that of a dank late autumn day. I think that the long orchestral prelude to Elgar's *The Dream of Gerontius* succeeds in conveying a deathly atmosphere, with its feverish restlessness and ponderous sense of finality. This atmosphere is conveyed partly by the music's use of the minor key and of descending scales.

Others have been concerned with the religious character of dying: R.C. Moberly wrote, 'We do not yet know the possibilities of humbling or of purifying discipline which may lie hid within the experience of dying.'[4] Countless Christians have regarded their own deaths as a participation in Christ's Passion, an understanding which Michael Wheeler finds articulated in Gerard Manley Hopkins' poem *The Wreck of the Deutschland*.[5]

Deathbed scenes were favourite ones for many Victorian novelists, e.g. Dickens in *The Old Curiosity Shop* and *Dombey and Son*. Modern novelists, however, do not usually attempt to describe the last hours of life or the moment of death in anything like this way (Evelyn Waugh's *Brideshead Revisited* is an obvious exception). For them, death seems rather to have three aspects: it is that towards which life is moving, it puts a seal on someone's whole life, and it may be the point at which accounts are settled, as it were, with other people.[6]

Wittgenstein remarked that death is not an event *in* life,[7] and Heidegger described human life as Being-towards-Death,[8] for human beings, unlike animals, *know* that they are going to die. Louis, in Mauriac's *The Knot of Vipers*, expects to die soon, and the

---

[4] R.C. Moberly, *Atonement and Personality*, p. 114.

[5] Michael Wheeler, *Death and the Future Life in Victorian Literature and Theology* (Cambridge, 1990), pp. 342–3. I think that this poem is the one amongst Hopkins' poems that deals most with soteriological themes.

[6] Some of this applies to films too: compare the treatment of Ester's approaching death in Ingmar Bergman's *The Silence* with the more complex handling of the subject in his later *Cries and Whispers*.

[7] Ludwig Wittgenstein, *Tractatus Logico-Philosophicus* 6.4311.

[8] Martin Heidegger, *Being and Time*, tr. J. Macquarrie and E. Robinson (London, 1962), esp. II.i.§§51–3 (pp. 296–311).

priest in Greene's *The Power and the Glory* knows that he risks being caught and executed; both of them are depicted as acting with reference to their likely deaths.

In a way, the priest's death in *The Power and the Glory* is necessary to the book, as it puts a seal on his life and enables the reader to assess it as a whole; similarly, with the death of the priest at the end of Bernanos' *The Diary of a Country Priest*. Of course, there is nothing particularly Christian in this idea. One would have to add also the idea that death is a fulfilment, for which life is a preparation, and a new beginning, rather than a tragedy or a 'full stop'. Bernanos' priest, early on in the book, reflects that the Christian God is not a vague 'Supreme Being', but the 'Risen Lord', 'a marvellous and living friend, who ... will share our last hour and receive us into His arms, upon His heart'.[9]

Louis' death is also necessary in Mauriac's *The Knot of Vipers*, to enable the reader to see the whole course of his life – though here it is a changed life. In the early part of the book, in which he is writing to his wife, Isa, Louis regards his imminent death as a time for settling scores with his family, especially her. But it is Isa who dies first, and Louis' own death is preceded by his conversion.

The deathbed conversion, like the suicide, is a special case. One can see it crudely in terms of a kind of insurance policy, or like renewing a driving-licence just in time. But there are more profound ways of looking at it. The priest in *The Power and the Glory* reflects:

He had heard men talk of the unfairness of a deathbed repentance – as if it was an easy thing to break the habit of a life whether to do good or evil. One suspected the good of the life that ended badly – or the viciousness that ended well.[10]

[9] Georges Bernanos, *The Diary of a Country Priest*, p. 26.
[10] Graham Greene, *The Power and the Glory*, p. 189.

The priest is doubting here whether there *are* any complete reversals of attitude at death. Similarly, Louis' change of heart at the end of *The Knot of Vipers* is hinted at earlier in the book, when he chided his wife for not living up to the teaching of the Gospel, and also when the Abbé Ardouin told him, 'You are a very good man', much to Louis' surprise.[11] Lord Marchmain's deathbed repentance, in Waugh's *Brideshead Revisited*, is difficult to assess, as we are not in a position to discern the motives of one who has played only a minor role in the novel up until the last chapter.

The life to come is not to be thought of by the Christian as 'more of the same', for this might turn out to be tedious. St Ambrose said that 'Deathlessness is no blessing but only a weariness if grace does not transfigure it.'[12] Janacek's opera *The Makropulos Affair*, in which a woman takes an elixir of immortality and comes to regret it, conveys such a tedium; as does Sartre's *Huis Clos*, in a different way. An envisaged *religious* afterlife is not regarded merely as survival, but as something higher and better; in the case of Christianity, it is envisaged as a new life, transformed by the Holy Spirit, in true holiness. Some have seen it more in terms of eternal growth and continued learning, activity, and loving,[13] in contrast to the traditional description of 'eternal rest'. Either way, such a life would be in the presence of God. The priest in Greene's *The Power and the Glory*, after his stay in prison, says to a self-righteous penitent, 'Loving God isn't any different from loving a man – or a child. It's wanting to be with Him, to be near Him.'[14] It would also be a communitarian life, as descriptions like 'the Communion of Saints' or 'the heavenly banquet' seek to suggest.

One would not expect novelists to try to depict such a life,[15] but rather to show how their characters behave as they do because

[11] François Mauriac, *The Knot of Vipers*, pp. 81, 85.

[12] Ambrose, *On the Death of his Brother Satyrus*, ii.47 (*P.L.*16:1327).

[13] E.g. Miguel de Unamuno in *The Tragic Sense of Life*, ch.10.

[14] Graham Greene, *The Power and the Glory*, p. 173.

[15] An exception is M. Scott Peck's *In Heaven as on Earth: A Vision of the After Life* (New York, 1997), a novel that seeks to convey a vision of what Purgatory might be like.

they live in expectation of it, and possibly also to depict what are taken to be anticipations of it here and now. For Greene, Mauriac, and many other writers, the possibility of salvation or damnation adds a seriousness to their characters' lives and actions: for them, as we saw in the last chapter, great issues are being decided here and now. There are of course, as we have seen, 'novels of resurrection', like Dostoevsky's *Crime and Punishment*, Tolstoy's *Resurrection*, or William Golding's *Darkness Visible*, but they too are concerned with ways in which people can be born again to a different kind of life in this world, hence I have included them under the wider heading of what I call 'novels of redemption'.[16] So, given what I have said, how can our final resurrection be represented?

Individual Resurrection

For St Paul the Resurrection of Christ heralds the redemption of the human race from death, and so anticipates our future resurrection and glorification. I have already mentioned how Eastern Christian depictions of it in icons and other paintings do something to convey this significance. We may compare and contrast such depictions not only with classical Western ones of Christ's resurrection but also with, for example, Stanley Spencer's *Resurrection* (in the Tate Gallery), in which the dead seem to be reviving or climbing out of their graves in Cookham Churchyard, rather like people waking up in the morning.

In Western theology it became common to distinguish between the judgement of the individual soul immediately after death, and the final judgement of all. Hence in Western art the general resurrection is usually combined with the Last Judgement, as in Michelangelo's fresco on the wall of the Sistine Chapel. This theological tradition is followed towards the end of Newman's *The Dream of Gerontius*, where the soul of the dead man is escorted by

[16] See again Richard Harries' essay 'The resurrection in some modern novels'.

an angel into the presence of God, after which Gerontius exclaims 'Take me away, and in the lowest deep/ There let me be ...'[17]

Whatever be the nature of our judgement by God, there are also the questions of what it is to believe in such a judgement, and of how the belief can be conveyed. Wittgenstein described belief in the Last Judgement as like living with a picture which regulates one's life; and he went on to mention the idea that believing in immortality is like having a task, the responsibility for which nothing, not even death, can remove.[18] Something of the latter understanding is conveyed in Solzhenitsyn's novel *The First Circle*, in which two people have to make decisions that have eternal consequences, in the sense that they transcend their own immediate circumstances and customary considerations. Nerzhin, who is in a 'special prison' with a relaxed regime, has the opportunity of having a love-affair with a fellow-prisoner, but decides to remain faithful to his wife, though he has no assurance of being released and rejoining her outside the prison. Volodin, the promising young diplomat, has privileged information and feels obliged to warn a friend that he is likely to be arrested, even though he knows that this tip-off may be traced back to him and may have serious consequences – which is what happens in due course, for he is found out, arrested, and sent to the Lubianka Prison. Solzhenitsyn does not, of course, try to imagine what these eternal consequences might be; the point, for him, is that there is a dimension to life and its decisions which a Marxist-Leninist or a hedonist would ignore. Similarly, in Bernanos' *The Diary of a Country Priest*, the priest confronts the countess with the thought that her refusal to love her daughter, and indeed her lovelessness in general, may result in eternal lovelessness.[19]

---

[17] John Henry Newman, *The Dream of Gerontius* (London, n.d.), p. 79.

[18] Ludwig Wittgenstein, *Lectures and Conversations on Aesthetics, Psychology, and Religious Belief*, ed. C. Barrett (Oxford, 1966), pp. 53–9, 70.

[19] Georges Bernanos, *The Diary of a Country Priest*, ch.5, esp. pp. 139–40. Conversely, the playwright and philosopher Gabriel Marcel saw love as having an eternal dimension: towards the end of his Gifford Lectures he quotes from one of his own plays, in which a character says, 'to love a being is to say, "Thou shalt not die".' Cf. his *The Mystery of Being*, vol.ii, tr. G.S. Fraser and R. Hague (London, 1951), p. 153.

Paintings of the Last Judgement may presumably fulfil a similar function, of warning people that their actions will have eternal consequences. Whether they are likely to be successful in performing this function is a moot question. Similarly with depictions of Hell and Heaven. Pictures of the former tend to be sadistic, grotesque, or fantastic; and those of the latter often fail to convey joy, and also the beauty that is believed to be possessed by glorified, risen bodies.[20] Writers too are often unconvincing: in particular, those who wish to depict Hell are best advised to concentrate on the inner penalty of loss [*poena damni*] and the sense of the absence of God. But music and poetry, again, may be more successful, e.g. Handel's *Messiah*, parts of Bach's B Minor Mass, and Dante's *The Divine Comedy*, because music can convey joy as well as sorrow in a direct way, and poetry is suggestive through its use of metaphor and image. Michael Wheeler thinks that it was no coincidence that Victorian theologians like F.W. Farrar and F.D. Maurice referred to the poets of their generation so often when re-assessing the traditional doctrine of Hell, for it was the latter who did most to explore the metaphorical nature of much of the language used.[21] Thus the poets influenced the theologians' treatment of the question.

More interesting, often, than treatments of Heaven or Hell are those of Purgatory. Dante's *Purgatorio* tends to receive less attention than his *Inferno* or *Paradiso*, but it contains some of his most interesting treatments, of virtues and vices, of repentance and purification (which Dante emphasizes more than satisfaction). Dorothy Sayers claimed that, in stressing the purgative and ameliorative aspect of Purgatory, Dante was laying the emphasis where the older, Greek tradition had laid it. She describes the way

---

[20] On which cf. St Augustine, *The City of God* 22:17, and John Meyendorff, *Christ in Eastern Christian Thought*, pp. 129*ff*. The latter cites the *Macarian Homilies* ii.5, where it is said that at the resurrection 'the body itself will be restored and glorified by the Light of the Lord which is already present in the soul.'
[21] Michael Wheeler, *Death and the Future Life*, p. 218; cf. pp. 187–9 with regard to my point about expressing the inner *poena damni*.

in which Dante brings out the purification of the heart and the consent of the will:

> You pay the price – but you pay it because you want to, and because that is the only means of expressing your love and sorrow: and in paying you grow clean and fit to receive the forgiveness freely offered and to return to that right relationship which nothing but your own folly ever disturbed ...
>
> Nobody comes to release the soul; it is its own judge, and when it *feels* that it is clean ... it simply gets up and goes.[22]

A similar idea is expressed also by Newman in *The Dream of Gerontius*, in which the painful purification of Purgatory is seen as something welcomed by the penitent, and as containing within it the seeds of growth and of hope. (Newman's treatment here was influenced by the work of St Catherine of Genoa, who emphasized the healing aspect of Purgatory.[23]) One can, of course, be concerned with the theme of purgation without specific reference to the Catholic doctrine of Purgatory: Nathan Scott describes T.S. Eliot's later work, especially *Ash Wednesday*, *The Family Reunion*, and the *Four Quartets*, as 'a poetry of purgation',[24] and sees Eliot's progression as analogous to Dante's. Many writers have sought to

---

[22] Dorothy L. Sayers, *Introductory Papers on Dante* (London, 1954), pp. 84, 88. C.A. Dinsmore takes a similar line, and sees such purification as the healing of the moral and spiritual blindness involved in sin (*Atonement in Literature and Life*, pp. 75, 84–5). See, however, Hans Urs von Balthasar, *The Glory of the Lord: A Theological Aesthetics*, vol.iii: *Studies in Theological Styles: Lay Styles*, tr. A. Louth et al. (Edinburgh, 1986), pp. 100–1, for a critique of Dante's treatment, e.g. in his failure to sufficiently stress the work of Christ here.

[23] Cf. Friedrich von Hügel, *The Mystical Element in Religion* (London, 1923), vol.i, p. 89; vol.ii, p. 245; and von Balthasar, *Theo-Drama* v, p. 362, who discusses briefly the role of free will here. More generally, see Paul S. Fiddes, *The Promised End: Eschatology in Art and Literature*, pp. 133–40, on the possibility of post-mortem growth and development, and the ways in which God can 'heal' time.

[24] Nathan A. Scott, Jr., *Rehearsals of Discomposure*, p. 228.

show how faults like selfishness and self-deception can be 'burnt away', even in this life.

A New Heaven and a New Earth

Now all that I have said so far is concerned mainly with the salvation of the individual. There is, however, another strand of Christian tradition, which is concerned with history and the corporate fate of the whole cosmos, with the final transformation of all things. Against Gnosticism and Docetism, which regarded matter as imperfect, and concluded that if Christ was truly God, he could not have had a material body, the early Church affirmed both the materiality of the Incarnation and the goodness of the whole creation. St Leo the Great, in a Christmas sermon, spoke of the birth of Christ as the prelude of a new creation, and exhorted his hearers:

> Use visible creatures as they should be used, as you use the earth, sea, sky, air, springs, and rivers; and whatever is beautiful and wonderful in them acknowledge to the praise and glory of the Creator.[25]

But what of the Fall? Has not the whole cosmos been affected by it? To quote the title of one of Tillich's sermons, 'Nature also mourns for a lost good'.[26]

Genesis 3 does not say exactly that nature is 'fallen', but it sees some kind of causal link between Adam's sin and the intractability of nature (vv. 18–19). Not surprisingly, therefore, prophecies of the peace of the Messianic age extend their message to nature: Isaiah envisages a restored order of the world, in which the wolf lives with the lamb, the calf and lion cub feast together, and the lion eats straw (Isa. 11.6–7). This text has become a favourite one for

---

[25] Leo the Great, *Serm. Nativ.* 7:6 (*P. L.* 54: 220–1).
[26] In Paul Tillich, *The Shaking of the Foundations* (London, 1949), pp. 76–86.

contemporary Christian ecologists: Alan Lewis describes it as a 'poetic vision of nature pacified, man and creature reconciled', a vision of a 'new creation, radiating out from redeemed men and women to embrace the creatures and suffuse the cosmos as a whole'.[27] He and other recent Christian writers on ecology have rediscovered an important strand of Biblical teaching and early tradition that has been ignored for several centuries, one which freed people from the ancient pagan fear of nature: for if it was created by God and redeemed by Christ, it shares in God's purposes and has a sacramental aspect, as manifesting divine glory. It also has its own final fulfilment: hence Jürgen Moltmann writes of 'eschatological ecology'[28] and he and other writers emphasize the duty incumbent on the human race (which Edward Echlin calls 'the responsible elder brother'[29]) to avoid 'ecological sin', and to heal and restore the cosmos. Such writers are seeing redemption as including the transformation of the world, rather than deliverance from it.

Mention of purpose and fulfilment leads to the consideration of another favourite text of the Christian ecological movement, Rom. 8.19–22, in which St Paul writes of the whole creation groaning in travail, awaiting its freedom from futility, in the hope that it 'will be set free from its bondage to decay and will obtain the freedom of the glory of the children of God'.[30] This is a difficult text to interpret: I follow commentators like George Caird and C.E.B. Cranfield in holding that in it 'creation' is not restricted to human beings, though Paul thinks that its liberation will come about through the latter (who, in turn, will be renewed through Christ).[31] Thus nature's redemption will come about

---

[27] Alan Lewis, *Theatre of the Gospel* (Edinburgh, 1984), p. 21.

[28] Jürgen Moltmann, *The Coming of God: Christian Eschatology*, tr. M. Kohl (London, 1996), pp. 277–9.

[29] Edward Echlin, *The Christian Green Heritage: World as Creation* (Nottingham, 1990), pp. 16, 24.

[30] Other relevant texts include Isa. 65.17, 25; 66.22; 1 Cor. 7.31; Col. 1.20.

[31] See George Caird, *Principalities and Powers*, pp. 76–7; C.E.B. Cranfield, *A Critical and Exegetical Commentary on the Epistle to the Romans* (Edinburgh, 1975), vol.i,

through the mediation of redeemed human beings. This is how the passage has commonly been interpreted traditionally. Just as Genesis 3 sees the fall of Adam as having somehow affected the world of nature, so it is fitting that the redemption of Adam's descendants should be instrumental in restoring nature and thus helping to further the 'new creation'. Liberation Theologians, not surprisingly, have seen this human mediation as involving political and social action. Thus Leonardo Boff claims that if Christ redeemed all reality and not just its spiritual sphere, then this all-embracing liberation must come about through social liberation.[32] Strictly speaking, this is a *non sequitur*, for the former liberation might be realized in some other way; but Boff might retort 'How else will it come about?'

There are, however, some other difficulties. What if the 'cussedness' of nature long anticipated the emergence of the human race? And is not Boff's interpretation not only political in its thrust, but also too anthropocentric? Why should the non-human cosmos not have its own purpose ordained by God, as well as being an environment for the human race? If we interpret Genesis 1.26–30 as enjoining stewardship rather than domination on Adam and his descendants, then we could allow that the human race has the task of furthering God's redemptive work in nature, whilst not restricting His concerns for it to ours.

There are some other Biblical texts that promise the restoration of all things, most notably Rev. 21.1–5, which prophesies 'a new

pp. 410–17; and Stanislas Lyonnet, 'The Redemption of the Universe', in G. Weigel et al., *The Church Readings in Theology* (New York, 1963), pp. 136–56.

For a similar opinion expressed in more general works, cf. Robert Murray, *The Cosmic Covenant*, pp. 165*ff*, and H. Paul Santmire, *The Travail of Nature: The Ambiguous Ecological Promise of Christian Theology* (Philadelphia, 1985), pp. 202*f*. (Santmire also notes Dante's lack of interest in such questions: earlier on, on p. 105, he describes the goal of Dante's pilgrimage as 'perfect, transparent spirituality, total release from the biophysical order'.)

[32] Leonardo Boff, 'The Future of the Church in Latin America', in K.-J. Kuschel and H. Häring (eds.), *Hans Küng: New Horizons for Faith and Thought* (London, 1993), p. 162.

heaven and a new earth' and a 'new Jerusalem, coming down out of heaven', and represents God as saying 'Behold I make all things new.'[33] Christian tradition has usually linked such texts to the resurrection of Christ (which is also mentioned by Paul shortly before the passage just discussed, in Rom. 8.11). Paul says of the risen Christ that all things hold together in him, and that he will reconcile all things to himself (Col. 1.17, 20).[34]

There are a number of themes here worthy of exploration by artists. I have already mentioned ways in which icon-painters have sought to bring out the cosmic aspects of the Resurrection, and linked this to a theology of the 'Cosmic Christ'. The West has tended, on the whole, to ignore the idea of the restoration of the cosmos until recently, when it has made something of a come-back through the ecological movement: Alan Lewis, for example, points to the way in which the Incarnation brought all fleshly, material reality into a new redemptive relationship with its Creator, and asks, if Jesus is the light of the world, i.e. the cosmos, 'should we be so reluctant to be ecological about redemption?'[35] Now if redemption means reclaiming what has been lost or spoilt and restoring a broken order, then it will involve beautifying or glorifying the cosmos.[36] Artists have sometimes sought to depict landscapes that might be called Paradisial, e.g. Samuel Palmer in some of his early Shoreham paintings, like *The Magic Apple Tree* (in the Fitzwilliam Museum, Cambridge) or the nineteenth-century American painter Edward Hicks, who sought again and again, obsessively, to express his vision of a 'Peaceable Kingdom', in which animals live at peace with each other and with the human race.[37]

[33] Cf. also Matt. 19.28, 1 Cor. 7.31, Phil. 2.10, and 2 Pet. 3.13.
[34] Cf. also Eph. 1.10, Phil. 2.9, and Col. 3.11.
[35] Alan Lewis, *The Theatre of the Gospel*, p. 24.
[36] Nicholas Berdyaev wrote, 'all beauty in the world is either a memory of paradise or a prophecy of the transfigured world', in *The Divine and the Human*, tr. R.M. French (London, 1949), p. 139.
[37] See Robert Murray, *The Cosmic Covenant*, ch.7.

Such depictions run the risk of merely fantasizing.[38] More common, however, are those that seek to portray something in this world which is taken to be an anticipation of the life to come – a 'first fruits' or 'earnest'. Many patristic writers drew attention to the principle of resurrection in the natural world,[39] from which they inferred that it was natural to look for it also in the supernatural, e.g. in the miracles of Christ, the Transfiguration, or grace-filled saints. Traditionally, Christ's miracles have been regarded as signs of his power and of his divinity, but many of them, especially healing the sick, calming the storm, and feeding the hungry, could be regarded as signs of the restoration of a disturbed order, and so, again, as an anticipation of cosmic regeneration.[40]

Lines of Continuity

The idea of the life to come being partially realized here and now by anticipation, expressed in Biblical metaphors like 'first fruits' and 'earnest', is important in the present context, because it provides us with some way of seeing a continuity between the three Acts of the Drama of Redemption, as well as pointing to the incompleteness of redemption so far. Without some such idea, the third Act seems to hang loose, or to be, as is said, 'pie in the sky'. In any case, my concern in this book has been more to discern what I have called 'rumours of redemption' than to imagine the final state. And the obvious pitfalls of trying to represent the future life, to which I have drawn attention, make it more natural for artists and writers to seek to discern its anticipations, than to try to depict its fruition. Writing of Dickens' *Our*

---

[38] One might regard much science fiction as a secularized version of eschatology. Conversely, however, C.S. Lewis used that genre for theological purposes in his trilogy, *Out of the Silent Planet, Perelandra*, and *That Hideous Strength*.

[39] D.S. Wallace-Hadrill, *The Greek Patristic View of Nature* (Manchester, 1968), p. 126.

[40] For this idea, cf. Walter Kasper, *Jesus the Christ*, pp. 95–6.

Mutual Friend Michael Wheeler says that the book's central conceit, of rising and falling, 'is underpinned with a theological understanding of the fall and of man's redemption through love, worked out in the here-and-now as an earnest of a future heavenly state'.[41]

Traditionally, theology has made causal links between the three Acts: because of Christ's life, death, and resurrection, the possibilities for our lives now are different; and if in this life we respond to him, our fate beyond death will be changed. The Holy Spirit has often been seen as a principle of continuity. For example, St Cyril of Alexandria says in his commentary on St John's Gospel,

> When the Maker of the universe designed, in a beautiful arrangement, to gather up all things in Christ and to restore again the nature of man to its pristine state, he promised along with the other gifts to give it also the Holy Spirit abundantly, because in no other way could it be reinstated in a peaceful and stable possession of good things.[42]

Cyril goes on immediately to refer to the coming of the Spirit on Christ at his baptism, 'as first-fruits of the renewed nature', given not for himself, but in order to renew all human nature through him and to restore its integrity. Elsewhere, he says that when Christ said to his disciples after the Resurrection 'Receive the Holy Spirit' (John 20.22), he renewed the beauty which human nature had lost through Adam's sin, and that we have the Spirit as an earnest (though we may lose it through sin).[43]

Cyril sees the lines of connection from Christ as going both backwards and forwards: backward to the Fall (for our fallen

---

[41] Michael Wheeler, *Death and the Future Life*, p. 282. On the other hand, one should also 'expect the unexpected', and leave room for novelty: see Paul S. Fiddes, *The Promised End*, pp. 167–8.

[42] Cyril of Alexandria, *In Joann.* v.2 (*P. G.* 73:752cd). He is referring also to the idea that Christ, the Second Adam, 'recapitulated' the history of the human race, and also its death. Cf. Irenaeus, *Adv. Haer.* v.1.2; 21.1; 23.2.

[43] Cyril of Alexandria, *In Matt.* xxiv.51 (*P. G.* 72:446c).

nature is restored through Christ), and forward to the coming of the Holy Spirit, which, in turn, anticipates the life of glory. There are other ways in which the lines of connection may be drawn. In Chapter 5 I used the phrase 'redeeming the past' to denote ways in which we can show up the past in a new light, for instance through practices like repentance and forgiveness. If we extend this idea eschatologically, we envisage that actions or events in the life to come might extend the 'picture' or 'weave' of our lives, and thus cause us to re-assess our earthly careers: I take it, for example, that some religious teachings about a future purification suggest how this might come about. As regards the lines of continuity going forward, the idea of a present 'first fruits' or 'earnest' has received an interesting recent development in the work of those Liberation Theologians, discussed earlier, who have written of the 'dangerous memory' of Christ, which inspires the overcoming of oppression and injustice in the world, as an anticipation of the coming of the Kingdom of God.

One might expect theology to be more concerned than art and literature are to work out the connections between the three Acts of the Drama of Redemption, and perhaps to be more successful in doing so. Nevertheless, the links between the three Acts of the Drama may be made artistically in a variety of ways. Dante's *Divine Comedy* is centred on Act III, but with constant reference back to the earlier Acts, especially the history of individuals in their lives on this earth. Novelists usually restrict themselves to Act II, but they may show what happens now as influenced by the work of Christ and as anticipating a future life. I have illustrated these ideas already, with reference to writers like Mauriac and Solzhenitsyn. I think, however, that we can take the idea of such an anticipation a little further and refine it by considering briefly the concept of an 'internal reward'.

If, for example, someone studies music and practises for long hours, day in and day out, he or she may become successful and eventually earn large sums of money. But this money is an 'external' reward, for it may not be desired, and it could as well have been acquired by becoming a footballer or a banker. If, however the reward is that the student becomes, say, the foremost Schubert interpreter of the age, then the reward is an 'internal' one, because it is what the student is aiming at, a fulfilment of his or her work, and because the reward could not be acquired in any other way than by study and constant practice. It is internal in the sense that there is an 'intentional' (i.e. directed towards something) relationship between the work and the reward, as well as a causal one. Presumably there can also be 'internal' punishments, i.e. ones which can be construed in some way as the implicit goals of evil-doing.

In religious terms, the life to come may be seen as the internal reward (or punishment) for the present life. For those who 'hunger and thirst after righteousness' (Matt. 5.6), the appropriate reward would be the achievement of what would satisfy them, righteousness.[44] For those whose aim is to build up a 'community of love' here on earth, in so far as it is possible, then the fitting 'internal reward' for their efforts would be to dwell in such a community hereafter.

It is difficult to convey the idea of an internal reward artistically. Negatively, Dostoevsky points out in *The Brothers Karamazov*, through Ivan, that even if the child torn to pieces by the landowner's dog were to be rewarded in some 'great harmony' in Heaven, this would still not entitle the mother to forgive their tormentor; for presumably it would be only an external reward. Positively, I think that some such idea is implicit in Dante's *Divine Comedy*: in his depiction of his relationship with Beatrice (seen against the background of his *Vita Nuova*), and in his attempts to show that some of the rewards and punishments that he depicts are the fulfilment of what people have done in this life, even though often they may not have been aware of the full implications of their actions.[45] The conversation between the priest and

---

[44] Thomas V. Morris' example, in his *Anselmian Explorations* (Notre Dame, 1987), pp. 210–12. See, more generally, Peter Byrne, *The Moral Interpretation of Religion* (Edinburgh, 1998), pp. 45–7.

[45] See Dorothy L. Sayers, *Introductory Papers on Dante*, pp. 13, 67*f*, 81, for this idea.

the countess in Bernanos' *The Diary of a Country Priest*, mentioned earlier, in which the former confronts the latter with the possibility of eternal lovelessness, is another obvious example. The idea of an internal punishment is also suggested in a different kind of example given by F.R. Leavis in a discussion of George Eliot's *Daniel Deronda*, with reference to Gwendolen Harleth's recovery of the diamonds that her husband Grandcourt had once given to his mistress, to which Gwendolen thought herself to be entitled. Leavis points out that the diamonds are her nemesis: as he puts it neatly, 'they are what Gwendolen married Grandcourt for, and her punishment is having to wear them'.[46] I think that some such notion of an internal connection is helpful in order to counter the crudity of those treatments of the afterlife that depict it in childish, hedonistic, or sadistic terms, and thereby contribute to the ridicule which the idea often receives today.

The special contribution of art and literature (especially the latter) here is that they can reveal the nature of such internal connections through concrete examples; and indeed, more generally, they can express and illustrate ideas that are elusive and that gain more from an imaginative than a discursive treatment. This suggests, again, that art and literature have their own contribution to make to religious understanding. In the next chapter I shall make some general remarks about how they do so, drawing together themes that have come up at several points in this study so far, and then compare their contribution to other sources of religious understanding.

[46] F.R. Leavis, *The Great Tradition* (2nd edn., London, 1960), p. 116.

CHAPTER NINE

Saying, Showing, and Understanding

Wittgenstein tells us on occasion, 'don't think, but look' (*Philosophical Investigations* §66). I am reminded of this advice when I read some recent writers on theological aesthetics who claim that art and literature can be primary expressions of religious ideas, i.e. ones which are not dependent on other modes of communication like preaching or theology. Thus Frank Burch Brown, as we saw in Chapter 1, says that the primary language of religion is 'markedly poetic, mythic, and otherwise aesthetic', so that 'it is with such language that theology repeatedly begins and ... it is to such language that theology must often return'.[1] Similarly, and more ambitiously, Aidan Nichols says in his book *The Art of God Incarnate* that 'art has a virtually sacramental power to bring the intangible within our touching', and that paintings should be 'revelatory after their own fashion, vehicles of presence'. These claims are traced back ultimately for their justification by Nichols to the teaching of the Seventh Ecumenical Council in 787 CE, which condemned iconoclasm. He notes that when the theological defence of icons was initiated by the Patriarch of Constantinople, St Germanus, the latter insisted that the making of artworks of the divine is endorsed by the Incarnation, for Christ's humanity was a form of God's self-expression. Nichols comments that it is odd that modern Christian theology has paid such scant attention to the visual arts, given the Biblical ideas that man is made in God's image and that Jesus is 'the image of the invisible God'.[2]

[1] Frank Burch Brown, *Religious Aesthetics*, p. 193.
[2] Aidan Nichols, *The Art of God Incarnate: Theology and Image in Christian Tradition* (London, 1980), pp. 5, 11, 83.

Nichols' main concern here is with the parallel between art (especially painting) and revelation. But mine now is with the question of religious understanding: if indeed a religion's art and architecture are part of what Ninian Smart calls its material dimension, it surely follows that an understanding of them, and of its music and literature too, will further our grasp of the nature of that religion.[3] Now the discussions of the last few chapters have provided us with numerous examples of soteriological themes in art and literature. We need to go on to ask therefore whether they succeed in conveying redemptive themes cogently, and so increase our religious understanding here. Do Bach and Grünewald help us to see the appalling cost of the Cross, and its significance? Does *The Dream of Gerontius* help us to envisage how human lives may continue beyond death? Likewise does *The Divine Comedy* do this, and also help us to understand the links between the three Acts of the Drama of Redemption?

More importantly for us, do writers like Dostoevsky and Mauriac convey successfully 'rumours of redemption', helping us to imagine redemptive powers working in people's lives here and now? I say that the last question is more important for us now, because I think that the arts and literature of redemption are most interesting and challenging when they are trying to show us present possibilities of redemption; that is why I have concentrated predominantly in this work on Act II of the Drama of Redemption.

In this chapter I shall first consider how works of art and literature show or express things, looking briefly at the distinction between primary expressions of religious ideas and illustrations (including those in words as well as in other media). My main concern is with primary expressions; but in the last part of the chapter I shall argue that the fact that something is an expression of a religious idea does not mean that it is beyond criticism or that it cannot clash with other expressions. Rather, the relation

[3] See, for example, Ninian Smart, *The World's Religions* (Cambridge, 1989), pp. 20–1.

between artistic and literary expressions is reciprocal: i.e. art and literature may help to shape theology, whilst theology may in turn influence art and literature.

Illustrations and Primary Expressions

I take it that the two writers whom I have cited, Brown and Nichols, are saying in different ways that art and literature can *show* us things. Someone who explicitly appealed to the idea of 'showing' here was Flannery O'Connor, who said, as we saw in Chapter 7, that 'Fiction writing is very seldom a matter of saying things; it is a matter of showing things.'[4] But there are different ways of showing people things; and in works of literature the ways may be subtle and complex, involving dramatization, allegory, and various other means of indirect communication. And what of music? Here the term 'express' seems more appropriate than 'show'. Moreover, some showings are dependent on something else for being understood, whilst others are not so, and so are what I call primary.

The basic distinction that I want to make, therefore, is between illustrations (of many different kinds) and primary expressions; that is, between things that are dependent on something else in order to convey their meaning, and things not so dependent. Some such distinction is needed if we consider the kind of questions that I have just raised about understanding. To ask now some more specific questions, do works like Grünewald's Isenheim altarpiece or Bach's *St Matthew Passion* increase our understanding of redemption and sacrifice, or support particular soteriological theories? Or are they simply illustrations which, although they may be vivid and imaginative in some cases, are

---

[4] Flannery O'Connor, *Mystery and Manners*, p. 93. In his *Triumphs of the Spirit in Russia* (London, 1997), p. 53, Donald Nicholl quotes the Russian theologian Pavel Florensky as saying, 'One showing is worth a thousand sayings.' Of course literature can also show us what difference a belief makes to a person's life.

dependent on other modes of expression, especially theology? In Canto vii of the *Paradiso* Dante gives a conventional Anselmian version of the doctrine of the Atonement, but does he increase the understanding of this approach for anyone who has read St Anselm? Does he show us anything new, or is it just 'versified Anselm'? Similarly, does Milton, in *Paradise Lost*, Book xii, add anything to what St Ambrose and others have said about the *felix culpa* of Adam's sin? Both Racine and Mauriac were influenced by Jansenism, but do they increase our understanding of it, or make it seem more attractive or plausible?

Sometimes, it seems, artistic and literary examples, whatever their merits, do not *add* anything to our religious or theological understanding. Indeed, on occasion, we need theology in order to understand art and literature, e.g. in the case of Spenser's *Amoretti* no.68 (a poem about the Cross), or many medieval illuminations, or even some well known works like the van Eyck brothers' Ghent Altarpiece. Sometimes signs and symbols lose their immediate power, and have to be explained.

On the other hand, some artists and writers, especially in a secular culture, have seen their task as being to foster religious understanding by producing primary expressions of religious ideas. Flannery O'Connor, for example, believed that redemption through Christ was a decisive event, but realized that she was writing for people who might well know no theology and who might find the very ideas of sin, grace, and redemption unfamiliar or absurd; since, however, as we have seen, she thought that fiction can show us things, it might well turn out to be the best way of expressing such ideas to many people today.

One difference between illustrations and primary expressions of religious ideas is that in the former case artists and writers often explicitly acknowledge a dependence on something else, e.g in the case of Botticelli's or Gustave Doré's illustrations of Dante's *Divine Comedy*; another is that they point a general moral, as in the case of Aesop's *Fables*. Of course both illustrations and primary expressions frequently shed light on something more general. But in the former case the connection is usually made explicit, often because the more general has been discovered already, and the illustration is used to bring it home or to clarify it. Whereas primary expressions are usually derived from people's own life experience and feelings. Even when they convey important general truths, this is rarely made explicit. Thus writers like Sophocles and Dostoevsky are praised for implicitly expressing and thereby anticipating the insights of a Freud or a Girard. So, writing of Dostoevsky's use of Christian symbolism, René Girard himself says,

> ... the truths painfully extracted from the psychological underground call for this symbolism ... The novelist does not attempt to 'illustrate' the principles of Christian faith, but he obeys the internal dynamics of his own creation.[5]

It is in this spirit that, as we have seen, Martha Nussbaum cautions against treating tragic dramas as merely sources of philosophical examples, or illustrations of moral theses; and more generally, advocates a conception of ethical understanding that gives priority to the perception of particular people and situations rather than abstract rules.[6] Putting both these points together, art and literature are for her especially appropriate methods of representation here, for they deal with moral particularities; moreover, at their best, they touch on what is most profound and moving in human life, with certain actions fraught with great significance, and with deep human responses. These are things which need to be shown before they are explained (if they can be explained).

Nussbaum has a lot to say about narratives at this point. For her they are especially suitable for capturing the time-bound character of human existence, and for showing the ways in which

---

[5] René Girard, *Feodor Dostoevsky: Resurrection from the Underground*, tr. J.G. Williams (New York, 1997), p. 100.
[6] Martha C. Nussbaum, *Love's Knowledge*, p. ix; idem, *The Fragility of Goodness: Luck and Ethics in Greek Tragedy* (Cambridge, 1986), pp. 12–17.

our beliefs, decisions, and policies are worked out over our lives. We saw in Chapter 7 the relevance of her discussion to 'novels of redemption'.

Unfortunately, however, Nussbaum does not discuss religious art and literature in the works mentioned, so we need to go on now and say a little more about religious 'showings' and other primary expressions, including narratives. We have here a variety of things to consider. The chorale '*O Haupt voll Blut und Wunden*' in Bach's *St Matthew Passion* is primarily an expression of pity, devotion, and love of Christ, rather than a statement of some truth. Similarly, the '*Agnus Dei*' in Beethoven's *Missa Solemnis* is a heartfelt prayer for mercy and peace: the composer called the '*dona nobis pacem*' 'a prayer for inner and outer peace'.[7] A picture of the Resurrection or a poem about the Cross is, however, trying to capture the religious meaning of events or actions, and perhaps of their consequences. They may also, of course, convey deep feelings about them. The aria 'I know that my Redeemer liveth' in Handel's *Messiah* both expresses Handel's faith in Christ and feelings of joy, peace, and reconciliation; similarly '*non confundar in aeternum*' in Berlioz's *Te Deum* is an expression of faith and a cry of hope. And again, images like those of Christ the Healer, the Good Shepherd, and the risen Christ both depict something and at the same time express people's deepest feelings and needs, e.g. to be healed, to be freed of their burdens, and to be given new hope.

In religious cases the distinction between primary expressions and illustrations would be between works that convey their message immediately to anyone familiar with the basic beliefs of a religion and the relevant artistic and literary idioms, and those requiring a lot of background information and explanation, and also a deeper knowledge of theology. But often it is a matter of degree. The 'Agnus Dei' of Beethoven's *Missa Solemnis* expresses Beethoven's prayers for mercy and peace, but a full understanding would require some knowledge of the Mass and of the background behind the phrase 'Lamb of God'; similarly,

[7] Wilfrid Mellers, *Beethoven and the Voice of God* (London, 1983), p. 305.

Grünewald's *Crucifixion* in his Isenheim altarpiece conveys the horrors of Christ's death more powerfully than most paintings of the subject. But there are varying degrees of understanding possible here, not just of the Gospel background, but of e.g. the lamb and the chalice at the foot of the Cross in the painting.

Often, too, the showing or primary expression presents something that is in a sense familiar to us, but in a new way. Thus, to take a different type of example, that of the novel, Colin McGinn claims, 'An effective work of fiction is precisely a refashioning of the obvious in such a way that we are enabled to experience it afresh'; for example, Mary Shelley in *Frankenstein* 'found a way of stating the obvious while appearing to tell of extraordinary events ... Thus the extraordinariness of the ordinary is brought home to us.'[8] McGinn instances the way in which Shelley uses the situation of Frankenstein's monster to show the nature of the human condition, especially our feelings of physical imperfection, of being 'thrown' into the world and isolated at times, or of being rejected and downtrodden.

In the case of religious art and literature what McGinn calls the 'obvious' might be the human condition, as in his example, or else the fundamental beliefs and practices of a religion. Thus the primary purpose of a painter depicting the Nativity or the Crucifixion might well be to encourage devotion among the beholders of the painting; likewise with a hymn-writer.[9] One of the problems of our time and culture, however, is that we can no longer assume any familiarity with religious beliefs and practices. And when paintings, illuminated manuscripts and so on are iconographically very sophisticated or complex, the problem is exacerbated. Even when people are religiously well informed, explanations may be required in a different age or context, e.g. for

---

[8] Colin McGinn, *Ethics, Evil, and Fiction*, pp. 169*f.*

[9] A hymn-writer may also wish to convey particular theological interpretations: Daniel Migliore matches up three hymns, 'A Mighty Fortress is Our God', O Sacred Head', and 'God of Grace and God of Glory' with three models of the Atonement, respectively victory, satisfaction, and moral influence. See his *Faith Seeking Understanding* (Grand Rapids, 1991), pp. 151–4.

some representations of the Cross, or of the Blessed Virgin Mary as the Second Eve. This is especially so when particular theologies are implicit in the works, e.g. concerning the connection between the death of Christ on the Cross and the Eucharist. This point applies also to literature: it requires considerable theological sophistication to understand the 'conceits' of seventeenth-century poets like Donne and Herbert.[10]

When a work of art or literature requires a lot of background information and explanation in order to be understood, it tends to be treated as an illustration rather than a primary expression. I should mention again that I do not regard the term 'illustration' as a derogatory one, for, etymologically, it is something that throws light on something else. It covers a wide variety of things: even the narrow category of book illustrations includes e.g. scenes in children's story books, engineers' drawings, diagrams in manuals on ball-room dancing, and miniatures in illuminated Books of Hours. Classical paintings are sometimes used as illustrations in modern Bibles or catechisms (thus showing that, although they are dependent on the text for being fully understood, they have an artistic importance lacking in ordinary book illustrations). Moreover, both mainly illustrative works of art or literature and primary expressions may incorporate powerful symbols which draw on subconscious responses and thereby have a healing effect. For symbols may move people without their quite knowing why or how: for example, to quote F.W. Dillistone again, 'In a mysterious way the Man upon the Cross retains His place in the human imagination as the timeless symbol of reconciliation through sacrifice.'[11] These points are specially relevant, I think, to symbols of redemption: since both Jews and Christians acknowledge that divine redemption has not been fully realized yet, it may be that we have to rely for understanding it more on images and signs than on the kind of clarity that theologians seek through argument.[12]

---

[10] See J.A.W. Bennett, *The Poetry of the Passion*, pp. 154*ff*.
[11] F.W. Dillistone, *The Christian Doctrine of the Atonement*, p. 399.
[12] I owe this point to Professor Paul Morris.

The evocative power of words and symbols is highly relevant to another area of religion, that of liturgy. At the beginning of his *The Shape of Soteriology* John McIntyre notes that the Eucharist was the first expression of the Church's view of the significance of Christ's death, and that soteriology, as such, was a late-comer on the theological scene (the first substantial treatise on it, St Anselm's *Cur Deus Homo*, did not appear until the eleventh century)[13]; now the Eucharist, and all liturgy, is a 'showing forth', a disclosing of presence. Like art and literature, liturgy derives a lot of its power from its use of symbols, which, because of their multi-dimensional nature, appeal to different levels of our being, especially the heart and the imagination. So here, again, we see the multi-faceted nature of 'showing'.

Primary Expressions of Redemption

To sum up so far: I have suggested two ways in which art and literature may foster religious understanding by showing or expressing things:

(i) they may provide illustrations of religious beliefs – at their best imaginative and illuminating ones;
(ii) they may be primary expressions of religious ideas (our main concern now).

I think that this distinction applies to narratives, too. Since Christians believe that redemption is worked out through historical events, the expression of this belief will include narratives, of various kinds: e.g. Gospels, biographies, and, as we have seen, novels. Some narratives may be classified as illustrations, if they are just using a story to reinforce a general thesis. But others are primary vehicles of religious ideas.

---

[13] J. McIntyre, *The Shape of Soteriology*, p. 9.

Of course, for Christians, the Bible is the primary text here. But that text includes different literary genres: prayers of repentance and supplication, narratives (especially those of Christ's Passion, death, and resurrection), and theological treatises in the form of letters; and so there are many ways of connecting it with our lives and experience. I have argued that a novel, a biography, or a drama may attempt to show how the process of redemption, which is described in the Bible in general terms as far as subsequent generations are concerned, is worked out in individual human lives here and now.

Primary expressions of redemption, in turn, fall into several different types, and can assist our understanding in a variety of ways. Our reflections in this work so far have suggested three main categories.

First, much art and literature expresses profound human reactions like repentance, pity, forgiveness, hope, the desire to atone for wrongdoing, and awareness of the need for purification. These particular reactions are found expressed in works like Rembrandt's painting, *The Return of the Prodigal Son*, Shakespeare's *Measure for Measure*, and Newman's *The Dream of Gerontius*. Such examples provide something like what Wittgenstein called a 'perspicuous representation',[14] and thereby further our understanding of such basic human reactions.

Second, going a step further, art and literature can attempt to show forth the true nature of human actions and transactions, and their consequences. Here narratives are pre-eminent. Among my examples, I have discussed Dostoevsky's depiction of the true nature of Raskolnikov's actions in *Crime and Punishment*, and Mauriac's description of himself as 'a metaphysician working in the concrete', making incarnate 'the sinner about whom the theologian gives us an abstract idea', and making 'visible, tangible, odiferous a world full of wicked pleasures – and of sanctity too'.[15]

---

[14] Ludwig Wittgenstein, *Philosophical Investigations*, §122.
[15] François Mauriac, *Journal* II, III, in *Oeuvres Complètes* xi, pp. 154, 262.

Third, the artist or writer (the latter especially) may try to show
forth the workings of grace, or something analogous to it,[16] in the
redemption of a sinner, or in the character of a saint, or, most
strikingly, a sinner turned saint (e.g. Mary Magdalen in popular
tradition, or Fr Zossima in *The Brothers Karamazov*). To quote again
from Mauriac's essay *God and Mammon*:

> What we call a beautiful character has become beautiful at
> the cost of a struggle against itself, and this struggle should
> not stop until the bitter end. The evil which the beautiful
> character has to overcome in itself and from which it has to
> sever itself, is a reality which the novelist must account for. If
> there is a reason for the existence of the novelist on earth it
> is this: to show the element which holds out against God in
> the highest and noblest characters – the innermost evils and
> dissimulations; and also to light up the secret source of purity
> in creatures who seem fallen.[17]

Sometimes, too, the most effective way in which a writer can illustrate the effects of grace is by representing its seeming absence,
depicting a 'graceless' world in need of redemption. Mauriac, as
we have seen already, does this in many of his works, e.g. the
earlier part of *The Knot of Vipers*, and so does Flannery O'Connor
sometimes in her novels and short stories. The latter sought also
to convey the costly nature of grace, and our resistance to it.

Novelists and dramatists, of course, have a restricted canvas:
the human heart and what stems from it, especially human
relationships. But perhaps that is as good a place as any to start

---

[16] Although grace is usually thought of as a Christian concept, we can find
similar ideas elsewhere, e.g. in Aeschylus' depiction of the cessation of the Furies'
pursuit of Orestes, and of Pallas Athene's establishment of the Areopagus in the
Eumenides, thus replacing the cycle of vengeance with the rule of justice; or in
Euripides' depiction of Hercules bringing back Alcestis from the dead after she
has died instead of her husband.

[17] François Mauriac, *God and Mammon*, pp. 78–9.

from, if one is trying to discern possibilities of redemption. We need, however, to relate this starting-point to our other sources.

A Clash of Understandings?

I want to go on, therefore, in the last part of this chapter to say a little more about the relationship between the understanding of redemption suggested by art and literature, and that provided by theology. If there can be primary expressions of religious ideas in art and literature, as well as illustrations, are those expressions subject to judgement by theology, or can they contribute to religious understanding independently of theology? Or is the relationship perhaps, as I shall argue, reciprocal? Although we bring our own views to bear in assessing any work of art or literature with a religious significance, one would expect that the quality of that work might well influence both our assessment of any theology implicit in it and our own religious stance. But if the relation is reciprocal, may not the two partners sometimes clash with each other?

We do not usually expect poets or novelists to propound theories of the Atonement (*pace* Dante), or to throw light on particular, sometimes rather technical, theological debates, e.g. that between Calvinists and Arminians on Predestination. It is much more likely that they will point to the inadequacy of a theology's understanding of human nature and action, or that they will implicitly challenge it on moral grounds. This is so, I believe, because of what we have just discussed, the role of art and literature in showing us things (as contrasted with arguing, or trying to prove a theological case), e.g. when a novel describes redemptive processes apparently being worked out through a person's life, or an icon shows us a particular interpretation of the Resurrection.

This is not to say, however, that the primary expressions are not subject to criticism, both in themselves as works of art or literature, and for the theology that may be implicit within them.

A more difficult and complex example is provided by Shakespeare in *Measure for Measure*. At the end of this play one who has caused a serious wrong, Angelo, twice asks for the punishment of death, whilst the ones who have suffered from his wickedness, Isabella and Mariana, ask for mercy for him. Here Shakespeare points to a spontaneous desire to atone for wrong-doing and to the costliness of being forgiven (being forgiven, I say, rather than forgiving). Hence Angelo's response puts a question-mark against theologies like Hans Küng's which brush aside questions of justice and reparation, and so rule out in advance traditional interpretations of the Atonement.[25]

Of course, Shakespeare does not offer us a theory of the Atonement: he is not trying to.[26] But he shows a profound under-standing of the human actions and responses that are at the root of concepts of guilt and atonement, an understanding which is, I believe, a prerequisite of any such theory. In his discussion of *Measure for Measure*, F.R. Leavis points out that Angelo begs for death when he 'stands condemned, not merely in the eyes of others, but in his own eyes, by the criteria upon which his self-approbation has been based'.[27] Moreover, his fall makes Isabella's warning to him earlier in the play turn out to be prophetic, when

[25] Hans Küng, *On Being a Christian*, pp. 419–36. See Hans Urs von Balthasar, *Theo-Drama* iii, pp. 239*f*, for a critique: he accuses Küng of failing to see the inseparable interrelation of divine righteousness and love; and also of making Jesus' mission and death a merely symbolic illustration of something that is already the case anyway, i.e. God's solidarity with us.

[26] Though Roy W. Battenhouse depicted the play as a 'parable of the Atonement', with the Duke representing God, in his '*Measure for Measure* and the Christian Doctrine of the Atonement', *Proceedings of the Modern Languages Association* lxi (1946), pp. 1029–59. But the play lacks any figure corresponding to Christ – unless, like Ulrich Simon, we see Mariana's intercession for Angelo as paralleling Christ's Cross (*Atonement*, p. 55).

[27] F.R. Leavis, 'The Greatness of "Measure for Measure"', *Scrutiny* x (1941–42), pp. 234–47, at p. 239. Harold Bloom observes that it is Isabella's holiness that sexually arouses Angelo: 'The pleasures of profanation are his deepest desire.' See Harold Bloom, *Shakespeare: The Invention of the Human* (London, 1999), p. 366.

she had pleaded with him to spare Claudio's life: 'If he had been as you, and you as he, / You would have slipped like him . . .'

In a more theological discussion, Charles Williams gives a different slant to the play: he too notes that Angelo *asks* for punishment; but he does so in the context of a consideration of pardon and Purgatory, in which Williams argues that pardoned souls are in Purgatory *because* they are pardoned: the will to reach God is counteracted by the desire for the compensation of sin.[28] Thus Williams is raising the question of what satisfaction does to us, rather than that of whether God's justice requires it (both questions are mentioned by St Anselm, who describes satisfaction as both a payment of what is due as satisfaction, and as a cleansing and a restoration of previous blessedness).[29] Thus it may seem to the sinner to be necessary, as an expression of penitence and as a means of purification.

Now whereas Anselm is, as Küng says correctly, concerned mainly with satisfaction, Shakespeare has suggested some further profound questions about what wrongdoing does to the sinner and about repentance. Why does Angelo *reject* forgiveness and mercy? Is it merely the consideration of satisfaction that leads him to want to atone? Or is he also rejecting something like what Bonhoeffer calls 'cheap grace'? Shakespeare, I think, grasps something of our need to take responsibility for our sins, to work

[28] Charles Williams, *The Forgiveness of Sins* (Grand Rapids, 1984), p. 89. One is reminded again of Gerontius' cry, on glimpsing the glory of God, 'Take me away . . .'

[29] See Anselm, *Cur Deus Homo* i.9. Küng misses this, as also, I think, does John Hick, in his essay 'Is the Doctrine of the Atonement a Mistake?' in Alan G. Padgett (ed.), *Reason and the Christian Religion: Essays in Honour of Richard Swinburne* (Oxford, 1994), pp. 247–63. After criticizing Swinburne's *Responsibility and Atonement,* Hick suggests that once we have offered penance and reparation to people we have injured, there is nothing further to be done towards God, except to accept His forgiveness as a free gift of grace (p. 252); he points out that the father does not require atonement from his son in the parable of the Prodigal Son (p. 256). But Hick fails to consider not only the claims of justice but also the expressive aspect of penitence. Might not the Prodigal Son have *wanted* to make atonement to his father, both as his due and as a demonstration of his sorrow?

through repentance, and to express sorrow; and thereby he shows up the inadequacy of a theology that is based on a too thin understanding of human nature. Hence Ulrich Simon says *Measure for Measure*, in its comprehension of guilt and of the possibilities of reconciliation, 'seems to grasp the whole subject more cogently than any dogmatic treatise'.[30] More generally, such examples may show up the inadequacies of some secular philosophies (as Dostoevsky also sought to show, e.g. in *Crime and Punishment*).

There are many other examples that one could give of art and literature implicitly criticizing theology.[31] But let us look now, by contrast, at the other side of the coin, at some of the ways in which theology may assess art and literature. The fact that something is a primary expression of a religious idea, e.g. of a particular model of redemption, does not mean that it is beyond criticism, for what it expresses may seem crude, shallow, perverted, and so on, and readers, listeners, and spectators may therefore reject what is shown to them. One can understand something, and yet find it objectionable!

Sometimes a person may object to the particular theology that is implicit in a work of art or literature. Thus Mary Grey criticizes Christina Rossetti's poem 'The Descent from the Cross' for its 'exaggerated image of the satisfaction view of atonement'.[32] But on occasion a more deep-rooted objection may surface, and this has occurred in the case of Goethe's *Faust*. At the end of that

---

[30] Ulrich Simon, *Atonement*, p. 6; cf. pp. 54–7.

[31] A third one might be William Styron's *Sophie's Choice*, as discussed by Kenneth Surin in his essay 'Atonement and moral apocalyptism: William Styron's *Sophie's Choice*', in his *Turnings of Darkness and Light: Essays in Philosophical and Systematic Theology*, pp. 102–16. Surin argues that the narration of the episode that gives the novel its title provides a basis for a critique of all 'subjective' theories of the Atonement, because the SS doctor is looking for a redemptive *experience*, following his 'unpardonable sin'. This may be so, but my problem with the episode is similar to my problem with Ibsen's *Brand*: are the doctor's character and conduct credible?

[32] Mary Grey, *Redeeming the Dream*, p. 118. She goes on to criticize some of Charles Williams' poetry likewise, for what she regards as its distorted theology (pp. 119–21).

work, Faust, instead of being consigned to Hell, is borne away by
angels, who sing, 'He who strives ever onwards, him we can
redeem.' Ulrich Simon contrasts the fate of Goethe's Faust with
that of Marlowe's, whose soul is lost, and he comments that
Goethe's ending 'lays to rest traditional interpretations of
atonement, and opens the way to salvation in a manner that was
to become normative for a century in Europe'; his Faust is a
'Promethean activist'. But, asks Simon, how can we condone 'the
acquittal and redemption of the unrepentant seducer and
murderer Faust, the prototype of the modern age?'[33] Simon
describes the loving intervention of Gretchen, in her intercession
for Faust, as producing 'a Catholic ending in which adoration and
thanksgiving blend in perfect harmony', and in which grace
'purifies, transforms, and welcomes the soul', and he raises doubts
about Goethe's theology:

> Theologically speaking, the Cross of Christ is not needed
> and reconciliation is obtained without sacrifice.
>   It is precisely this secularisation of redemption which
> endeared Goethe's Faust to the liberal optimistic sentiment
> of European enlightenment.[34]

I am not sure that there is a 'Catholic ending' here (there is
Gretchen's intercession for Faust, yes; but what of Purgatory?);
but I think that Simon is right to emphasize the absence of repentance and atonement in *Faust*. Another critic, Richard Kroner,
likewise draws attention to Faust's apparent lack of contrition,
and concludes:

---

[33] Ulrich Simon, *Atonement*, pp. 35–6. In a similar spirit, George Steiner writes in
The Death of Tragedy of Goethe's 'evasion of tragedy' in his 'sublime melodrama'
(pp. 133, 135); cf. pp. 166–9, 266–70. See also von Balthasar's discussion of the
play in his *Theo-Drama* i, pp. 470–2; and, more generally, on Goethe's attitude to
Christianity, Karl Löwith, *From Hegel to Nietzsche*, tr. D.E. Green (London, 1964),
pp. 14–24. Löwith accuses both Goethe and Hegel of humanizing Luther's
theology of the Cross in different ways.

[34] Ulrich Simon, *Atonement*, p. 38. Cf. von Balthasar, *Theo-Drama*, i, p. 191.

How infinitely humbler are the great voyagers and pilgrims
of spiritual history! ... when we think of figures like Orestes
or Oedipus, must we not conclude that even in Antiquity the
human spirit was capable of being far more deeply smitten
by a sense of its moral inadequacy than it seems possible for
Germany's greatest poet to have been?[35]

Different generations, it would seem, often see things in different
ways, and so vary in their estimate of classic works. The kind of
optimism that appealed to Goethe may seem shallow to those like
Simon, Steiner, and Kroner, who lived through the dark history of
the mid-twentieth century; and other, more personal, factors can
also influence people in their assessment of works of art as true to
life, profound, and morally or religiously adequate. I shall return
to this question in my Conclusion. But let me end the present
discussion by looking briefly at the third possibility mentioned
earlier, that the religious understandings gained from theology
and from art and literature may complement each other, a possibility well expressed by Edward Yarnold:

The artist and the theologian need each other. The artist
needs the theologian to check the exuberance of his vision
and to rescue it from isolation and subjectivity by linking it
with the consciousness of the Church. The theologian needs
the artist to enrich his thinking and rescue it from aridity and
irrelevance by linking it with the aspirations of humanity.[36]

Yarnold is writing about the visual arts. As regards literature,
many people have written of the way in which T.S. Eliot's later
work was closely integrated with his theology. Thus in a

[35] Richard Kroner, 'The Tragedy of Titanism', in Nathan A. Scott, Jr. (ed.), *The
Tragic Vision and Christian Faith*, pp. 153–73, at p. 173. To be fair to Goethe, it is
worth noting that the Doctor Marianus speaks of repentance in his prayer at the
end of *Faust*. But there is little sign of it, as yet, in Faust himself.
[36] Quoted in Tom Devonshire Jones (ed.), *Images of Christ: Religious Iconography in
Twentieth Century British Art* (Northampton, 1993), p. 11.

comparison of Samuel Beckett's *Endgame* and T.S. Eliot's *Ash Wednesday* (both of which works begin with a decisive experience of the truth of the Book of Ecclesiastes), Stanley Cavell remarks that Eliot, as it were, moves up from this beginning, and 'his belief is organizing his art and his art is testing his belief'.[37]

In the case of Eliot, we are dealing with the work and the theology of a single person. But there are also cases where those of two different people may complement each other. A good example of such a reciprocity is provided by Simon J. Taylor in an article in which he relates the film *Dead Man Walking* to R.C. Moberly's *Atonement and Personality*.[38]

In this film a nun, Sister Helen Prejean, is counselling a condemned murderer, Matthew Poncelet, and her aim is to get him to take responsibility for what he has done. Taylor compares her stance with Moberly's similar understanding of punishment as meant to produce penitence in the criminal, rather than as retribution, and he argues that the logic of such a view should have led Moberly to an absolute rejection of capital punishment. Without the death penalty, it is true, Poncelet would not have reflected on his crime in the way that he does; but the film leaves us with the impression of a man who has only begun to live fully as a responsible human being just as he is about to die. Where the film fails theologically, according to Taylor, is in its inability to show us how the relatives of Poncelet's victims, whose problems and sufferings are not removed by his execution, may achieve salvation, too; though the film does indeed show us clearly that Poncelet's actions have deeply wounded them. Hence Taylor ends his article by suggesting that Moberly's stress on the importance of pneumatology for the Doctrine of the Atonement contains further resources for reflection on the issues raised by the film: for Moberly saw that people cannot be saved as isolated individuals, and that they only find fulfilment in life with others. He also saw

[37] Stanley Cavell, *Must we Mean What we Say?*, p. 162.
[38] Simon J. Taylor, '"A Searching Experience": Salvation in the Film *Dead Man Walking*', *Theology* ci (1998), pp. 104–11.

that salvation is not a single event, but a *process* in which, through the Holy Spirit, we are united to Christ and to His Church. Hence, Taylor says, 'We are thus enabled to make theological sense of the open-endedness with which we are left at the end of *Dead Man Walking*' (p. 108).

Of course the envisaged conversation between the film and the book could be prolonged, with further contributions from either side. And, as in the case of Goethe's *Faust*, future generations may see things differently: Moberly's book, with all its virtues and its faults, is very much of its time (nearly a century before the film was made), and *Dead Man Walking* may well affect future generations in a way different from its contemporaries.

In the next chapter I shall mention a few of the factors which influence people's assessment of works of art and literature that have a theological significance. What the examples that I have just discussed show is that art and literature may put a question-mark against theology, whilst the latter may, in turn, criticize them for their moral, religious, or theological inadequacy; or, thirdly, the process may be two-way. Thus the relationship between the primary religious expressions found in art and literature, and other expressions, e.g. theology, is complex, and the process of acquiring understanding is many-sided. But this complexity, and the fact that there are the three possibilities that I have outlined, stems, I believe, from what I discussed in the first part of this chapter, the subtle and varied ways in which art and literature can express or show us things.

CHAPTER TEN

Conclusion

It is now time to sum up the contribution that this study may have made to our seeing how the 'arts of redemption' can contribute to religious and theological understanding. We have seen, at least, that ideas of repentance, forgiveness, and reconciliation have often played a central role in Western literature, and in art, too, (see, for example, Rembrandt's well-known painting *The Prodigal Son* in the Hermitage, St Petersburg, and his drawing of the same subject [Plate 3]); that Christian concepts of redemption and salvation have been a leading theme there for many centuries; and that much art and literature have sought to convey some sense of 'the Drama of Redemption' (a drama that I have sought to break down into three 'Acts'), and of grace working through human life and history. On occasion, too, particular soteriological theories and models have been expressed; and differences between some churches and traditions, despite their common acceptance of certain fundamental teaching, have emerged on some issues, e.g. the Protestant preference for word over image, the Orthodox emphasis on the final transfiguration of all things, and the Catholic doctrine of Purgatory.

In my Preface I invited readers to supplement the examples of the arts and literature of redemption that I discuss with ones of their own, and to assess how much they contribute to our understanding here. It would seem that any generation's art and literature reveal something of its spirituality, for they show wherein people seek fulfilment or transformation – and so they may reveal a loss of depth, too. They may also, of course, challenge or criticize the spirit of the age, and seek to disassociate themselves from it: when Daumier said 'We must follow our own time', Ingres replied, 'What if the time is wrong?'[1] Those of our own time rarely, perhaps, engage with explicitly soteriological themes, in any traditional sense, though I have mentioned some examples in this work. But modern art and literature, and music too,[2] have often shown an overwhelming concern with the great evils of the age, and with our desire to be free of them: with the horrors of modern war, genocide, racial strife and persecution, concentration camps, and the loneliness and alienation of much urban life. As F.W. Dillistone says,

> Man is estranged within himself, divided, in conflict, and therefore anxious, even in despair. Who shall deliver? What process can deliver? ... These are the great questions of modern literature, of modern plays, of modern medicine, of modern psycho-therapy.[3]

Even when there is no explicit religious message, 'redemptive' themes often surface. The modern cinema, for example, has many examples of people sacrificing themselves for others, of their learning through suffering, of the guilty seeking atonement, or of visions of a transformed world. Those who dismiss such works as embodying secularized versions of religious themes, or as substitutes for religion, may, I have argued, be assuming too narrow an account of what constitutes salvation.

Showing Forth

The most obvious feature of the arts and literature of redemption is that they exhibit religious images and ideas of redemptive

---

[1] Ernst Gombrich, *A Lifelong Interest: Conversations on Art and Science with Didier Eribon* (London, 1993), p. 164.
[2] I am thinking especially here of much British music inspired by the two World Wars, e.g. Benjamin Britten's *War Requiem*.
[3] F.W. Dillistone, *The Christian Understanding of Atonement*, p. 350.

powers in an immediate way: as I have said, they show and express things directly. This was already realized by those who defended the use of icons in the eighth and ninth centuries: Paul Evdokimov quotes the Fourth Council of Constantinople in AD 860 as affirming, 'What the Gospel tells us by the word, the icon announces to us by colours and makes present to us', and he goes on to say, 'The icon does not demonstrate anything but shows it.'[4]

In their capacity to thus present things to us, art and literature play a role analogous to religious revelation, which is commonly regarded as God's manifesting something or showing forth His presence and power (the Latin *revelatio*, like the Greek *apocalypsis* means literally 'uncovering'), or stating a truth. Only at a later stage do theorizing and arguing arise. In like manner, aesthetics and literary criticism come later. If someone objects to the vision of life implicit in a work of art or literature, the most direct response is to present an alternative vision. I take it that Alexander Solzhenitsyn was presenting an alternative to official Communist ideology in his earlier works, while, conversely, Thomas Hardy, in some of his novels, was presenting what might be called a nonredemptive vision of the world. Neither of them was *arguing* a case, or trying to prove a theory. The question for the reader, therefore, is: who has seen life more fully and deeply, and portrayed it more convincingly?

Different models of redemption are often implicit in the examples we have discussed. Two that I have singled out are Eastern depictions of the Resurrection, which convey its significance as the beginning of the redemption of the human race and of the renewal of the cosmos, and the recurrence of the figure of a Suffering Servant in many plays and novels. Other models include the Good Shepherd, the Lamb of God, the scapegoat, and the cosmic victory of good over the powers of evil. Sometimes the choice of model has been deliberate, sometimes it has appealed to the artist or writer for reasons of which he or she may not have been fully aware. Different models appeal to

[4] Paul Evdokimov, *L'Art de l'icône*, p. 157.

different people, for personal, artistic, religious or artistic reasons; and certain models appeal especially to certain eras – that of the Good Shepherd, for example, was particularly attractive to the early Church. Of course, religious traditions influence people's choices here, but those traditions are, in turn, moulded and changed by the experience of each generation. In a similar way, theology is affected by history and experience: Ian Bradley argues that the tendency of many twentieth-century theologians to locate suffering within the Godhead was influenced by the two World Wars.[5]

Wittgenstein wrote of life forcing certain concepts on us.[6] It would seem, however, that the process may often take several centuries, and that its beginnings may be lost in the mists of time. When Helmuth Graf von Moltke wrote to his wife in August 1941 that the likely defeat of Germany would leave it with 'a bloodguilt that cannot be atoned for in our lifetime and can never be forgotten', and asked 'Will men arise capable of distilling contrition and penance from this punishment, and so, gradually, a new strength to live?',[7] he was articulating feelings that might be traced back not only through the Christian centuries but also to ancient Greece and Israel (which is not to say that they are universal to all humanity: earlier on I raised the question of whether Western concepts of atonement, redemption, and reconciliation are comprehensible in Eastern cultures and religions – a question with which Shusaku Endo was wrestling in many of his novels, or whether they should be subsumed under some wider heading, e.g. purification, or the restoration of a moral order).

[5] Ian Bradley, *The Power of Sacrifice*, ch.7.
[6] Ludwig Wittgenstein, *Culture and Value*, p. 86e.
[7] Helmuth James von Moltke, *Letters to Freya 1939–1945*, tr. B. Ruhm von Oppen (London, 1991), p. 156.

Assessing the Arts of Redemption

How then are we to assess such art and literature? One obvious answer is that they must have stood the test of time, i.e. be continuously convincing, not ephemeral or eccentric, and so be in some sense classical.[8] But this answer is a kind of appeal to authority, even if it is the authority of tradition (which G.K.Chesterton called 'the democracy of the dead'[9]); and such authority must ultimately appeal to individuals' assessment. But how do we decide now, in the light of our own experience? Since the arts and literature of redemption are usually concerned with deep and difficult issues of good and evil, it would seem to be a matter of our deciding what is most profound and cogent: what these works say and show should relate to our natural instincts and to our tendencies to feel deeply about certain things, and should disclose sometimes a compelling truth about the world, which fosters our understanding of human life.

I said earlier on that if we read authors as diverse as Hardy and Solzhenitsyn the questions arise of who has seen and portrayed life more fully, profoundly, and convincingly, and of who has expressed our deepest needs and discerned possibilities of meeting them. No doubt personal experience will affect each reader's judgement, but certain faults will render a work of art or literature suspect to many people, and make it unlikely to survive 'the test of time': I am thinking especially of shallowness, vulgarity, triviality, cynicism, and sentimentality. Moreover, although 'the uses of adversity' is a perennial theme in art and literature, any seeming belittling of human suffering is suspect to people today: life is hard enough, and art and literature should do justice to this fact. Superficiality is as bad here as it is in the theodicies of some philosophers or theologians. This is part of what the

---

[8] See Anthony Savile, *The Test of Time* (Oxford, 1982), esp. ch.7 ('Depth'); and David Tracy, *The Analogical Imagination: Theology and the Culture of Pluralism* (London, 1981), ch.3, for the use of these criteria in aesthetics and theology.
[9] G.K. Chesterton, *Orthodoxy* (London, 1909), p. 83.

critics of Goethe's *Faust* mentioned in the last chapter were getting at: was the poet taking evil seriously enough?

Many people today, including a lot of Christians, find Holman Hunt's *The Light of the World* (much admired by Ruskin and many Victorians) too cloying; or at any rate, they are not moved by it. Some modern readers find Victor Hugo's *Les Misérables* sentimental; while others may say that the fault lies more in the emotional coldness or shallowness of such readers, and that the novel is outstanding in its conveying of the power of self-sacrificing love. Many people today accept Philip Larkin's view of life (and death), but Seamus Heaney obliquely suggests a question similar to the one that I have just asked about profundity when he contrasts Larkin's attitude to death with that of W.B. Yeats.[10]

Sometimes writers set out deliberately to present a vision of life that is at odds with that of their surrounding culture or of other writers. Flannery O'Connor's letters and essays reveal such a resolve. I have also mentioned Malcolm Scott's thesis that many French Catholic novelists of the early twentieth century were consciously rejecting the Naturalism of Zola and others, and presenting a different view of life, an 'alternative realism'. Of course, not every reader is convinced: Rayner Heppenstall, for example, found Mauriac's vision both unappealing and unconvincing, and quotes a French critic, Benjamin Crémieux, as saying that Mauriac compels us to accept his vision by poisoning our lungs, but that after a deep breath we see that it is 'the creation of a bourgeois world, stupidly enslaved by anti-natural superstitions, absurd prejudices, irremediably sick and putrid'.[11] But that response, in turn, may strike one as flippant or superficial, after reading Mauriac at his best; and talk of 'anti-natural superstitions' might alert us to the fact that something more than literary

---

[10] Cf. again Seamus Heaney, *The Redress of Poetry*, pp. 146–63.
[11] Rayner Heppenstall, *The Double Image*, p. 57. Heppenstall also accuses D.H. Lawrence of oversimplifying, but by presenting the opposite myth to that of Mauriac's 'Jansenist gloom', the myth that 'man is naturally good, the flesh wholly innocent, and the world beautiful' (pp. 60–2).

criticism is going on here! Mauriac himself no doubt would reply that such responses indicate the loss of a sense of sin, or a lack of depth, thereby suggesting a false picture of life: so-called realism may impose a restricted vision of 'reality'.[12]

Personal tragedies, or events like the Holocaust and the two World Wars, may also affect people's judgement of past works of art and literature: they may feel that such evil is incompatible with God's love and providence, or that such events are irredeemable; or they may think that neither literature nor theology can understand them. Elie Wiesel remarked that the great post-War novelists like Malraux, Mauriac, Faulkner, Silone, Mann, and Camus chose to keep away from the theme of the Holocaust: 'they chose not to describe something they could not fathom'.[13] The writers who did so, e.g. Leon Wells and Anne Frank, were, Wiesel says, chroniclers and witnesses, whose desire was to remember and to bear witness to what had happened, rather than to use their imaginations (modestly, Wiesel does not mention his own work; and in the years since he wrote this essay, there has been more of an attempt by imaginative writers to tackle the subject).

A writer may, however, seek to show that such situations are not wholly irredeemable: there are 'cosmic optimists' who are not Panglossian, such as Dostoevsky. There are those, too, who seek to present what Aldous Huxley called 'the whole truth', as opposed to the 'distillation' of tragedy.[14] But, again, they must avoid the

[12] Mauriac describes the style of the Goncourt brothers' *Journal* as mirroring only the surface of things, like those painters who see everything and understand nothing. Similarly, he accuses Zola of denying grace, and Balzac and Proust of ignoring it and so depicting a graceless world. Whereas he himself had, he says, 'a sense of the drama of salvation above everything, and of an invisible but real realm, of nature penetrated by grace'. See his *Mémoires intérieurs*, pp. 97, 244; and more generally on the different kinds of realism to be found in novels, see again T.R. Wright, *Literature and Theology*, pp. 110–28.

[13] Elie Wiesel, 'Art and Culture after the Holocaust', in Eva Fleischner (ed.), *Auschwitz: Beginning of a New Era?*, p. 412.

[14] Aldous Huxley, 'Tragedy and the Whole Truth', in his *On Art and Artists*, pp. 60–8.

faults of shallowness, sentimentality, callousness, and cynicism; and their readers must judge how profound and convincing they find what is written, in terms of their own experience and understanding of life and their deepest convictions.

More difficult, perhaps because less discussed, is the situation facing Christians today who are faced by the 'salvation optimism' of much modern theology: by this I mean the tendency to preach that all people will be saved (traditionally known as Universalism), or at any rate that we can hope and pray that they *may* be saved. John Hick is an exponent of the former position: in his book *Death and Eternal Life* he envisages God as the divine psychotherapist who will work on his patients over several lifetimes, so that they eventually make the right decisions and choose Him (a strange combination of the Eastern doctrine of reincarnation and the Catholic doctrine of Purgatory).[15] Karl Rahner is probably the best-known modern exponent of the latter position, through his thesis of 'Anonymous Christianity': whilst he does not exclude the possibility of damnation, Rahner argues that all men and women are open to God's grace, so we can never be certain in the concrete case that we have to deal with 'pure nature', i.e. nature without grace; hence they may be open to God's word, Christ, and therefore merit the name 'Christian', even without realizing it.[16] Those who are convinced by such theologies may find it hard to fully appreciate much traditional Christian art and literature, which presents damnation as a real possibility – they may regard these works as sado-masochistic. Yet Greene praised Mauriac for presenting his characters as real people with souls to save or lose, and, as we have seen, commented (perhaps thinking of the endings of his own *Brighton Rock* and *The Heart of the Matter*, in

[15] John Hick, *Death and Eternal Life* (London, 1976), pp. 455–64. In his more recent work, Hick eschews such theistic formulations.
[16] See again, Karl Rahner, 'Nature and Grace', in his *Theological Investigations* iv, pp. 165–88; and also 'Christianity and non-Christian Religions' in his *Theological Investigations* v, tr. K.-H. Kruger (London, 1966), pp. 115–34. Of course many other modern theologians besides Hick and Rahner exhibit salvation optimism, e.g. Barth and von Balthasar.

which both Pinkie's and Scobie's widows are comforted by priests who appeal to God's mercy), 'Mauriac's characters sin against God, whereas mine, try as they may, never quite manage to.'[17] Greene evidently shrank from accepting the possibility of final damnation. Similarly, someone brought up on what J.C. Whitehouse calls a 'horizontal' view of the relation between human beings and God, i.e. one which emphasizes that our salvation will depend on our relationships with other people, may find it difficult to appreciate fully some literature of the recent past, which saw the former relation more as a 'vertical' one.[18]

Again, however, someone who champions Mauriac's theology or that of earlier generations might claim that literature can show up the shallowness and superficiality of some modern theology. If indeed Mauriac depicts life as it really is, with all the depths of human evil, then he refutes any easy optimism about final salvation, and also perhaps questions those modern views of redemption that emphasize recreation in glory more than sin and atonement.[19] This is another example of the thesis for which I argued in the last chapter, that the relationship between theology and art or literature is reciprocal, and that each may criticize the other. I do not think that art and literature can directly establish or refute theories of redemption *qua* theories – that is not their business (though they may show us the soil out of which such theories grow). But they can show up inadequate underlying accounts of human nature and experience, and also, possibly, deficient accounts of divine nature and actions. This is true whether the authors of such accounts be St Anselm or John Hick.

Art and literature can also present us with alternative visions to those we find lacking. When Dostoevsky described himself as a

[17] Philip Stratford, *Faith and Fiction*, pp. 19, 237.
[18] J.C. Whitehouse, *Vertical Man: the human being in the Catholic novels of Graham Greene, Sigrid Undset, and Georges Bernanos* (London, 1999), pp. 14–22.
[19] Though Mauriac himself responded in conversation with Philip Stratford to Greene's remark about sinners, 'We all sin against God. Any sin is a sin against God. But there is the mercy of God which is greater than all that.' Cf. again Philip Stratford, *Faith and Fiction*, p. 237.

'realist in the higher sense', he signalled his desire to create a persuasive alternative to the average Monday morning view of life. He did not simply 'read off' his vision from the world out there, but used his imagination to recreate it. The persuasiveness of such recreations depends a lot on unconscious factors in the reader. Thus Mary Grey, after criticizing some 'poems of Atonement' by Christina Rossetti and Charles Williams for their distorted theology, remarks that since their ideas are rooted psychically rather than rationally, 'It is therefore at the subliminal level of image and symbol that the healing must begin.'[20] The convincing communication of a powerful and profound image of salvation or 'rumour of redemption', therefore, is the best answer both to a superficial or unconvincing one and to the messages of darkness and despair that we find so often today.

[20] Mary Grey, *Redeeming the Dream*, p. 121.

Bibliography

Allen, Diogenes, 'Acting Redemptively', *Theology Today*, vol.41 (1984–85), pp. 267–70.

Anselm, St, *Cur Deus Homo*, in S.N. Deane (tr.), *Saint Anselm: Basic Writings* (La Salle, ILL., 1962).

Aquinas, St Thomas, *Summa Theologiae*, 3a.46–52, ed. and tr. Richard T.A. Murphy (London, 1965).

Aulén, Gustaf, *Christus Victor: An Historical Study of the Three Main Types of the Idea of the Atonement*, tr. A.G. Herbert (London, 1931).

Bal, Mieke, *Reading Rembrandt: Beyond the Word-Image Opposition* (Cambridge, 1991).

Balthasar, Hans Urs von, *Mysterium Paschale*, tr. A. Nichols (Edinburgh, 1990).

—— *Theo-Drama: Theological Dramatic Theory*, tr. G. Harrison (San Francisco, 1988–98).

Barth, Karl, *Church Dogmatics*, vol.4, part 1, *The Doctrine of Reconciliation*, tr. G.W. Bromiley (Edinburgh, 1956).

Barton, Stephen and Stanton, Graham (eds.), *Resurrection: Essays in Honour of Leslie Houlden* (London, 1994).

Begbie, Jeremy S., *Theology, Music and Time* (Cambridge, 2000).

Bennett, J.A.W., *The Poetry of the Passion* (London, 1982).

Bergonzi, Bernard, *The Myth of Modernism and Twentieth-Century Literature* (Brighton, 1986).

Berlin, Isaiah, *Two Concepts of Liberty* (Oxford, 1958).

Boff, Leonardo, *Jesus Christ Liberator*, tr. P. Hughes (London, 1980).

—— *Passion of Christ, Passion of the World*, tr. R.R. Barr (Maryknoll, NY, 1989).

Bradley, Ian, *The Power of Sacrifice* (London, 1995).

Brown, Frank Burch, *Religious Aesthetics: A Theological Study of Making and Meaning* (Princeton, 1989).

Browning, Don, *Atonement and Psychotherapy* (Philadelphia, 1966).

Caird, George, *Principalities and Powers: A Study in Pauline Theology* (Oxford, 1956).

Cavell, Stanley, *Must we Mean What we Say?* (New York, 1969).

Cooke, Deryck, *The Language of Music* (Oxford, 1959).

Crites, Stephen, 'The Narrative Quality of Experience', *Journal of the American Academy of Religion*, vol.39 (1971), pp. 291–311.

Daly, Gabriel, *Creation and Redemption* (Delaware, 1989).

Deacy, Christopher, 'An application of the religious concept of redemption in *film noir*', *Scottish Journal of Religious Studies* xviii (1997), pp. 197–212.

—— 'Screen Christologies: An Evaluation of the Role of Christ-Figures in Film', *Journal of Contemporary Religion* xiv (1999), pp. 325–37.

de Gruchy, John W., *Christianity, Art and Transformation: Theological Aesthetics in the Struggle for Justice* (Cambridge, 2000).

Derbes, Anne, *Picturing the Passion in Late Medieval Italy: Narrative Painting, Franciscan Ideologies, and the Levant* (Cambridge, 1996).

Detweiler, Robert (ed.), *Art/Literature/Religion: Life on the Borders*, J.A.A.R. Thematic Studies 49/2 (Chico, CA, 1983).

Dillistone, F.W., *The Christian Understanding of Atonement* (London, 1968).

—— *The Novelist and the Passion Story* (London, 1960).

Dixon, John W., *Nature and Grace in Art* (Chapel Hill, NC, 1964).

Drury, John, *Painting the Word: Christian Pictures and their Meanings* (New Haven, 1999).

Eliot, T.S., *Complete Poems and Plays of T.S. Eliot* (London, 1969).

—— *Selected Essays* (3rd edn., London, 1969).

Evdokimov, Paul, *L'Art de l'icône: Théologie de la beauté* (Paris, 1970).

—— 'Nature', *Scottish Journal of Theology* xviii (1965), pp. 1–22.

Fiddes, Paul S., *Past Event and Present Sacrifice* (London, 1989).

—— *The Promised End: Eschatology in Theology and Literature* (Oxford, 2000).

Fleischner, Eva (ed.), *Auschwitz: Beginning of a New Era? Reflections on the Holocaust* (New York, 1977).

Florovsky, Georges, *Creation and Redemption* (Belmont, MA, 1976).

Ford, David, *Self and Salvation: Being Transformed* (Cambridge, 1999).

Forsyth, Peter Taylor, *Christ on Parnassus* (London, 1911).

—— *Religion in Recent Art* (London, 1901).

Fox, Matthew, *The Coming of the Cosmic Christ: The Healing of Mother Earth and the Birth of a Global Renaissance* (San Francisco, 1988).

—— *Creation Spirituality: Liberating Gifts for the Peoples of the Earth* (San Francisco, 1991).

—— *Original Blessing: A Primer in Creation Spirituality* (Santa Fé, 1983).

Fry, Roger, *Vision and Design* (Harmondsworth, 1937).

Gibbons, Robin, 'Celebration and Sacrament: Holy Place and Holy People', *New Blackfriars*, vol.77, no.904 (1996), pp. 234–43.

Girard, René, *Feodor Dostoevsky: Resurrection from the Underground*, tr. J.G. Williams (New York, 1997).

—— *Things Hidden since the Foundation of the World*, tr. S. Bann and M. Metzer (London, 1987).

Green, Martin, *Yeats's Blessing on von Hügel: Essays on Literature and Religion* (London, 1967).

Greene, Graham, *Collected Essays* (Harmondsworth, 1970).

Grey, Mary, *Redeeming the Dream: Feminism, Redemption and Christian Tradition* (London, 1989).

Gunton, Colin, *The Actuality of the Atonement: A Study of Metaphor, Rationality and Christian Tradition* (Edinburgh, 1988).

—— 'Universal and Particular in Atonement Theology', *Religious Studies* xxviii (1992), pp. 453–66.

Gutierrez, Gustavo, *A Theology of Liberation*, tr. C. Inda and J. Eagleson (2nd edn., London, 1988).

Handelman, Susan, *Fragments of Redemption: Jewish Thought and Literary Theory in Benjamin, Scholem, and Levinas* (Indiana, 1989).

Harries, Richard, 'The resurrection in some modern novels', in E. Russell and J. Greenhalgh (eds.), *'If Christ be not risen': Essays in resurrection and survival* (London, 1986), pp. 40–55.

Hart, Trevor, 'Redemption and Fall', in Colin Gunton (ed.), *The Cambridge Companion to Christian Doctrine* (Cambridge, 1997), pp. 189–206.

Hauerwas, Stanley, *Dispatches from the Front: Theological Engagements with the Secular* (Durham, NC, 1994).

Heaney, Seamus, *The Redress of Poetry* (London, 1995).

Hengel, Martin, *The Atonement: The Origins of the Doctrine in the New Testament*, tr. John Bowden (London, 1980).

Heppenstall, Rayner, *The Double Image: mutations of Christian mythology in the work of four French Catholic writers of today and yesterday* (London, 1947).

Hick, John, *An Interpretation of Religion* (London, 1989).

—— 'Is the Doctrine of the Atonement a Mistake?', in Alan G. Padgett (ed.), *Reason and the Christian Religion: Essays in Honour of Richard Swinburne* (Oxford, 1994), pp. 247–63.

—— 'On Grading Religions', *Religious Studies* xvii (1981), pp. 451–67.

Higgins, Jean, 'The Inner Agon of Shusaku Endo', *Cross Currents*, Winter 1984–85, pp. 414–26.

Hillman, James, *Healing Fiction* (Woodstock, CT, 1983).

—— *Suicide and the Soul* (Dallas, 1978).

Hodges, H.A., *The Pattern of Atonement* (London, 1955).

Horne, Brian, *Imagining Evil* (London, 1996).

Hospers, John, *Meaning and Truth in the Arts* (Hamden, CT, 1964).

Huxley, Aldous, *On Art and Artists* (London, 1960).

James, William, *The Varieties of Religious Experience* (Fontana edn., London, 1960).

Jasper, David, *The Study of Literature and Religion: An Introduction* (London and Basingstoke, 1989).

—— (ed.), *Images of Belief in Literature* (London and Basingstoke, 1984).

Jasper, David J., and Crowder, Colin (eds.), *European Literature and Theology in the Twentieth Century: The Ends of Time* (London, 1990).

Jones, L.Gregory, *Embodying Forgiveness* (Grand Rapids, 1995).

Kartsonis, Anna, *Anastasis: The Making of an Image* (Princeton, 1986).

Kasper, Walter, *Jesus the Christ*, tr. V. Green (London, 1976).

—— *Theology of Christian Marriage*, tr. D. Smith (London, 1980).

Küng, Hans, *On Being a Christian*, tr. E. Quinn (London, 1977).

Leavis, F.R., *The Common Pursuit* (London, 1962).

—— *The Great Tradition* (2nd edn., London, 1960).

Lewis, Alan, *Theatre of the Gospel* (Edinburgh, 1984).

Lossky, Vladimir, *In the Image and Likeness of God* (London, 1974).

Loughlin, Gerard, *Telling God's Story: Bible, Church, and Narrative Theology* (Cambridge, 1996).

Lovejoy, Arthur, *Essays in the History of Ideas* (Baltimore, 1948).

Lucas, J.R., *Freedom and Grace* (London, 1976).

McGinn, Colin, *Ethics, Evil, and Fiction* (Oxford, 1997).

MacGregor, Neil, with Erika Langmuir, *Seeing Salvation: Images of Christ in Art* (London, 2000).

MacIntyre, Alasdair, *After Virtue* (2nd edn., London, 1984).

McIntyre, John, *The Shape of Soteriology: Studies in the Doctrine of the Death of Christ* (Edinburgh, 1992).

MacKinnon, Donald, *Borderlands of Theology and Other Essays* (London, 1968).

—— *Explorations in Theology* (London, 1979).

—— *The Problem of Metaphysics* (London, 1974).

—— *The Stripping of the Altars* (London, 1969).

Marsh, Clive and Ortiz, Gaye (eds.), *Explorations in Theology and Film: Movies and Meaning* (Oxford, 1987).

Mauriac, François, *God and Mammon* (London, 1936).

—— 'Le Roman', in his *Oeuvres Complètes* viii (Paris, 1963), pp. 263–84.

—— 'Le Romancier et ses personnages', in *Oeuvres Complètes* viii (Paris, 1963), pp. 287–328.

May, John R. (ed.), *Image and Likeness: Religious Visions in American Film Classics* (New York, 1992).

Mellers, Wilfrid, *Bach and the Dance of God* (London, 1980).

—— *Beethoven and the Voice of God* (London, 1983).

Metz, Johann Baptist, *Faith in History and Society: Toward a Practical Fundamental Theology* (London, 1981).

Meyendorff, John, *Christ in Eastern Christian Thought* (New York, 1975).

—— 'New Life in Christ: Salvation in Orthodox Theology', *Theological Studies* 1 (1989), pp. 481–99.

Mink, Louis O., 'History and Fiction as Modes of Comprehension', *New Literary History* i (1969–70), pp. 541–58.

—— 'Narrative Form as a Cognitive Instrument', in R.H. Canary and H. Kosicki (eds.), *The Writing of History: Literary Form and Historical Understanding* (Madison, 1978), pp. 129–49.

Moberly, R.C., *Atonement and Personality* (London, 1901).

Moeller, Charles, *Man and Salvation in Literature*, tr. C.U. Quinn (Notre Dame, 1970).

Moltmann, Jürgen, *The Coming of God: Christian Eschatology*, tr. M. Kohl (London, 1996).

—— *The Crucified God: The Cross of Christ as the Foundation and Criticism of Theology*, tr. R.A. Wilson and J. Bowden (London, 1974).

Morris, Thomas V., *Anselmian Explorations* (Notre Dame, 1987).

—— 'A Response to the Problem of Evil', *Philosophia* xiv (1984), pp. 173–85.

Murphy, Daniel, *Christianity and Modern European Literature* (Dublin, 1997).

Murray, Robert, *The Cosmic Covenant* (London, 1992).

Nelson, Mark T., 'Temporal Wholes and the Problem of Evil', *Religious Studies* xxix (1993), pp. 313–24.

Newman, John Henry, *An Essay in Aid of a Grammar of Assent* (4th edn., London, 1874).

Nichols, Aidan, *The Art of God Incarnate: Theology and Image in Christian Tradition* (London, 1980).

Niebuhr, Reinhold, *Beyond Tragedy: Essays on the Christian Interpretation of History* (London, 1938).

Nussbaum, Martha, *The Fragility of Goodness: Luck and Ethics in Greek Tragedy* (Cambridge, 1986).

—— *Love's Knowledge: Essays on Philosophy and Literature* (New York, 1990).

O'Connor, Flannery, *Mystery and Manners* (London, 1972).

Ogden, Schubert, *Faith and Reason: Towards a Theology of Liberation* (Belfast and Ottawa, 1979).

Orwell, George, *Collected Essays* (London, 1962).

Ouspensky, Leonid, *Theology of Icons* (Crestwood, NY, 1978).

Pattison, George, *Art, Modernity and Faith: Restoring the Image* (2nd edn., London, 1998).

Pavelin, Alan, *Fifty Religious Films* (Chislehurst, 1990).

Porter, Stanley, et al., *Images of Christ Ancient and Modern* (Sheffield, 1997).

Rahner, Karl, 'Nature and Grace', in his *Theological Investigations* iv, tr. K. Smyth (London, 1974), pp. 165–88.

Reutersward, Patrik, *The Visible and the Invisible in Art: Essays in the History of Art* (Vienna, 1991).

Ricoeur, Paul, *Time and Narrative*, vols.i and ii, tr. K. McLaughlin and D. Pellauer (Chicago, 1984, 1985); vol.iii, tr. K. Blamey and D. Pellauer (Chicago, 1988).

Robinson, H. Wheeler, *Redemption and Revelation: In the Actuality of History* (London, 1942).

Root, Michael, 'The Narrative Structure of Soteriology', *Modern Theology* ii (1986), pp. 145–58.

Savile, Anthony, *The Test of Time* (Oxford, 1982).

Sayers, Dorothy L., *Introductory Papers on Dante* (London, 1954).

Schillebeeckx, Edward, *Christ: The Experience of Jesus as Lord*, tr. John Bowden (London, 1980).

Schiller, Gertrud, *Iconography of Christian Art*, vol.ii, tr. J. Seligman (London, 1972).

Schwager, Raymund, *Jesus in the Drama of Salvation: Toward a Biblical Doctrine of Salvation*, tr. J.G. Williams and P. Haddon (New York, 1989).

Scott, Malcolm, *The Struggle for the Soul of the French Novel: French Catholic and Realist Novels, 1850–1970* (London, 1989).

Scott, Nathan A., Jr., *Rehearsals of Discomposure: Alienation and Reconciliation in Modern Literature* (London, 1952).

—— (ed.), *The Tragic Vision and The Christian Faith* (New York, 1957).

Sherrard, Philip, *The Sacred in Life and Art* (Ipswich, 1990).

Sherry, Patrick, 'Redeeming the Past', *Religious Studies* xxxiv (1998), pp. 165–75.

—— 'Redemption, Atonement, and the German Opposition to Hitler', *Theology* xcviii (1995), pp. 431–40.

—— *Spirit and Beauty: An Introduction to Theological Aesthetics* (Oxford, 1992).

—— 'Novels of Redemption', *Literature and Theology* xiv (2000), pp. 249–60.

Simon, Ulrich, *A Theology of Auschwitz* (London, 1967).

—— *Atonement: From Holocaust to Paradise* (Cambridge, 1987).

Sobrino, Jon, *Jesus the Liberator: A Historical-Theological Reading of Jesus of Nazareth*, tr. P. Burns and F. McDonagh (London, 1993).

—— *The Spirituality of Liberation: toward a political holiness*, tr. R.R. Barr (Maryknoll, NY, 1988).

Steiner, George, *The Death of Tragedy* (London, 1961).

—— 'A Note on Absolute Tragedy', in *Literature and Theology* iv (1990), pp. 147–56.

Stratford, Philip, *Faith and Fiction: Creative Process in Greene and Mauriac* (Notre Dame, 1964).

Stroup, George, *The Promise of Narrative Theology* (London, 1984).

Surin, Kenneth, *Turnings of Darkness and Light: Essays in Philosophical and Systematic Theology* (Cambridge, 1989).

Sutherland, Stewart, 'Christianity and Tragedy' in *Literature and Theology* iv (1990), pp. 157–68.

Swanston, Hamish, *Handel* (London, 1990).

Swinburne, Richard, *Responsibility and Atonement* (Oxford, 1989).

Sykes, Stephen (ed.), *Sacrifice and Redemption: Durham Essays in Theology* (Cambridge, 1991).

—— *The Story of the Atonement* (London, 1997).

Tanner, Michael, *Wagner* (London, 1996).

Taylor, Simon J., ' "A Searching Experience": Salvation in the Film *Dead Man Walking* and R.C. Moberly', *Theology* ci (1998), pp. 104–11.

Temple, William, *Mens Creatrix* (London, 1917).

Templeton, Elizabeth, *The Strangeness of God* (London, 1993).

Tillich, Paul, *On Art and Architecture*, ed. John and Jane Dillenberger (New York, 1987).

—— *Systematic Theology* ii (London, 1957).

Trinité, Philippe de la, *What is Redemption?*, tr. A. Armstrong (London, 1961).

Turnell, Martin, *Modern Literature and the Christian Faith* (London, 1961).

Turner, H.E.W., *The Patristic Doctrine of Redemption: A Study of the Development of Doctrine during the First Five Centuries* (London, 1952).

Weinandy, Thomas, 'Gnosticism and Contemporary Soteriology: Some Contemporary Confusions', *New Blackfriars*, vol.76, no.898 (1995), pp. 546–54.

Whale, J.S., *Victor and Victim: The Christian Doctrine of Redemption* (Cambridge, 1960).

Wheeler, Michael, *Death and the Future Life in Victorian Literature and Theology* (Cambridge, 1990).

White, Vernon, *Atonement and the Incarnation* (Cambridge, 1991).

Williams, Charles, *The Forgiveness of Sins* (Grand Rapids, 1984).

Wittgenstein, Ludwig, *Culture and Value*, tr. Peter Winch (Oxford, 1980).

—— *Philosophical Investigations*, tr. G.E.M. Anscombe (Oxford, 1953).

Wolterstorff, Nicholas, *Art in Action: Toward a Christian Aesthetic* (Grand Rapids, 1980).

Woodman, Thomas, *Faithful Fictions: The Catholic Novel in British Literature* (Milton Keynes, 1991).

Wright, T.R., *Literature and Theology* (Oxford, 1988).

Young, Frances M., *Sacrifice and the Death of Christ* (London, 1975).

Plates

1. Mathis Grünewald, *The Resurrection* (wing of the Isenheim Altarpiece, Unterlinden Museum, Colmar)
2. *The Resurrection* (mural, St Saviour in Chora, Istanbul)
3. Rembrandt van Rijn, *The Return of the Prodigal Son* (drawing, Teyler Museum, Haarlem)
4. Rembrandt van Rijn, *Christ Preaching to the Poor* (etching)

Mathis Grünewald, *The Resurrection* (wing of the Isenheim Altarpiece). Unterlinden Museum, Colmar

The Resurrection (mural, St Saviour in Chora, Istanbul)

Rembrandt van Rijn, *The Return of the Prodigal Son* (Teyler Museum, Haarlem)

Rembrandt van Rijn, *Christ Preaching to the Poor* (etching)

Index